CM13005571
06/13
£23.99
363.2 532SMA

Blackstone's

Police Q&A

Road Policing 2014

Blackstone's
Police Q&A

Road Policing 2014

Twelfth edition

Huw Smart and John Watson

OXFORD
UNIVERSITY PRESS

OXFORD
UNIVERSITY PRESS

Great Clarendon Street, Oxford, OX2 6DP,
United Kingdom

Oxford University Press is a department of the University of Oxford.
It furthers the University's objective of excellence in research, scholarship,
and education by publishing worldwide. Oxford is a registered trade mark of
Oxford University Press in the UK and in certain other countries

© Huw Smart and John Watson, 2013

The moral rights of the authors have been asserted

First published in 2013

Impression: 1

Crown copyright material is reproduced under Class Licence
Number C01P0000148 with the permission of OPSI
and the Queen's Printer for Scotland

Published in the United States of America by Oxford University Press
198 Madison Avenue, New York, NY 10016, United States of America

British Library Cataloguing in Publication Data

Data available

ISBN 978–0–19–968208–9

Printed and bound in Great Britain by
CPI Group (UK) Ltd, Croydon, CR0 4YY

Contents

Introduction

Before you get into the detail of this book, there are two myths about multiple-choice questions (MCQs) that we need to get out of the way right at the start:

1. that they are easy to answer;
2. that they are easy to write.

Take one look at a professionally designed and properly developed exam paper such as those used by the Police Promotion Examinations Board or the National Board of Medical Examiners in the US and the first myth collapses straight away. Contrary to what some people believe, MCQs are not an easy solution for examiners and not a 'multiple-guess' soft option for examinees.

That is not to say that *all* MCQs are taxing, or even testing—in the psychometric sense. If MCQs are to have any real value at all, they need to be carefully designed and follow some agreed basic rules.

And this leads us to myth number 2.

It is widely assumed by many people and educational organisations that anyone with the knowledge of a subject can write MCQs. You need only look at how few MCQ writing courses are offered by training providers in the UK to see just how far this myth is believed. Similarly, you need only to have a go at a few badly designed MCQs to realise that it *is* a myth nonetheless. Writing bad MCQs is easy; writing good ones is no easier than answering them!

As with many things, the design of MCQs benefits considerably from time, training and experience. Many MCQ writers fall easily and often unwittingly into the trap of making their questions too hard, too easy or too obscure, or completely different from the type of question that you will eventually encounter in your own particular exam. Others seem to use the MCQ as a way to catch people out or to show how smart they, the authors, are (or think they are).

There are several purposes for which MCQs are very useful. The first is in producing a reliable, valid and fair test of knowledge and understanding across a wide range of subject matter. Another is an aid to study, preparation and revision for such examinations and tests. The differences in objective mean that there are slight differences in the rules that the MCQ writers follow. Whereas the design of fully validated MCQs to be used in high stakes examinations which will effectively determine who passes and who fails have very strict guidelines as to construction, content and style, less stringent rules apply to MCQs that are being used for teaching and revision. For that reason, there may be types of MCQ that are appropriate in the latter setting which would not be used in the former. However, in developing the MCQs for this book, the authors have tried to follow the fundamental rules of MCQ design but they would not claim to have replicated the level of psychometric rigour that is—and has to be— adopted by the type of examining bodies referred to previously.

These MCQs are designed to reinforce your knowledge and understanding, to highlight any gaps or weaknesses in that knowledge and understanding and to help focus your revision of the relevant topics.

I hope that we have achieved that aim.

Good luck!

Blackstone's Police Q&As—Special Features

References to Blackstone's Police Manuals

Every answer is followed by a paragraph reference to Blackstone's Police Manuals. This means that once you have attempted a question and looked at an answer, the Manual can immediately be referred to for help and clarification.

Unique numbers for each question

Each question and answer has the same unique number. This should ensure that there is no confusion as to which question is linked to which answer. For example, Question 2.1 is linked to Answer 2.1.

Checklists

The checklists are designed to help you keep track of your progress when answering the multiple-choice questions. If you fill in the checklist after attempting a question, you will be able to check how many you got right on the first attempt and will know immediately which questions need to be revisited a second time. Please visit www.blackstonespolicemanuals.com and click through to the Blackstone's Police Q&As 2014 page. You will then find electronic versions of the checklists to download and print out. Email any queries or comments on the book to: police.uk@oup.com.

Acknowledgements

This book has been written as an accompaniment to Blackstone's Police Manuals, and will test the knowledge you have accrued through reading that series. It is of the essence that full study of the relevant chapters in each Police Manual is completed prior to attempting the Questions and Answers. As qualified police trainers we recognise that students tend to answer questions incorrectly either because they don't read the question properly, or because one of the 'distracters' has done its work. The distracter is one of the three incorrect answers in a multiple-choice question (MCQ) and is designed to distract you from the correct answer, and in this way discriminate between candidates: the better-prepared candidate not being 'distracted'.

So particular attention should be paid to the *Answers* sections, and students should ask themselves, 'Why did I get that question wrong?' and, just as importantly, 'Why did I get that question right?'. Combining the information gained in the *Answers* sections together with re-reading the chapter in the Police Manual should lead to a greater understanding of the subject matter.

The authors wish to thank all the staff at Oxford University Press who have helped put this publication together. We would particularly like to dedicate these books to Alistair MacQueen who sadly passed away in 2008. It was his vision and support that got this project off the ground. Without his help neither Huw nor John would have been able to make these Q&As the success they are. We would also like to show appreciation to Fraser Sampson, consultant editor of Blackstone's Police Manuals, whose influence on these Q&As is appreciated.

Huw would like to thank Caroline for her constant love, support and understanding over the past year—and her ability to withstand the pressures of being the partner to a workaholic! Special thanks to Lawrence and Maddie—two perfect young adults. Last but not least, love and special affection to Haf and Nia, two beautiful young girls.

John would like to thank Sue, David, Catherine and Andrew for their continued support, and the occasional use of the computer.

1 | Definitions and Principles

Please note that the questions in this chapter relate to material in the Blackstone's Police Manuals which has been excluded from the Inspectors' Exam syllabus for 2014.

STUDY PREPARATION

The definitions and principles set out in road traffic legislation are critical to understanding and proving many—if not all—the relevant offences. There is little point in knowing that a particular offence can only be committed by a motor vehicle, for instance, if you don't recognise a 'motor vehicle' when you come across one.

The definitions addressed in this chapter are therefore the building blocks for the rest of the subjects that follow—so they are well worth careful study.

QUESTIONS

Question 1.1

PARKER has retired and bought a 100-year-old steam engine, which he has rebuilt. PARKER only uses the steam engine off-road, in fields during carnivals and parades, supporting local charities.

Could PARKER's steam engine be classed as a mechanically propelled vehicle in these circumstances?

A Yes, and PARKER would bear the burden of showing that the vehicle did not meet the requirements of being 'mechanically propelled'.

B Yes, but the prosecution would bear the burden of showing that the vehicle meets the requirements of being 'mechanically propelled'.

C No, a steam engine will not be classed as 'mechanically propelled' in any circumstances.
D No, because PARKER is not using it on the road.

Question 1.2

NEWBERRY removed the engine from his car, and arranged for his friend, SIM-MONDS, to help him tow the car to a garage to have a new engine fitted. They were stopped by the police while towing the car on a road.

Which of the following statements is correct, in relation to the status of the vehicle under the Road Traffic Act 1988?
A It was both mechanically propelled and a motor vehicle.
B It was still mechanically propelled, but was not a motor vehicle.
C It was still a motor vehicle, but was not mechanically propelled.
D It was neither a motor vehicle nor mechanically propelled.

Question 1.3

NICHOL owns a Mini vehicle, which was manufactured for use on the road. NICHOL has decided to take up auto-cross racing, which will take place off roads and has completely rebuilt the vehicle to use in the races. NICHOL has no intention of using the Mini on the road again.

Would NICHOL's Mini be classed as a motor vehicle at this time, under s. 185(1) of the Road Traffic Act 1988?
A No, because NICHOL does not intend to use it on the road.
B Yes, because it has retained its original character of a vehicle intended to be used on a road.
C No, because NICHOL has changed its character so that it is no longer suitable for use on the road.
D Yes, because it was the manufacturer's intention that the vehicle would be used on the road.

Question 1.4

The police in a city centre area are conducting a road safety exercise in relation to petrol-driven and electrically assisted scooters. Members of the public have complained that an increase in their use by commuters has become dangerous to pedestrians and drivers. Prior to the exercise, Sergeant BATEMAN is due to conduct a briefing to staff about the status of such scooters, as vehicles on the road.

What decisions have the courts made in respect of such vehicles, which could be included in the briefing?

A That a petrol-driven scooter is a motor vehicle and an electrically assisted scooter is a mechanically propelled vehicle.

B That a petrol-driven scooter is a motor vehicle, but an electrically assisted scooter is neither a motor vehicle nor a mechanically propelled vehicle.

C That both types of scooter are motor vehicles.

D That both types of scooter are mechanically propelled vehicles.

Question 1.5

SEXTON's car had broken down on the driveway and was left there for a number of months and during this time the insurance expired. SEXTON sold the car to STEPHENS and agreed to help tow it to STEPHENS's house. STEPHENS towed the car, while SEXTON sat in it and steered.

Should SEXTON's car have been insured while it was being towed?

A No, although it remained a motor vehicle, it was exempt for the purposes of insurance while it was being towed.

B Yes, it was still a motor vehicle and was not exempt from the requirement for insurance while it was being towed.

C No, it was not a motor vehicle while it was being towed; it was classed as a trailer, which is exempt from the requirement for insurance.

D Yes, it was classed as a mechanically propelled vehicle while it was being towed and was not exempt from the requirement for insurance.

Question 1.6

CLIFFORD was driving his car and his wife LISA was in the front passenger seat. CLIFFORD's mobile phone rang, but it had fallen behind his seat. CLIFFORD asked LISA to steer the car while he reached for his phone. LISA took hold of the wheel, but the car veered across the carriageway and collided with a lamp post, causing substantial damage to it.

Who may be charged in relation to 'driving' in these circumstances?

A LISA is not liable, as only one person may be the driver of a vehicle at any one time.

B LISA and CLIFFORD could both be held to be the driver of the vehicle.

C LISA and CLIFFORD could both be held to be the driver of the vehicle, provided they are not charged with dangerous driving.

D Either LISA or CLIFFORD could be held to be the driver, but to charge both is not permitted in relation to road traffic offences.

Question 1.7

MICHAELS was driving his car on a road when his mobile phone rang. He did not have a hands-free kit; therefore he stopped at the side of the road. MICHAELS answered the phone while his car was stationary, with the engine still running. He remained in this position for ten minutes, before completing the call and driving off.

In these circumstances, would MICHAELS have been the driver of the motor vehicle, while it was stationary?

A No, as the vehicle was stationary, he was no longer a driver.

B Yes, he will be a driver until the end of his journey.

C No, the vehicle was stationary only for a short period of time.

D Yes, it's irrelevant how long the vehicle was stationary for.

Question 1.8

REID was sitting in a car on a road with a steep gradient—the vehicle was pointing downhill. It had been snowing heavily and there was ice on the road. REID tuned on the engine and released the handbrake and was about to set off slowly, however, the vehicle started sliding down the hill. REID had no control over the vehicle and was trying to apply the brakes, or turn the vehicle into the skid, but it continued sliding sideways down the hill and collided with a wall.

Could REID be held to have been 'driving' in these circumstances?

A No, at no time was REID in full control of the propulsion of the vehicle.

B Yes, even though REID did not have full control of the propulsion of the vehicle, the engine was running and this amounts to driving.

C No, a person may not be 'driving' when they are only attempting to control the movement of the vehicle.

D Yes, whether or not the engine is running is irrelevant when deciding if a person is driving; it's whether they have some control of the propulsion of the vehicle that counts.

Question 1.9

KELLY was drunk and decided to drive home. He opened his car door and sat in the driver's seat. However, when KELLY tried to start the car, he could not do so because he was using his house keys. Eventually KELLY managed to find the correct key, but the car would not start, as the battery was flat.

In these circumstances, which would be the first point at which KELLY has 'attempted' to drive his car?

A He did not attempt to drive the car at any time.

B When he tried to start the car with the correct key.

C When he first sat in the driver's seat.

D When he tried to start the car with the house key.

Question 1.10

WATKINS borrowed his friend's car one evening and went out drinking. On his way home, he went to a takeaway restaurant. WATKINS was overheard by CARTER, boasting about driving home. It was obvious that WATKINS was drunk and CARTER telephoned the police. WATKINS was leaving the premises when the police arrived.

In relation to the proof required to establish whether a person is 'in charge' of a vehicle, which of the following is true?

A WATKINS must show that there was no likelihood of him resuming control of the vehicle while he was drunk.

B The prosecution must show that WATKINS intended to drive the vehicle in the future.

C WATKINS must show that he had no intention of resuming control of the vehicle while he was drunk.

D The prosecution must show that there was a likelihood of WATKINS driving the vehicle in the future.

Question 1.11

SHAWCROSS was driving a motor vehicle and was involved in an accident, having injured a pedestrian in the car park of a large out-of-town shopping area. The police were called and it transpired that SHAWCROSS was a disqualified driver. The location had the traditional appearance of a car park, with parking bays either side of a carriageway for vehicles to pass to various shops in the vicinity and road markings and directional signs to assist motorists. The accident occurred in one such carriageway.

Given that under s. 103 of the Road Traffic Act 1988 a person is guilty of an offence if, while disqualified, they drive a motor vehicle on a road, which of the following statements is correct as to whether this location could qualify as a 'road'?

A   A car park would not generally be a road, but the road markings and directional signs will establish the location as a road.

B   A car park will not generally be a road, but it may be declared as one in exceptional circumstances.

C   A car park will not generally be a road, but if the court finds that the carriageway is a road in these circumstances, it will transform the rest of the location into a road.

D   A car park is provided for parking vehicles and could not be a road in any circumstances.

Question 1.12

VIVIER arranged a Scout fête, and was given permission to use a field belonging to GILES, a local farmer. On the day of the fête, entry was restricted to members of the local Scout groups, and drivers of vehicles were charged £1 each for entry.

In relation to road traffic offences, would GILES's field qualify as a 'public' place in these circumstances?

A   No, as entry to the field was restricted to certain people.

B   Yes, as members of the public were allowed access.

C   Yes, people were using the field with GILES's permission.

D   No, as the people using the field were charged for entry.

Question 1.13

TANNER was stopped by Constable CHEN one evening as she drove her vehicle in an access road leading to a block of flats. Constable CHEN suspected that TANNER had been drinking and asked her to supply a specimen of breath, which proved positive. She was later charged with driving with excess alcohol. At a later court appearance, she pleaded not guilty. TANNER relied on the defence that the access road on which she was driving belonged to a local housing department and that it was not a public place. There were signs at the entrance to the access road saying 'Private Residents Only'.

What would the prosecution need to show, in order to prove that the road was, in fact, a public place?

A The prosecution would need to provide clear evidence that the road was used by motorists other than residents.

B The prosecution would not be able to show that the access road was a public place, because of the signs that were in place.

C The prosecution would need to provide some evidence that the road was used by motorists other than residents.

D The prosecution would not be able to show that the access road was a public place, because a private place cannot become a public place in any circumstances.

Question 1.14

RICHLEY was stopped by police officers in the car park of the Red Lion public house at 9.30 pm, and asked to provide a specimen of breath for analysis, which was positive. The car park had a sign up saying 'customers only'.

Is this car park a 'public place' at this time?

A Only if the prosecution can adduce clear evidence showing who uses the car park, when and for what purpose.

B No, as only a 'special class of public', i.e. customers, are allowed to park there.

C Yes, even if the prosecution do not adduce evidence that the car park was a public place.

D No, as no invitation or permission was given to the public in general, only to persons wishing to use the public house.

Question 1.15

BAKER was driving a tractor and towing a trailer laden with hay on a road, on behalf of his employer, RICHARDSON. Constable SHAH stopped BAKER for having an insecure load, as some of the bales had fallen off the trailer and on to the road. Constable SHAH reported BAKER for the offence and later spoke to RICHARDSON, who denied responsibility as BAKER had loaded the trailer himself. RICHARDSON stated he would not have authorised the load to be carried in such a manner.

Would RICHARDSON be guilty of 'using' a vehicle in these circumstances?

A No, as he did not authorise BAKER to use the vehicle in such a way.

B No, as BAKER was not acting in the course of his employment.

C No, as BAKER was drawing a trailer, only he could 'use' it.

D Yes, he would be guilty in these circumstances alone.

Question 1.16

In certain circumstances an offence of 'using' a vehicle may be committed.

In relation to the term 'using' a vehicle, which of the following is correct?

A   If a vehicle is on a road and is in an unroadworthy condition, the owner cannot be said to be using it.
B   The passenger in a vehicle cannot be guilty of using it in any circumstances.
C   A trailer attached to a vehicle can never be 'used'.
D   Only if an employee is driving the vehicle can an employer be said to be using it.

Question 1.17

PRICE is the transport manager of a haulage company. He knows that most of his drivers make false entries on their tachograph sheets. PRICE has not instructed them to do this, but as it means that the drivers work longer hours on behalf of the company, he does not stop them. HILLMAN, the owner of the company, is unaware of what is happening.

Is either PRICE or HILLMAN guilty of 'causing' offences in relation to drivers' hours in these circumstances?

A   Yes, PRICE only, as he has turned a blind eye to what is happening.
B   No, neither person is guilty of 'causing' offences in these circumstances.
C   Yes, HILLMAN only as the owner of the company.
D   Yes, both people would be 'causing' offences in these circumstances.

Question 1.18

SILVER has recently re-applied for a driving licence following a period of disqualification, but has been unable to afford to buy a new car because of the high cost of insuring it. SILVER has asked to borrow STAENBERG's car for the day. STAENBERG is aware of the recent disqualification but agrees to lend SILVER the car. STAENBERG has not discussed whether or not SILVER has insurance to drive the car on the road legally.

If SILVER does not have insurance and drives it on a road, which of the following would have to be proved, if STAENBERG were to be guilty of permitting the use of the vehicle without insurance?

A   That STAENBERG knew SILVER did not have insurance and that the motor vehicle would be driven on a road.

B Only that STAENBERG knew SILVER would drive the motor vehicle on a road.

C That STAENBERG knew or believed SILVER did not have insurance and that the motor vehicle would be driven on a road.

D That STAENBERG knew SILVER did not have insurance or that the motor vehicle would be driven on a road.

Question 1.19

WILSON is a driving test examiner and was in the passenger seat of a vehicle being driven by CORY, who was sitting a driving test. On several occasions during the test, CORY was involved in incidents with other vehicles, which nearly amounted to collisions. Eventually, CORY was involved in an actual collision with a pedestrian, having mounted the kerb while turning a corner. The police were called and CORY was reported for driving without due care and attention, contrary to s. 3 of the Road Traffic Act 1988.

In these circumstances, could WILSON be guilty of aiding and abetting CORY to commit the offence of driving without due care and attention?

A No, driving test examiners cannot be classed as 'supervisors', and therefore cannot be guilty of aiding and abetting examinees.

B No, WILSON cannot be guilty of aiding and abetting CORY simply by failing to intervene; the court would require evidence of active participation.

C Yes, even though WILSON would not be classed as a 'supervisor', driving test examiners can be guilty of aiding and abetting examinees.

D Yes, driving test examiners always have a duty to act as 'supervisors' because of their role; WILSON could be guilty of aiding and abetting CORY.

Question 1.20

LEES has been involved in a long-standing dispute with her neighbour, GREEN, over parking outside their houses. One morning, LEES was leaving for work. However, GREEN had parked his car bumper to bumper with her own, making it difficult for her to get out of her parking space. LEES deliberately drove into GREEN's car to try to move it forward, to give herself some space. As a result, damage was caused to both vehicles.

In these circumstances, what test would a court have to apply, in determining whether an 'accident' has taken place, under the Road Traffic Act 1988?

A That an ordinary person would think an accident has taken place.

B None. An accident has not taken place, as the act was deliberate.

C That LEES realised at the time that an accident was taking place.

D That a reasonable person would think an accident has taken place.

Question 1.21

MARTIN owed BELL a considerable amount of money. BELL threatened to set fire to MARTIN's car if the money was not paid immediately. MARTIN persuaded his brother to lend him the money and he drove to BELL's house. On his way, MARTIN was stopped by the police, who discovered he was a disqualified driver. MARTIN claimed he was acting under duress, and would not have driven had it not been for the threat made by BELL.

Would MARTIN be entitled to claim a defence of duress in these circumstances?

A No, the defence will apply only where death is threatened.

B No, the defence will apply only where death or serious injury are threatened.

C Yes, the defence will apply where serious damage has been threatened.

D No, the defence will not apply in a case of disqualified driving.

Question 1.22

JOHN and BARBARA were divorced and had a 12-year-old daughter who lived with BARBARA. JOHN was concerned for the welfare of his daughter as BARBARA had been displaying violent tendencies towards her. One evening, he was in the pub when he received a text message from his daughter saying that BARBARA had threatened to harm her with a knife. JOHN drove to BARBARA's house despite the fact that he had consumed six pints of beer. He then drove his daughter to his mother's house, five miles away, and attended a local police station to report the incident. The officer receiving the report realised that JOHN had been drinking and requested a sample of breath. JOHN was later found to be over the limit and was charged with driving with excess alcohol.

Would JOHN be able to claim the defence of necessity, because of the circumstances leading to his arrest?

A Yes, because his daughter had been at risk of serious harm.

B No, because it was his daughter who was at risk of serious harm and not JOHN himself.

C No, because of the distance JOHN drove after picking up his daughter.

D Yes, because his daughter was at risk of serious harm and the driving was not disproportionate to the harm threatened.

Question 1.23

HAWKINS was involved in a road traffic collision. HAWKINS was to blame, having travelled through a red traffic light. When the police arrived, HAWKINS told the officer that she was diabetic and had blacked out momentarily, having suffered a hypoglycaemic episode.

Would HAWKINS be able to rely on this as a defence in these circumstances?
A No, HAWKINS has no defence in these circumstances.
B Yes, such an attack would provide an automatic defence.
C Yes, provided she could show the attack was unforeseen.
D No, even though the element of *mens rea* is not present, the *actus reus* is.

Question 1.24

O'TOOLE was driving an ambulance to a serious injury road traffic accident. O'TOOLE had activated the siren and flashing lights and was approaching a junction control-led by traffic lights, which were showing red. O'TOOLE slowed down on her approach, but drove through the red light. KEYSE, a pedestrian, stepped off the pavement into the path of the vehicle and was struck by the ambulance, sustaining injuries as a result.

In relation to O'TOOLE's driving, which of the following statements is correct?
A Emergency service crews are entitled to pass through red lights, and O'TOOLE may rely on this exemption to defend her driving.
B O'TOOLE will not be liable for the injuries caused to KEYSE in these circumstances, as she warned the pedestrian of her approach.
C O'TOOLE may be guilty of driving without due care and attention, but may have a defence because of the serious nature of the accident she was attending.
D O'TOOLE will be liable for the injuries caused to KEYSE in these circumstances, even though she warned the pedestrian of her approach.

Question 1.25

Constable SAUNDERS had recently left the Roads Policing Department and was a Grade I advanced police driver. The officer was on duty in a police vehicle in the early hours of the morning, following a vehicle driving on a trunk road (speed limit 60 mph), which was driving at speeds in excess of 100 mph. The pursuit manager consid-ered that Constable SAUNDERS was adequately trained, and authorised the pursuit to continue. However, the officer lost control of the police vehicle on a bend and collided with a wall. Constable SAUNDERS's force submitted a file to the Crown Prosecution Service (CPS), seeking advice as to whether the officer should be prosecuted for dangerous driving.

Should the CPS take Constable SAUNDERS's training into account, when determining whether or not the officer's driving was dangerous?

A No, Constable SAUNDERS is not entitled to have this training taken into account.

B Yes, depending on how recently Constable SAUNDERS was declared professionally competent to take part in pursuits.

C Yes, Constable SAUNDERS was in an authorised pursuit situation and is entitled to have this training taken into account.

D Yes, Constable SAUNDERS was on duty and is entitled to have this training taken into account.

ANSWERS

Answer 1.1

Answer **B** — A mechanically propelled vehicle is, quite simply, a vehicle that is constructed so that it can be propelled mechanically. This is regardless of what the vehicle is being used for and for that reason answer D is incorrect.

'Mechanically propelled' does not include electrically assisted pedal cycles, but it generally *does* include steam and electrically powered vehicles (see *Elieson* v *Parker* (1917) 81 JP 265). Answer C is therefore incorrect.

Finally, the prosecution bears the burden of showing that a vehicle meets the requirements of being 'mechanically propelled' (*Reader* v *Bunyard* [1987] RTR 406). Answer A is therefore incorrect.

Road Policing, para. 3.1.4

Answer 1.2

Answer **A** — Removing an engine from a vehicle does not stop it from being 'mechanically propelled', if you can show that the engine can easily be replaced (*Newbury* v *Simmonds* [1961] 2 All ER 318). Answers C and D are therefore incorrect.

A vehicle that is being towed by another will still be a motor vehicle (*Cobb* v *Whorton* [1971] RTR 392). Answers B and D are therefore incorrect.

Road Policing, paras 3.1.4, 3.1.5

Answer 1.3

Answer **B** — The test as to whether a vehicle is intended or adapted for use on roads is an objective one—would a reasonable person say that one of its uses would be general use on a road? It has nothing to do with the owner's or manufacturer's intention. Answers A and D are therefore incorrect.

A good example of this approach can be seen in *Nichol* v *Leach* [1972] RTR 476, where the owner of a Mini car rebuilt it solely for 'auto-cross' racing, never intending it to be used on a road. Nevertheless, it was held to have retained its original intended road use character and remained a 'motor vehicle'. Answer C is therefore incorrect.

Road Policing, para. 3.1.5

Answer 1.4

Answer **C** — The Divisional Court has held that a petrol-driven micro-scooter was a motor vehicle according to s. 185(1) of the Road Traffic Act 1988 (see *Chief Constable of North Yorkshire Police* v *Saddington* [2001] RTR 227).

In *DPP* v *King* [2008] EWHC 447 (Admin), the defendant was stopped by the police while riding a 'City Mantis' electric scooter on a public road. The scooter looked like a bicycle except that it did not have any pedals or other means of manual propulsion and it was capable of speeds up to 10 mph. The defendant was charged with driving a motor vehicle while disqualified and with no insurance. At trial, the issue arose regarding whether the scooter was a motor vehicle. The defendant was acquitted but, following the case being passed to the High Court, the case was remitted with a direction to convict as the court decided that the scooter was a motor vehicle (see also *Coates* v *CPS* [2011] EWHC 2032 (Admin), where an electrically powered 'Segway Personal Transporter' was also found to be a 'motor vehicle' by the court).

Since both are motor vehicles, answers A, B and D are incorrect.

Road Policing, para. 3.1.5

Answer 1.5

Answer **B** — When motor vehicles are being towed by other vehicles, they remain 'motor vehicles' (answers C and D are therefore incorrect). As a result, trailers require insurance when used on roads and public places (*Cobb* v *Whorton* [1971] RTR 392). Answer A is therefore incorrect.

Road Policing, para. 3.1.5

Answer 1.6

Answer **B** — It is possible for more than one person to be the 'driver' of a vehicle as s. 192(1) of the Road Traffic Act 1988 makes provision for the 'steersman' to be a 'driver'. This was confirmed in the case of *Tyler* v *Whatmore* [1976] RTR 83, when one person was sitting in the driver's seat and the other leaned across and operated the steering wheel. Answer A is therefore incorrect.

The only situation where this rule does not apply is in a case of causing death by dangerous driving under s. 1 of the 1988 Act. Answer C is incorrect, as the rule *will* apply in the case of dangerous driving.

Answer D is incorrect because the rule does allow for both to be charged, subject to the exception mentioned.

Road Policing, para. 3.1.6

Answer 1.7

Answer **B** — For the purposes of road traffic offences, a person who takes out a vehicle remains the 'driver' of it, and he or she will be 'driving', until he or she has completed that journey. Therefore, even if the vehicle is stationary for some time, the person may still be the 'driver' if he or she has not completed the journey (see *Jones* v *Prothero* [1952] 1 All ER 434) (answer C is therefore incorrect).

A person may still be 'driving' although the vehicle is stationary, when he is buying a newspaper or when he is changing a wheel (*Pinner* v *Everett* [1969] 1 WLR 1266); therefore, answer A is incorrect.

In *Edkins* v *Knowles* [1973] QB 748, it was emphasised that the reason for stopping is relevant as it might be part of the journey, e.g. stopping at a set of traffic lights or a junction, or may mark a break in the journey; however, the court did state that the length of the break and whether the driver leaves the vehicle is important and the court must consider the period of time and the circumstances before making its decision. Answer D is therefore incorrect.

Road Policing, paras 3.1.6, 3.1.7

Answer 1.8

Answer **B** — There are many different cases ruling on whether or not a person is 'driving' a vehicle. In *DPP* v *Alderton* [2003] EWHC 2917 it was held that operating the controls of a car (accelerator, clutch and steering) which was parked on a grass verge and wheel spinning was 'driving' even though there was no movement of the vehicle. Further, a person may be 'driving' even though they are only attempting to control the movement of the vehicle. In *Rowan* v *Merseyside Chief Constable* (1985), *The Times*, 10 December, the defendant knelt on the driving seat, released the handbrake and thereafter attempted to re-apply it to stop the movement of the vehicle—he was held to be 'driving'. Answers A and C are therefore incorrect.

The Divisional Court has accepted a finding that a person sitting in the driver's seat of a car with the *engine running* had been 'driving' (*R (On the application of Planton)* v *DPP* [2001] EWHC Admin 450). This has been extended in *Mason* v *DPP* [2010] RTR 120, where the Divisional Court suggested that 'driving' would occur when turning on the engine. This can be compared to the situation where the person sitting in the driving seat of a stationary motor vehicle with hands on the steering wheel and the *engine off*, was held *not* to be 'driving' (*Leach* v *DPP* [1993] RTR 161). Therefore, whether or not the engine is running *is* relevant when deciding if a person is driving and answer D is incorrect.

Road Policing, para. 3.1.7

Answer 1.9

Answer **D** — Acts which are merely preparatory will not amount to attempting to drive. Merely sitting in a car would not be sufficient, as this is still a preparatory act. Answer C is therefore incorrect.

It has been held that, where a defendant sits in the driver's seat of a car and tries to put his or her house keys in the ignition, that behaviour may be enough to prove a charge of 'attempting to drive' (*Kelly* v *Hogan* [1982] RTR 352). Answer A is therefore incorrect.

The fact that the vehicle is incapable of being driven will not prevent a charge involving an 'attempt' to drive (*R* v *Farrance* [1978] RTR 225). Answer B is incorrect because the question asks for the first point at which the defendant could be guilty of 'attempting' to drive.

Road Policing, para. 3.1.8

Answer 1.10

Answer **A** — The case of *DPP* v *Watkins* [1989] 2 WLR 966 outlines the principles to be applied when considering whether or not a person is 'in charge' of a vehicle.

Where the defendant is the owner of the vehicle, *or* where he or she has recently driven it, it will be for him or her to show that there was no likelihood of his or her resuming control while he or she was drunk.

Where the defendant is not the owner, or has not recently driven the vehicle, the prosecution will only need to show that the defendant was in voluntary control of the vehicle, or intended to become so in the immediate future. Answers B and D are incorrect for this reason.

Answer C is incorrect, as the defendant must show that it is *unlikely* that he will drive while unfit, not that he had no *intention* of doing so—a slight difference in wording, but nevertheless important in the context of the case.

Road Policing, para. 3.1.9

Answer 1.11

Answer **B** — The situation regarding car parks becoming roads was reviewed as a result of two cases, namely, *Cutter* v *Eagle Star Insurance Co Ltd* [1997] 1 WLR 1082 and *Clarke* v *Kato* [1998] 1 WLR 1647.

In *Cutter*, it was found that while it remained a question of fact in every case, a 'road' had the physical character of a defined or definable route or way, with ascertained or ascertainable edges, leading from one point to another with the function of serving as a means of access enabling travellers to move conveniently from one point to another along that route. The proper function of a car park was to enable stationary vehicles to stand and wait. In the ordinary use of language, a car park was not a road; they have separate and distinct characters. Where legislation referred to 'a road or other public place', the express addition of the words 'or other public place' clearly indicates that, where the word 'road' stands alone, it bears its ordinary meaning and does not extend to places such as car parks.

However, in *Clarke* it was conceded that in exceptional circumstances a car park *could* become a road (answer D is therefore incorrect), but in the event of a carriageway being found to exist within its bounds which does so qualify, the remaining area will retain its integrity as a car park. Answer C is therefore incorrect.

There is no mention in either case of road markings and directional signs establishing the location as a road and therefore answer A is incorrect.

Road Policing, para. 3.1.10

Answer 1.12

Answer **A** — In order for a place to be a 'public place', it must be shown by the prosecution that:

- the people admitted to the place are members of the public and are admitted for that reason, and not because they belong to a certain or special class of the public; *and*
- those people are so admitted with the permission, express or implied, of the owner of the land

(*DPP* v *Vivier* [1991] RTR 205).

This case shows that the place in question must be open to *all* members of the public, without restriction (answer B is therefore incorrect). It is irrelevant whether the people are there with permission if only restricted members of the public are present. The two requirements from the *Vivier* case go hand in hand and answer C is therefore incorrect.

The fact that people had to pay to enter the land is completely irrelevant as to whether it is a public place. It is the *class of people* that are allowed entry (or not) that is important. If the fête had been open to *all* members of the public and they had all been made to pay, it would have been a public place. (Answer D is therefore incorrect.)

Road Policing, para. 3.1.11

Answer 1.13

Answer **A** — The circumstances in the question mirror those in the case of *R* v *DPP, ex parte Taussik* [2001] ACD 10. In this case, the Divisional Court took the view that the evidence provided by the police was very thin, and that they had not shown that motorists other than residents used the access road regularly. This meant that the court could not find that the road was a public place. The court held that such a road *could* become a public place (therefore answers B and D are incorrect), but it was essential that the prosecution provided *clear* evidence that the road was used by motorists other than residents and that they should present factual details of who used the road and for what purpose. Answer C is incorrect for this reason.

Road Policing, para. 3.1.11

Answer 1.14

Answer **C** — In order to prove that a place is in fact a 'public place' for the purposes of road traffic offences, it must be shown by the prosecution that:

- those people who are admitted to the place in question are members of the public and are admitted as such, not as members of some special or particular class of the public (e.g. people belonging to an exclusive club) or as a result of some special characteristic that is not shared by the public at large; *and*
- those people are so admitted with the permission, express or implied, of the owner of the land in question

(*DPP* v *Vivier* [1991] RTR 205).

Customers of this pub are members of the general public who are invited to use it by the licensee, therefore making it public and not a 'special class' of persons, e.g. members of a club, and therefore answers B and D are incorrect.

The importance of police officers providing enough evidence to show that a particular location amounted to a public place was highlighted in *R v DPP, ex parte Taussik* [2001] ACD 10. In that case the defendant was stopped as she drove out of an access road leading from a block of flats. The road was a cul-de-sac leading off a highway and was maintained by the local housing department. At the entrance to it there was a large sign saying 'Private Residents Only'. As there was no evidence from the officers themselves that they had seen motorists (other than residents) using the road, the court was unable to conclude that the road was anything other than a private one. Contrast this with *R (On the application of Lewis)* v *DPP* [2004] EWHC 3081 (Admin), where the court held it was not necessary for the prosecution to adduce evidence that a pub car park was a public place, given that it was attached to the public house and given a general invitation to use it by the licensee. Therefore answer A is incorrect.

Road Policing, para. 3.1.11

Answer 1.15

Answer **D** — Offences relating to 'using' a vehicle are generally committed by the driver and the driver's employer. For the employer to commit the offence of 'using', the person driving the vehicle must be doing so in the ordinary course of his or her employer's business (*West Yorkshire Trading Standards Service* v *Lex Vehicle Leasing Ltd* [1996] RTR 70). It must be proved that:

- the employer owned the vehicle;
- the driver was employed by the employer; *and*
- the driver was driving in the ordinary course of his or her employment

(*Jones* v *DPP* [1999] RTR 1).

It is immaterial that the employer has not specifically authorised the employee to use the vehicle in such a way (*Richardson* v *Baker* [1976] RTR 56). Answers A and B are therefore incorrect.

The owner of a trailer who is responsible for putting it on a road will not escape liability by arguing that it was being drawn and therefore 'used' by someone else (*NFC Forwarding Ltd* v *DPP* [1989] RTR 239).

Answer C is therefore incorrect.

Road Policing, para. 3.1.12.1

Answer 1.16

Answer **D** — If a vehicle is shown to be a 'motor vehicle' and it is on a road, it may be said to be in 'use', even if it is in such a state that it cannot be driven (*Pumbien* v *Vines* [1996] RTR 37). Therefore answer A is incorrect.

It is generally the case that a passenger in a car does not 'use' the vehicle. However, if a passenger arranges to travel in or on a vehicle for his or her benefit, he or she will 'use' the vehicle (*Cobb* v *Williams* [1973] RTR 113). A passenger can also 'use' a vehicle if there is an element of 'joint enterprise' (*O'Mahoney* v *Jollife and Motor Insurers' Bureau* [1999] RTR 245). Answer B is therefore incorrect.

The Divisional Court has applied a broader interpretation to the meaning of 'use' when considering offences involving trailers. The court held that the owner of a defective trailer who is responsible for putting it on a road should not be able to escape liability for its condition simply by arguing that it was being drawn—and therefore 'used' by someone else (*NFC Forwarding Ltd* v *DPP* [1989] RTR 239). Therefore answer C is incorrect.

If a person driving a vehicle is doing so in the ordinary course of his or her employer's business, the employer is using the vehicle (see, e.g. *West Yorkshire Trading Standards Service* v *Lex Vehicle Leasing Ltd* [1996] RTR 70). In such a case you must prove that:

- the defendant (employer) actually owned the vehicle;
- at the relevant time, the driver was employed by the defendant; and
- the driver was driving the vehicle in the ordinary course of his or her employment

(*Jones* v *DPP* [1999] RTR 1).

If the driver is not an employee then the employer is not using the vehicle, even if that driver is a partner of the firm or has been asked to drive the vehicle by the employer (*Crawford* v *Haughton* [1972] 1 WLR 572).

Road Policing, paras 3.1.12.1, 3.1.12.2

Answer 1.17

Answer **B** — 'Causing' will involve some degree of dominance or control, or express mandate from the 'causer'.

Causing requires both positive action and knowledge by the defendant (*Price* v *Cromack* [1975] 1 WLR 988). Therefore it is not enough that the person in charge is aware an offence is being committed; he or she must have done something to contribute to it. Neither person in the scenario could meet these criteria, as neither 'ordered' the offences to be committed (one person was unaware of what was going on).

Further, wilful blindness by employers to their employees' unlawful actions is not enough to amount to 'causing' the offence (*Redhead Freight Ltd* v *Shulman* (1989) RTR 1). Answers A, C and D are incorrect for these reasons.

Road Policing, para. 3.1.12.3

Answer 1.18

Answer **A** — Generally in order to prove a case of 'permitting' there must be proof of knowledge by the defendant of the vehicle's use *and* of the unlawful nature of that use. In other words, there must be proof that the defendant knew the vehicle was being used and that the driver was committing an offence by using it (i.e. by driving it on a road without insurance). Answers B, C and D are incorrect for this reason.

Road Policing, para. 3.1.12.4

Answer 1.19

Answer **C** — It is possible for someone to aid and abet another to commit an offence under ss. 1 to 3 of the Road Traffic Act 1988. The supervisor of a learner driver may commit such an offence if he or she fails to supervise the other person properly (*Rubie* v *Faulkner* [1940] 1 All ER 285).

However, a driving test examiner is in the vehicle for a different purpose to a 'supervisor' and will not generally be liable for the driver's behaviour (*British School of Motoring Ltd* v *Simms* [1971] 1 All ER 317). Answer D is therefore incorrect.

However, although driving test examiners are not generally 'supervisors' or instructors, there are occasions where the driving of the examinee may be so incompetent that it would be a danger to other road users to allow it to continue. As such, the examiner may be liable as an accessory to any relevant offence by failing to intervene. Support for this view can be found in an unreported appeal to the Crown Court at Burnley (*R* v *Hoyle (Charles)* [1980] unreported), where the judge upheld the examiner's conviction of aiding and abetting the offence of driving without due care and attention. Answer A is therefore incorrect.

The offence may be committed by a person who fails to intervene and the court would not necessarily require evidence of active participation. Answer B is incorrect for this reason.

Road Policing, para. 3.1.13

Answer 1.20

Answer **A** — The general test which a court will apply is whether an *ordinary person* (not a reasonable person) would say that there had been an accident in all the circumstances. Answer D is therefore incorrect. It is immaterial what the driver of the vehicle thought at the time, and therefore answer C is incorrect.

The term 'accident' *will* include a deliberate act committed by the driver of a vehicle, such as ramming a gate (*Chief Constable of Staffordshire v Lees* [1981] RTR 506). Consequently, answer B is incorrect.

Road Policing, para. 3.1.14

Answer 1.21

Answer **B** — The defence(s) of duress and *necessity* will apply to cases of dangerous driving, careless and inconsiderate driving *and* driving while disqualified (*R v Martin* [1989] RTR 63 and *R v Backshall* [1998] 1 WLR 1506). Answer D is therefore incorrect. The defence of duress will only apply where the defendant was forced to commit an offence to avoid death or serious injury (*R v Conway* [1989] RTR 35). The defence *will not* apply in cases of criminal damage or where criminal damage has been threatened, no matter how serious. Answers A and C are therefore incorrect.

Road Policing, para. 3.1.15.1

Answer 1.22

Answer **C** — A person may claim the defence of 'necessity' when charged with a drink driving offence. The situation was considered in the cases of *DPP v Tomkinson* [2001] EWHC Admin 182 and *DPP v Hicks* [2002] EWHC 1638 (Admin). In *Hicks*, the court found that the defence would be available only if:

- the driving was undertaken to avoid consequences that could not otherwise have been avoided;
- those consequences were inevitable and involved a risk of serious harm to the driver *or someone else for whom he or she was responsible*;
- the driver did no more than reasonably necessary to avoid harm; *and*
- the danger of so driving was not disproportionate to the harm threatened.

This ruling followed the earlier *Tomkinson* case, when the Divisional Court found that the defendant had driven a far greater distance than was necessary to avoid the relevant danger and that the defence would not be available. In the case examined in the question, unquestionably the daughter had been threatened with serious harm, which was unlawful. However, the harm threatened must also be immediate. If JOHN had been stopped by the police on the way to picking his daughter up, he may have been able to claim the defence of 'necessity', but by removing his daughter from the scene, he also removed the immediate danger from her. By continuing to drive five miles away from the danger, he did more than was 'reasonably necessary to avoid the harm', as quoted in *Hicks* mentioned previously. It could be argued that because of the distance JOHN travelled after picking up his daughter, the danger of driving while under the influence was disproportionate to the harm threatened and that he could have stopped at some point to call the police, which is why answer C is correct and answers A and D are incorrect.

The defence *may* be used where a person other than the driver is threatened, therefore answer B is incorrect.

Road Policing, para. 3.1.15.1

Answer 1.23

Answer **C** — When a person's movements are beyond his or her control, or his or her actions are involuntary, he or she will not generally be liable in criminal law as the element of *actus reus* is not present. It is also highly likely that because there is no willed action or omission by the defendant, he or she will not have the required state of mind (*mens rea*). A defence is provided in such circumstances, namely 'automatism'. Answers A and D are therefore incorrect.

There is no automatic defence of *automatism*; it will be available only in certain circumstances (answer B is therefore incorrect). If a person has a particular medical condition, which is likely to occur when he or she is driving, he or she has a duty to take reasonable steps to avoid driving when the symptoms are likely to arise (*R v Sibbles* [1959] Crim LR 660). This case is supported by *Moses v Winder* [1981] RTR 37 (which relates specifically to a diabetic undergoing a hypoglycaemic attack).

Road Policing, para. 3.1.15.3

Answer 1.24

Answer **B** — There is no special exemption for emergency drivers with regard to standards of driving (*R v O'Toole* (1971) 55 Cr App R 206), and they will be judged against the standards of care which apply to *all* drivers. There is an exemption which allows emergency drivers to pass through red lights under the Traffic Signs Regulations and General Directions 2002 (SI 2002/3113), reg. 36(1)(b). However, this *does* *not* exempt emergency drivers from having to drive with due care and attention. Answer A is therefore incorrect.

Answer C is incorrect because of the case of *DPP* v *Harris* [1995] RTR 100, where the driver of a police surveillance vehicle following a suspect drove through a red light. The court held that even though the suspects were being followed to the scene of an armed robbery, the seriousness of the circumstances did not provide an exemption.

Answer D is incorrect (and consequently answer B is correct), because of the ruling in the case of *Keyse* v *Commissioner of the Metropolitan Police* [2001] EWHC Civ 715. This was a case defended on behalf of a police driver, but would presumably apply to other emergency service drivers. The court held that the police driver, who was driving with the vehicle's visual and audible warning equipment in operation, was not liable for the injuries to a pedestrian who stepped off the pavement into the path of the vehicle.

Road Policing, para. 3.1.15.5

Answer 1.25

Answer **A** — In *Milton* v *CPS* [2007] EWHC 532, the Administrative Court examined the case of a Grade I advanced police driver, who was charged with dangerous driving under s. 2 of the Road Traffic Act 1988 and exceeding the speed limit. The officer was acquitted of the speeding offences, having successfully argued that he was entitled to have his 'expert' driving skills taken into account in deciding whether or not the driving was dangerous. It was held that expert driving skills amounted to a circumstance that *should* be taken into account in determining whether or not a particular piece of driving was dangerous and it was observed that although the driving was dangerous for a driver of ordinary skill, such driving would not have been dangerous for a man of exceptional skill.

However, in *R* v *Bannister* [2009] EWCA Crim 1571, the Court of Appeal overruled the previous authority of *Milton* and held that an advanced police driver with highly developed driving skills was *not* entitled to have that ability taken into account when deciding whether or not the driving in question was dangerous.

The statutory test is based simply on the standard of the competent and careful driver, who is not to be vested with any particular level of skill or ability not found in the ordinary motorist.

Answers B, C and D are therefore incorrect.

Road Policing, para. 3.1.15.5

2 | Key Police Powers

STUDY PREPARATION

This chapter examines several essential policing powers relating to road traffic matters. While many sections of the Road Traffic Act 1988 contain their own specific powers (such as breath test legislation), those discussed in this chapter are at the core of everyday policing for operational officers.

We will be examining powers to stop vehicles, to demand production of documents, to seize and retain vehicles and finally to require information regarding the identity of drivers and the associated legislation.

QUESTIONS

Question 2.1

Constable DURSTOW attended a report of a person having been knocked over and injured in a leisure centre car park, by a person driving a dumper truck. As the officer arrived, witnesses stated that they believed the driver, COLLINS, was drunk. Constable DURSTOW saw the vehicle at the far side of the car park and drove over, activating the blue lights on the police car. COLLINS drove off through the car park, failing to stop for the officer. He drove around the car park a few times, eventually abandoning the vehicle and running off through nearby woods.

> Given that the car park is a public place and the vehicle was not intended or adapted for use on roads, would COLLINS be guilty of failing to stop in these circumstances, under s. 163(3) of the Road Traffic Act 1988?
>
> **A** Yes, because COLLINS was involved in an accident which caused injury to another person.
> **B** No, this offence can only be committed by a person driving a motor vehicle on a road.

C Yes, regardless of the accident; COLLINS was driving a mechanically propelled vehicle in a public place.

D No, this offence can only be committed by a person driving a mechanically propelled vehicle on a road.

Question 2.2

Constable ELIAS had been tutoring Constable CHIDIKE for four weeks and had identified that the officer needed more experience in dealing with breathalysers. On a night shift, Constable ELIAS decided to set up a checkpoint on a housing estate with the intention of stopping all vehicles that came along. The plan was for Constable CHIDIKE to speak to the drivers to identify whether they had been drinking and, hopefully, to conduct some breath test procedures.

Would the officers' actions be lawful in these circumstances?

A Yes, it is perfectly acceptable randomly to stop vehicles to train newly appointed officers in traffic procedures.

B No, they must at least anticipate detecting an offence or a crime before stopping the vehicle.

C No, this represents random breath testing, which is unlawful.

D Yes, it is perfectly acceptable to stop vehicles to conduct random breath tests.

Question 2.3

Constable HERSI was on duty when she stopped BELL, a learner driver, who was driving a motor vehicle on a road. BELL was accompanied by MARTIN, who was supervising him. Constable HERSI asked BELL and MARTIN to produce their driving licences. However, only MARTIN had his with him.

From whom could Constable HERSI require a date of birth in these circumstances?

A Either, but only if she suspects BELL has committed an offence.

B Either, but only if she suspects that MARTIN is under 18.

C From BELL, as MARTIN has produced a driving licence.

D From either, but only if she suspects that MARTIN is under 21.

Question 2.4

POULTEN has been stopped by Constable GREGORY while driving a motor vehicle on a road. Constable GREGORY conducted a Police National Computer (PNC) check on her BlackBerry, which revealed that POULTEN's vehicle was uninsured. POULTEN had bought the vehicle two days before the stop check and stated that he had received an email from the insurance company, with the certificate of insurance attached. POULTEN offered to show the officer the copy of the certificate on his iPhone.

What is POULTEN required to do, in order to comply with the production of a certificate of insurance, under s. 165 of the Road Traffic Act 1988?

A POULTEN must provide Constable GREGORY with electronic access to a copy of the certificate.

B POULTEN must either produce a legible printed copy of the certificate there and then, or within seven days.

C POULTEN must email the electronic version of the certificate to Constable GREGORY, provided this can be viewed on the BlackBerry.

D POULTEN must produce a legible printed copy of the certificate within seven days.

Question 2.5

BRIARS was involved in a non-injury road traffic collision which the police attended. BRIARS was issued with an HORT/1 form to produce a driving licence and certificate of insurance. BRIARS was due to go on holiday the next day for a week and asked a friend, HAGGER, to take the documents to the station with the HORT/1 form.

In relation to the production of both documents, which of the following statements is correct?

A HAGGER may not produce these documents; they must both be produced by BRIARS.

B HAGGER may produce the driving licence, but BRIARS must produce the certificate of insurance.

C HAGGER may produce both the driving licence and the certificate of insurance.

D HAGGER may produce the certificate of insurance, but BRIARS must produce the driving licence.

Question 2.6

Constable HOLDSWORTH attended a road traffic collision in the High Street. One of the vehicles was being driven by SAUNDERS, a provisional licence holder. The officer was told that another vehicle had driven into the rear of SAUNDERS's car, while it was stationary at a set of traffic lights. At the time, SAUNDERS was being supervised by AMIN, a full licence holder. Both SAUNDERS and AMIN produced driving licences at the scene, but neither could produce a certificate of insurance. Constable HOLDS-WORTH issued SAUNDERS with an HORT/1 form for the production of this document.

> What is Constable HOLDSWORTH entitled to ask of AMIN, according to s. 165(5) of the Road Traffic Act 1988 (requirement to produce insurance)?
> A Constable HOLDSWORTH is entitled to ask for AMIN's name, address and date of birth, and the name and address of the owner of the vehicle.
> B Constable HOLDSWORTH is entitled to ask for AMIN's name, address and date of birth, but only if it is suspected that SAUNDERS has committed an offence.
> C Constable HOLDSWORTH is entitled to ask AMIN whether or not SAUNDERS was insured to drive the motor vehicle on a road.
> D Nothing, the duties under s. 165 only apply to the *driver* of a motor vehicle on a road.

Question 2.7

JORDAN is a designated police community support officer (PCSO) working on a housing estate. Numerous complaints have been received about a motor cycle being ridden around the estate by NEAL. JORDAN saw NEAL sitting astride the motor cycle outside a shopping centre and conducted a Police National Computer (PNC) check on the vehicle, which showed that the vehicle was uninsured.

> Does JORDAN have the power to seize NEAL's motor cycle under s. 165A of the Road Traffic Act 1988, in these circumstances?
> A No, only a constable has the power to seize vehicles under this section.
> B Yes, JORDAN has the power to seize and remove the vehicle in these circumstances.
> C No, only a constable in uniform or an authorised vehicle examiner has the power to seize vehicles under this section.
> D No, only a constable in uniform has the power to seize vehicles under this section.

Question 2.8

Constable GREEN was on mobile patrol following a vehicle being driven by STONE, who was unaccompanied at the time. The officer conducted a Police National Computer (PNC) check on the vehicle, which showed that it was uninsured. STONE began to make off and, not being pursuit trained, Constable GREEN stood down from following the vehicle. The officer traced the vehicle about two hours later, outside

STONE's house. STONE produced a certificate of insurance, which was dated the day before and the officer concluded that PNC had not yet been updated; however, STONE did admit to only being a provisional driving licence holder.

Does Constable GREEN have the power to seize STONE's vehicle under s. 165A of the Road Traffic Act 1988, in these circumstances?

A Yes, the vehicle can be seized because the driver failed to stop, and Constable GREEN has reasonable grounds for believing the vehicle was being driven other-wise than in accordance with a licence.

B No, STONE has produced a valid certificate of insurance, which was the original reason for stopping the vehicle.

C No, STONE is no longer 'driving' the vehicle.

D Yes, the vehicle can be seized simply because the driver failed to stop, without any of the other conditions being met.

Question 2.9

Constable BRIGHT was on mobile patrol and was attempting to stop a vehicle, which made off without stopping. The officer conducted a Police National Computer (PNC) check, which showed that the vehicle did not have insurance. Constable BRIGHT attended the address of the registered owner, HANSON, a short while later and spoke to HANSON, who admitted that the vehicle was uninsured. HANSON stated that the vehicle was parked in the detached garage in the grounds of the house.

Would Constable BRIGHT be entitled to seize the vehicle, under s. 165A(1) of the Road Traffic Act 1988, in these circumstances?

A No, because the vehicle was in a private dwelling house.

B Yes, because the vehicle was not in a private dwelling house.

C Yes, a constable may enter any premises in order to exercise this power.

D No, because the vehicle was on private property.

Question 2.10

Constable KEYS stopped a motor vehicle being driven by GIANNI. A Police National Computer (PNC) check revealed that the vehicle was registered to SCHAFFER, and it was listed as being uninsured. GIANNI admitted not being insured to drive the vehicle; therefore, Constable KEYS seized it using powers under s. 165A of the Road Traffic Act 1988. Constable KEYS provided GIANNI with a notice outlining the reasons for the seizure, and gave a further notice to SCHAFFER the following day.

What must be outlined in the notice given to GIANNI and SCHAFFER in respect of claiming the vehicle?

A It must be claimed no later than seven days from the time the seizure notice was given to SCHAFFER.

B It must be claimed no later than seven days from the time the seizure notice was given to GIANNI.

C It must be claimed within 14 days from the time the vehicle was seized, or from the time the seizure notice was given to GIANNI, whichever was the soonest.

D It must be claimed no later than 14 days from the time the seizure notice was given to SCHAFFER.

Question 2.11

A vehicle which is owned by PEARSON was seized by the police under s. 165A of the Road Traffic Act 1988. The vehicle was being driven at the time by McCAULEY. The vehicle is being stored in a garage owned by a firm employed by the local council. PEARSON has been given a seizure notice, but is about to go away on business and is unable to attend to recover the vehicle.

Would PEARSON be able to nominate McCAULEY to recover the vehicle in these circumstances?

A Yes, but PEARSON must first produce a current certificate of insurance and a driving licence at the police station; McCAULEY must then produce such valid documents at the garage.

B No, only PEARSON may recover the vehicle, by producing a current certificate of insurance, first at the police station and then at the garage.

C No, only PEARSON may recover the vehicle, by producing a current certificate of insurance and a driving licence, first at the police station and then at the garage.

D Yes, McCAULEY may recover the vehicle, by producing a current certificate of insurance and a driving licence, first at the police station and then at the garage.

Question 2.12

Constable PIERCE was dealing with a road traffic accident, which involved serious injuries to one driver. The driver of the other vehicle left the scene without stopping. A Police National Computer (PNC) check revealed that the registered keeper of the vehicle, LOWE, lived nearby. Constable PIERCE attended LOWE's address immediately to ascertain who was driving the vehicle.

What does s. 172 of the Road Traffic Act 1988 say in relation to Constable PIERCE's ability to ascertain these details?

A A request may be made verbally by Constable PIERCE, and LOWE has 28 days in which to reply.

B A request may only be made by post, and LOWE would have 28 days in which to reply.

C A request may be made verbally by Constable PIERCE, and LOWE must reply immediately.

D Constable PIERCE may not make the request: this power is restricted to people authorised by the Chief Officer of Police.

ANSWERS

Answer 2.1

Answer **D** — Section 163(1) of the Road Traffic Act 1988 states that a person driving a mechanically propelled vehicle on a road must stop the vehicle on being required to do so by a constable in uniform or a traffic officer. Any person who fails to do so commits an offence (s. 163(3)).

It is irrelevant that the driver was involved in an injury accident: the power relates to a person driving a mechanically propelled vehicle on a road and answers A, B and C are therefore incorrect.

Road Policing, para. 3.2.2

Answer 2.2

Answer **A** — Section 163(1) of the Road Traffic Act 1988 states that a person driving a mechanically propelled vehicle on a road must stop the vehicle on being required to do so by a constable in uniform or a traffic officer. This is a power for an officer in uniform randomly to stop vehicles. That said, like any power available to the police its use must be able to be justified. In *Stewart* v *Crowe* 1999 SLT 899, it was said that the power under s. 163 represented a necessary and proportionate response to the prevention of crime and that the only limit on the power is that it should not be used whimsically or oppressively.

In *Chief Constable of Gwent* v *Dash* [1986] RTR 41, vehicles were being randomly stopped in order to give a police officer further experience of the breath test procedure under the supervision of her senior. The court held that the actions of the police were not an abuse of power and did not amount to malpractice; therefore, the requirement of a breath specimen and the subsequent procedure were lawful. Random stopping of cars for the purpose of ascertaining whether their drivers have alcohol in their bodies is perfectly permissible; random breath testing, however, is not. This case adds yet another reason for a police officer to stop a vehicle—to train newly appointed officers in traffic procedure. Answers B and D are therefore incorrect.

In *Miller* v *Bell* 2004 GWD 26–564, it was held that the requirement to stop the vehicle is a legal one and as a result of a response given by the driver and/or the officer's observations, a suspicion may form in the officer's mind that the driver has alcohol in their body and they may require the driver to take a preliminary test. This is a random stop but *not* a random preliminary test. Answer C is therefore incorrect.

Road Policing, para. 3.2.2

Answer 2.3

Answer **D** — The power to demand a person's date of birth in these circumstances is given by s. 164(2) of the Road Traffic Act 1988. If a person is driving a vehicle, and fails to produce a driving licence as requested, the officer may ask for his or her date of birth. There is no requirement to suspect that an offence has been committed. Answer A is therefore incorrect.

A constable may also demand a date of birth from a person who is supervising a driver, if he or she suspects that person to be under 21 years of age. Answer B is therefore incorrect. This power would also apply even if the person has produced a driving licence, provided the constable had reason to suspect that he or she is under 21. Answer C is therefore incorrect.

Road Policing, para. 3.2.3.2

Answer 2.4

Answer **A** — Section 165(4)(a) of the Road Traffic Act 1988 states that a person will not be convicted of an offence of failure to produce any certificate if he or she shows that:

> within seven days after the date on which the production of the certificate or other evidence was required it was produced at a police station that was specified by him at the time when its production was required...

However, s. 165(2B) states that in the case of a certificate transmitted to a person as described in s. 147(1A)(a) of this Act, the person is to be treated for the purposes of this section as producing the relevant certificate of insurance if—

(a) using electronic equipment...he provides the constable or examiner with electronic access to a copy of the certificate, or
(b) he produces a legible printed copy of the certificate.

Therefore, the person *may* comply with this section by simply providing the constable or vehicle examiner with electronic access to a copy of the certificate there and then, without the requirement of producing a legible printed copy of the certificate (at the time or within seven days). Answers B and D are therefore incorrect.

Section 165(2D) states that nothing in subs. (2B) or (2C) requires a constable or examiner to provide a person with electronic equipment for the purpose of compliance with a requirement imposed on the person by this section. Therefore, production in these circumstances is not dependent on the officer having a suitable electronic device to receive the certificate, and for that reason answer C is incorrect.

Road Policing, para. 3.2.3.4

Answer 2.5

Answer **D** — Under s. 164(8)(a) of the Road Traffic Act 1988, the person must show that within seven days after the production of his or her licence and its counterpart was required, he or she produced them *in person* at a police station that was specified by him or her at the time their production was required.

On the other hand, under s. 165(4)(a), the person must show that within seven days, the certificate of insurance *was produced* at a police station, removing the requirement for it to be produced in person.

Since answer D is the only one containing the correct combination, answers A, B and C are incorrect.

Road Policing, para. 3.2.3.4

Answer 2.6

Answer **A** — Section 165(5) of the Road Traffic Act 1988 states that a person:

(a) who supervises the holder of a provisional licence granted under Part III of this Act while the holder is driving on a road a motor vehicle, or

(b) whom a constable or vehicle examiner has reasonable cause to believe was supervising the holder of such a licence while driving, at a time when an accident occurred owing to the presence of the vehicle on a road or at a time when an offence is suspected of having been committed by the holder of the provisional licence in relation to the use of the vehicle on a road,

must, on being so required by a constable or vehicle examiner, give his name and address and the name and address of the owner of the vehicle.

Since the officer may ask the supervisor for these details, answer D is incorrect.

Constable HOLDSWORTH may ask for these details if the vehicle was involved in an accident on the road or if it is suspected that SAUNDERS has committed an offence. Answer B is therefore incorrect.

There is no power under this section to deal with the supervisor in respect of insurance issues. These duties belong to the driver and therefore answer C is incorrect.

Road Policing, para. 3.2.4

Answer 2.7

Answer **D** — Vehicles may be seized under s. 165A of the Road Traffic Act 1988, subject to certain conditions being satisfied. The first condition is where a constable in *uniform* requests that a person produces evidence that a motor vehicle is or was not being driven in contravention of s. 87(1) of the Act (driving otherwise than in accordance with a licence); the second condition is that a similar request is made for evidence that the vehicle was not being driven in contravention of s. 143 (driving without insurance). Where the person fails to produce such evidence, provided the constable has reasonable grounds for believing that the vehicle was being so driven, he or she may seize the vehicle.

The power is restricted to police officers, in uniform, and is not given to authorised vehicle examiners or PCSOs.

Answers A, B and C are therefore incorrect.

Note that PCSOs do have a power to seize a motor vehicle under s. 59 of the Police Reform Act 2002 (using a motor vehicle in an anti-social manner).

Road Policing, para. 3.2.5

Answer 2.8

Answer **A** — Vehicles may be seized under s. 165A of the Road Traffic Act 1988, subject to certain conditions being satisfied. Under s. 165A, the first condition is where a constable in uniform requests that a person produces evidence that a motor vehicle is or was not being driven in contravention of s. 87(1) of the Act (driving otherwise than in accordance with a licence); the second condition is that a similar request is made for evidence that the vehicle was not being driven in contravention of s. 143 (driving without insurance).

There is a third condition attached to s. 165A, which is when a constable in uniform requires a person driving a motor vehicle to stop (under s. 163); the person fails to stop the vehicle, or to stop it for long enough, for the constable to make such lawful enquiries as he or she considers appropriate, and the constable has reasonable grounds for believing that that vehicle is or was being driven in contravention of s. 87(1) or s. 143.

If any of these conditions apply, and the person fails to produce evidence that the vehicle was not being driven in contravention of these two sections, provided the constable has reasonable grounds for believing that the vehicle was being so driven, he or she may seize the vehicle, notwithstanding that the person is no longer driving it. Answer C is therefore incorrect.

The vehicle may be seized if one condition is not met (i.e. the driver has insurance) and the other condition is (i.e. he or she has no driving licence). Answer B is therefore incorrect.

Finally, a vehicle cannot be seized simply because the driver failed to stop. The constable must have reasonable grounds for believing that at least one of the other conditions is met. Answer D is therefore incorrect.

Road Policing, para. 3.2.5

Answer 2.9

Answer **B** — Vehicles may be seized under s. 165A of the Road Traffic Act 1988, subject to certain conditions being satisfied. Under s. 165A(4), where a constable in uniform has required a person to stop a motor vehicle and the person fails to do so, the constable may seize the vehicle where the constable has reasonable grounds for believing the vehicle is or was being driven contrary to s. 143 of the Act.

For the purposes of exercising the power under s. 165A, a constable may enter any premises other than a private dwelling house on which he or she has reasonable grounds for believing the vehicle to be. Answer C is therefore incorrect.

Under s. 165A(9)(d), the definition of a 'private dwelling house' does *not* include any garage or other structure occupied with the dwelling house or land belonging to it. Since a garage is not a private dwelling house, answer A is incorrect.

This exception refers to private dwelling houses and not private property, therefore if the vehicle had been parked on property which was private, but not a dwelling, it could have been seized and therefore answer D is incorrect.

(Note that the powers referred to in s. 165A also apply to circumstances where a person is believed to be driving a vehicle contrary to s. 87(1) of the Act (driving otherwise than in accordance with a licence).)

Road Policing, para. 3.2.5

Answer 2.10

Answer **A** — The relevant regulations are the Road Traffic Act 1988 (Retention and Disposal of Seized Motor Vehicles) Regulations 2005 (SI 2005/1606) and they set out the procedures to be followed by the police in exercising the seizure power.

On seizing a vehicle using powers under s. 165A of the Road Traffic Act 1988, the constable must give the driver a seizure notice unless it is impracticable to do so (reg. 4(1)). Where the driver is not the owner or registered keeper of the vehicle, the police officer or agent must take reasonably practicable steps to give a seizure notice to the keeper (and to the owner, if that is someone different) unless he or she is satisfied that this has already been done or the vehicle has been released in accordance with the regulations (reg. 4(2)).

The seizure notice must give specified details about the seizure and retention of the vehicle, including a requirement that the owner (or keeper) claims it within a specified period of time *not being less than seven working days from the day when the notice is given to the registered keeper or owner* as the case may be.

Answers B, C and D are therefore incorrect.

(Note, where a vehicle is not released, it cannot be *disposed of* until at least 14 days after the date on which it was seized.)

Road Policing, para. 3.2.5.1

Answer 2.11

Answer **D** — The relevant regulations are the Road Traffic Act 1988 (Retention and Disposal of Seized Motor Vehicles) Regulations 2005 (SI 2005/1606) and they set out the procedures to be followed by the police in exercising the seizure power.

The owner or keeper of the vehicle must be given a seizure notice, which must give specified details about the seizure and retention of the vehicle. These details will include an indication that a person must pay any relevant charges and must produce at a specified police station a valid licence and proof of insurance in respect of their use of the vehicle (or nominate a third person who can produce those documents in respect of that person's use of the vehicle to whom the vehicle can be released) (reg. 4(3)–(4)).

Specific provision is made for cases where the person claiming the vehicle can demonstrate that they are the owner and pay the required fee, but they nominate a third person who produces a valid certificate of insurance covering their use of that vehicle and a valid driving licence authorising them to drive that vehicle. In such circumstances, the authorised person must permit that person to remove the vehicle (reg. 5(2)).

Therefore, a nominated person *may* recover the vehicle (answers B and C are incorrect for this reason). The nominated person may also produce the documents at a police station (reg. 4) and subsequently at the place where the vehicle is being held (reg. 5). Answer A is therefore incorrect.

Road Policing, para. 3.2.5.1

Answer 2.12

Answer **C** — Under s. 172(2) of the Road Traffic Act 1988, where the driver of a vehicle has committed an offence to which the section applies (this includes ss. 3 and 170 (accidents)), the keeper of the vehicle shall give information as to the identity of the driver as required by or on behalf of a chief officer of police.

There is no mention of a person having to be authorised to make such a request on behalf of the chief officer and therefore it can be assumed that as Constable PIERCE is acting in the course of his duties, he is acting on behalf of the chief officer. Answer D is therefore incorrect.

When a request is made by post, the keeper has 28 days in which to reply. The 1988 Act does not state that *all* requests must be made by post and answer B is therefore incorrect. On the contrary, the case of *Lowe* v *Lester* [1987] RTR 30 indicates that requests may be made verbally, and the information must be provided within a reasonable time, which may in the prevailing circumstances mean *immediately*. Therefore, answer A is incorrect.

Road Policing, para. 3.2.6

3 | Offences Involving Standards of Driving

QUESTIONS

Question 3.1

Fifty cars were gathered in a supermarket car park one evening, racing in an unauthorised 'max power' rally. GLEESON was driving one of the cars at high speed and KRAMER was in the front passenger seat. GLEESON lost control of the car and crashed into a shelter. GLEESON survived the crash, but KRAMER did not. The car park was only open to the public when the supermarket was open. A barrier prevented vehicular access outside these hours, but the people attending the rally damaged it to gain access.

Could GLEESON be found guilty of causing death by dangerous driving, under s. 1 of the Road Traffic Act 1988 in these circumstances?

A No, GLEESON was not driving on a road.

B Yes, because GLEESON was trespassing, the offence could be complete.

C No, GLEESON was not driving on a road or public place.

D Yes, there are no restrictions on where the offence may take place.

Question 3.2

GRAHAM is appearing in court having been charged with an offence under s. 1A of the Road Traffic Act 1988 (causing serious injury by dangerous driving). GRAHAM is accused of driving at high speeds through a housing estate and seriously injuring a pedestrian when the vehicle mounted a pavement. The prosecution has evidence from witnesses that GRAHAM had drunk at least eight pints of lager before driving the vehicle and had staggered out of the pub 15 minutes before the accident; however, they have no evidence of the proportion of alcohol in GRAHAM's body, because the defendant managed to evade arrest for three days after the accident.

Would the evidence that GRAHAM consumed alcohol prior to driving be relevant to the issue in proving dangerous driving?

A No, the prosecution is unable to produce direct evidence of whether GRAHAM was over the limit at the time of the accident.

B Yes, the amount of alcohol consumed before the accident would be sufficient in itself to convict GRAHAM of this offence.

C Yes, the evidence *may* be relevant to the issue of whether GRAHAM drove dangerously.

D No, the evidence is unlikely to be allowed because its prejudicial nature outweighs its probative value.

Question 3.3

HENNIGAN was driving a stolen vehicle and WEBB was a passenger. They were driving at 60 mph, approaching a junction, when HENNIGAN told WEBB to pull the handbrake up. He tried to do a handbrake turn, but lost control when WEBB pulled the handbrake, and collided with a wall. WEBB was killed in the accident, but HENNIGAN survived.

Would HENNIGAN be guilty of causing the death of WEBB by dangerous driving in these circumstances?

A Yes, If It can be shown he was a substantial cause of WEBB's death.

B No, as WEBB contributed substantially to his own death.

C Yes, if it can be shown he was the sole cause of WEBB's death.

D Yes, if it can be shown he contributed in some way to WEBB's death.

Question 3.4

DALEY was driving her car on the approach to a zebra crossing when some children were crossing the road. When DALEY applied her brakes, they failed and she knocked over a child, injuring her. DALEY's car was examined and it was found that her brake discs were worn so much that they did not work. DALEY stated that she had heard the brakes squealing earlier in her journey, but had not realised how bad they were.

What further evidence, If any, would be required In order to convict DALEY of driving dangerously?

A That it would have been obvious to a competent and careful driver that driving the vehicle in that condition would be dangerous.

B No further evidence is required; DALEY may be convicted on these facts alone.

C DALEY could not be convicted of dangerous driving, as she was unaware of the dangerous condition of her car.

D That It should have been obvious to DALEY that driving the vehicle in that condition would be dangerous.

Question 3.5

SCULLY has been arrested for an offence under s. 1A of the Road Traffic Act 1988 (causing serious injury by dangerous driving). SCULLY works for a skip hire company and was driving a vehicle which was carrying a skip full of building materials to a refuse tip. The load was insecure and a large piece of metal fell off the skip, seriously injuring a pedestrian. SCULLY claimed in interview that he was an experienced driver and had securely fastened the load and inspected it before setting off, something which he had done thousands of time before. SCULLY maintained that he had done all he could and that he could not be held liable for a freak accident such as this.

In considering whether or not SCULLY should be charged with this offence, which of the following statements is correct in relation to his 'inspection' of the vehicle before driving?

A It must be shown that had a component and careful driver inspected the vehicle closely, it should have been obvious to them that the way in which it was loaded would make driving it dangerous.

B It must be shown that had a component and careful driver seen the load, it should have been obvious to them that the way in which it was loaded would make driving it dangerous.

C It must be shown that it should have been obvious to SCULLY, after careful inspection, that the way in which the vehicle was loaded would make driving it dangerous.

D SCULLY may not be charged under this legislation; an offence under s. 1A may only be charged when the circumstances relate to the standard of a person's driving.

Question 3.6

CALVIN is appearing in Crown Court for an offence of dangerous driving. Witnesses saw CALVIN speeding towards a junction on a housing estate and failing to brake in time. The defendant's vehicle shot through the junction and collided with another vehicle. A nearby resident, REID, has also provided a written statement stating that she saw CALVIN doing handbrake turns in the road shortly before the collision, before the vehicle sped off out of her sight towards the junction where the collision occurred. In her statement, REID has stated that CALVIN was well known on the estate for the dangerous way he drove and she had heard from other residents that there had been several other near misses such as the current case.

Would the prosecution be able to admit REID's evidence in asking the court to decide whether CALVIN is guilty of dangerous driving?

A Yes, the court may hear the evidence of CALVIN's driving immediately before the incident, but the information regarding previous bad driving is hearsay and inadmissible.

B Yes, the court may hear all of REID's testimony—hearsay evidence such as this is admissible in cases of dangerous driving.

C No, only an expert witness could give this evidence and REID will not be regarded as such.

D No, REID's entire evidence is hearsay, which would not be admissible in this case.

Question 3.7

HIGGINSON has been charged with causing death by dangerous driving in relation to a road traffic collision.

In relation to the actual causes of the collision, which of the following is true?

A Any police officer may give an opinion, but it *must* be supported with factual evidence.

B A police officer who has experience in collision investigation may give such opinion.

C A police officer who has experience in collision investigation may give such opinion, but it *must* be supported with factual evidence.

D Only factual evidence in relation to the dangerous driving is allowed. Opinion as to the cause of the collision is not.

Question 3.8

O'BRIEN has been convicted of an offence of dangerous driving and is awaiting sentence by the court.

In relation to disqualification and having to take an extended driving test (re-test), which of the following is true?

A O'BRIEN must be disqualified and discretionary re-test.

B O'BRIEN must be disqualified and compulsory re-test.

C O'BRIEN should be disqualified unless special reasons exist, if disqualified discretionary re-test.

D O'BRIEN should be disqualified unless special reasons exist, if disqualified compulsory re-test.

Question 3.9

McCRONE was involved in a road traffic accident when he drove into a parked car, having lost concentration momentarily. The collision resulted in VERITY, who was sitting in the passenger seat of the parked car, suffering from a whiplash injury.

In relation to McCRONE's state of mind, what would the prosecution need to prove in order to convict him of driving without due care and attention?

A Either that McCRONE knew, or was aware of the fact that his driving fell below the required standard.

B The prosecution has nothing to prove in relation to McCRONE's state of mind, provided it can be shown his driving fell far below the required standard.

C That McCRONE was aware of the fact that his driving fell below the required standard.

D The prosecution has nothing to prove in relation to McCRONE's state of mind; there is no requirement to prove any knowledge or awareness by the defendant.

Question 3.10

TYLER is appearing before the court on a count of careless driving contrary to s. 3 of the Road Traffic Act 1988. TYLER collided with a car in front, while driving in traffic on a motorway. At the time, the police were clearing the scene of a serious accident on the opposite carriageway. TYLER's defence was that he was distracted by the activity and because he was driving at 65 mph, had no time to react.

Which of the following statements is correct, in relation to whether the court should take account of TYLER's claims to have been distracted?

A The court may take account of distraction as a defence, depending on any other hazards on the road at that time.

B The court may only take account of distraction as a defence in a case where the driver was responding to an emergency situation.

C The court may take account of distraction as a defence, but the speed at which a vehicle was travelling will not be a factor for consideration.

D The court may not take account of distraction as a defence; the driver is always responsible for his or her own actions.

Question 3.11

WARE was driving his car on the road in heavy rain in a built up area. There were several puddles at the side of the road and WARE deliberately drove through these, in order to soak pedestrians who were using the pavement. As a result of WARE's actions, several pedestrians and a pedal cyclist were soaked by water from the puddles; however, the water missed other pedestrians who were protected by a bus shelter.

Against which people, if any, might WARE have committed an offence under s. 3 of the Road Traffic Act 1988 (driving without due consideration to other road users)?

A The pedal cyclist and all pedestrians, as there was potential for them to be affected by WARE's actions.

B None of the people, as no motor vehicles were affected by WARE's actions.

C The pedal cyclist and the pedestrians who were soaked, as they were actually affected by WARE's actions.

D The pedal cyclist only, as the only person 'using' the road.

Question 3.12

LEIGH was driving a motor vehicle behind FOGG, on the approach to a pelican crossing. LEIGH saw a pedestrian on the pavement next to the crossing, but was in a hurry and hoped to get through the green light before the pedestrian pushed the 'stop' button. FOGG anticipated that the pedestrian might push the button and slowed down, stopping short of the crossing even though the lights were still green. LEIGH was not concentrating and drove into the rear of FOGG's vehicle.

Which of the following statements is correct, in relation to the proof required for an offence of driving without due care and attention, contrary to s. 3 of the Road Traffic Act 1988?

A Any breach of road traffic regulations will provide conclusive evidence for this offence.

B Colliding with another vehicle will provide conclusive evidence for this offence.

C Colliding with another vehicle will not provide conclusive evidence for this offence, but a breach of pedestrian crossing regulations will.

D Neither colliding with another vehicle nor breaching pedestrian crossing regulations will provide conclusive evidence for this offence; further evidence is required.

Question 3.13

RICHARDS was unconscious in hospital, having been involved in a road traffic collision with another vehicle. The driver of the other vehicle was killed during the collision. Constable HOULIE suspected that RICHARDS caused the collision by driving without due care and attention, and was guilty of an offence under s. 3A of the Road Traffic Act 1988. Using powers under s. 7A of the Act, Constable HOULIE arranged for a blood sample to be taken from RICHARDS. Upon waking, RICHARDS refused to give permission for the blood sample to be sent for a laboratory test.

Would RICHARDS be guilty of an offence under s. 3A(1)(d) of the Road Traffic Act 1988 (causing death by careless driving when under the influence of drink or drugs) in these circumstances?

A Yes, provided it was suspected that RICHARDS has been drinking.

B No, but RICHARDS would commit an offence under s. 7A of the Act.

C Yes, if RICHARDS did not have a reasonable excuse for failing to give permission.

D Yes, provided the request was made within 18 hours of the accident.

Question 3.14

CAGE works for a building company and has a drug habit. CAGE turned up for work while under the influence of drugs and was fired. To get revenge, CAGE stole a dumper truck from the site, intending to take it to the head office and cause damage. On the way, CAGE was involved in a road traffic collision, where a pedestrian walked into the road in front of the dumper truck, and was killed. CAGE was still under the influence of drugs at this time.

Has CAGE committed an offence under s. 3A of the Road Traffic Act 1988, in these circumstances?

A No, CAGE was not under the influence of drink at the time of the accident.

B No, it must be shown that CAGE drove without due care and attention or without due consideration to other road users.

C No, he was not driving a motor vehicle at the time of the accident.

D Yes, he was driving a mechanically propelled vehicle on a road while under the influence of drugs.

Question 3.15

ADAMS was driving a motor vehicle on a road. An elderly person stepped out from behind a parked car and into the path of ADAMS's vehicle. ADAMS's vehicle collided with this person, and the collision turned out to be fatal. It was discovered by the police officer investigating the case that ADAMS had a full driving licence, but did not have a certificate of insurance.

Would ADAMS be guilty of an offence under s. 3ZB of the Road Traffic Act 1988 (causing the death of another person) in these circumstances?

A No, because ADAMS had a full driving licence.

B No, unless it could be proved that ADAMS was also driving without due care and attention.

C No, because ADAMS was not a disqualified driver.

D Yes, ADAMS would be guilty of the offence in these circumstances alone.

Question 3.16

KEENAN is appearing in Crown Court for causing death by dangerous driving. KEENAN had been driving on a motorway and had driven into the rear of the car in front. This resulted in a multiple pile-up, during which the occupants of the car in front died. Witnesses stated that KEENAN had caused the accident by driving too close to the vehicle in front and when it braked, KEENAN was unable to react quickly enough.

Would the prosecution be entitled to introduce the stopping distances shown in the Highway Code, to assist in establishing KEENAN's liability for the offence?

A No, the provisions of the Highway Code may only be introduced in proceedings by the defence, to negate the defendant's liability.

B No, the failure by a person to observe a provision of the Highway Code may only be introduced in civil proceedings.

C Yes, the failure by a person to observe a provision of the Highway Code may be introduced in any civil or criminal proceedings.

D Yes, but the failure by a person to observe a provision of the Highway Code may only be introduced in certain criminal proceedings.

Question 3.17

MULLER was riding a bicycle along the road, approaching a junction. In order to avoid stopping at the junction, MULLER decided to ride across the pavement. In doing so, MULLER collided with HOLLAND, a pedestrian. MULLER was in a hurry and started to ride away, but HOLLAND tried to obtain the cyclist's name and address. MULLER refused to do so and rode off.

Has MULLER committed an offence by refusing to provide these details?

A Yes, but only if HOLLAND was injured during the incident.

B Yes, MULLER has committed an offence in these circumstances alone.

C No, this power is only given to police officers.

D Yes, provided it can be shown MULLER was guilty of an offence of dangerous cycling.

Question 3.18

Sergeant AZIZ stopped a vehicle which had been circulated after it had been involved in an incident of dangerous driving. Sergeant AZIZ asked the male driver for his name and address for the purposes of summonsing him for the offence. When asked, the male said nothing and just stood looking at the officer. Sergeant AZIZ eventually arrested the person using powers under s. 24 of the Police and Criminal Evidence Act 1984.

In the circumstances as outlined, has an offence under s. 168 of the Road Traffic Act 1988 been committed?

A No, the offence is only committed by those who refuse to give or give false details and this has not occurred in these circumstances.

B Yes, silence has been held to be a refusal in these circumstances.

C Yes, as failure to give details amounts to refusal.

D No, the offence is only committed by those who refuse to give details and this has not occurred in these circumstances.

ANSWERS

Answer 3.1

Answer **C** — The offence of causing death by dangerous driving under s. 1 of the Road Traffic Act 1988 may be committed by a person driving a mechanically propelled vehicle *on a road or public place*. The Act gives a wide meaning to the types of vehicle that may commit the offence (including dumper trucks, cranes and quad bikes), and the location. Answers A and D are therefore incorrect.

A place will only be public if people are admitted with the permission, express or implied, of the owner of the land in question (see *DPP v Vivier* [1991] RTR 205). Because drivers of the vehicles were trespassing, the offence will *not* be complete as it may only take place on a road or public place and therefore answer B is incorrect.

Road Policing, paras 3.3.2, 3.1.11

Answer 3.2

Answer **C** — In some circumstances the condition of the driver will be relevant. In *R v Pleydell* [2005] EWCA Crim 1447, the court found that the mere presence of a controlled drug (such as cocaine) in a driver's blood may of itself be relevant to the issue of whether a person drove dangerously—even if there is no specific evidence as to the drug's effect on the person's driving.

Turning to drink-related matters, in *R v Woodward* [1995] RTR 130, the courts held that evidence of drink will be admissible in an offence of causing the death of another by dangerous driving (under s. 1 of the Act) where the quantity of it may have adversely affected the quality of the defendant's driving. Answer D is incorrect for this reason.

There is no requirement to prove whether the defendant was above or below the prescribed limit, as that is not an element of the offence (*R v Mari* [2010] RTR 192); evidence of the amount of alcohol consumed and said to affect the defendant's ability to drive suffices. Answer A is therefore incorrect.

On the other hand, in *R v Webster* [2006] 2 Cr App R 103, it was held that the fact that a driver was adversely affected by alcohol is a circumstance relevant to the issue of dangerous driving, but is not in itself determinative to prove the offence. Answer B is therefore incorrect.

Road Policing, paras 3.3.2, 3.3.2.2

Answer 3.3

Answer **D** — To prove an offence under s. 1 of the Road Traffic Act 1988 (causing death by dangerous driving), it must be shown that a person other than the defendant died. The driving by the defendant must be shown to have been a cause of the death. It is not necessary to show that it was the sole or even a substantial cause of death (*R* v *Hennigan* [1971] 3 All ER 133). Answers A and C are therefore incorrect.

It is irrelevant whether or not the person killed contributed to the incident which resulted in his or her death. Answer B is therefore incorrect.

Road Policing, para. 3.3.2.1

Answer 3.4

Answer **A** — Section 2A(2) of the Road Traffic Act 1988 states:

(2) A person is also to be regarded as driving dangerously for the purposes of sections 1 and 2 above if it would be obvious to a competent and careful driver that driving the vehicle in its current state would be dangerous.

The test is an objective one which looks at the manner of driving and *not* at the defendant's state of mind. It must be proved that:

- the dangerous condition would itself have been obvious to a competent and careful driver; *or*
- the defendant actually *knew* of its condition

(*R* v *Strong* [1995] Crim LR 428).

Answer B is incorrect as the prosecution has to prove one of these requirements.

Answer C is incorrect for the same reason.

Answer D is incorrect as the dangerous driving must have been obvious to a competent and careful driver—not simply to DALEY herself.

However, see the case of *R* v *Marchant and Muntz* [2003] Crim LR 806, where the prosecution failed to convince the Court of Appeal that a vehicle was dangerous as a result of its being 'manufactured' in that way.

Road Policing, paras 3.3.2.2, 3.3.2.3

Answer 3.5

Answer **B** — Section 2A(2) of the Road Traffic Act 1988 states that a person is to be regarded as driving dangerously for the purposes of ss. 1, 1A and 2 if it would be obvious to a competent and careful driver that driving the vehicle in its current state would be dangerous. Therefore, an offence may be charged under s. 1A when the dangerous driving relates to the current state of the vehicle (answer D is therefore incorrect) and the standard of 'observation' required is what a 'competent and careful' driver would consider to be dangerous, and not the defendant. Answer C is therefore incorrect.

In relation to the dangerous state of a vehicle being 'obvious', no special definition is required and such an observation could arise from an inspection which is something between a fleeting glance and a long look (*R v Marsh* [2002] EWCA Crim 137). Since there is no need for that component and careful driver to have inspected the vehicle closely, answer A is incorrect.

Road Policing, paras 3.3.2.2, 3.3.2.3, 3.3.3

Answer 3.6

Answer **A** — Evidence showing how the particular vehicle was being driven before the incident itself *may* be given in support of the charge of dangerous driving.

However, care needs to be taken by the prosecution not to seek to adduce inadmissible evidence about the defendant's past bad driving (*R v McKenzie* [2008] EWCA Crim 758). Answer B is therefore incorrect.

The evidence REID is able to give of CALVIN's driving immediately before the incident is direct evidence and could be admitted in this case—even though REID is not an expert witness. On the other hand, the information regarding previous bad driving is hearsay and inadmissible. Answers C and D are therefore incorrect.

Road Policing, para. 3.3.4

Answer 3.7

Answer **B** — Whether a witness is properly qualified in the subject calling for expertise is a question for the court. Such competence or skill may stem from formal study or training, experience, or both.

In *R v Oakley* [1979] Crim LR 657, a police officer who had attended a course, passed an exam as a collision investigator, and attended more than 400 accidents was entitled to give expert evidence as to the cause of a collision. Answers A and D are therefore incorrect.

The investigation of road traffic collisions is a science that has professional qualifications attached to it, and mathematical calculations that would not look out of place on a rocket scientist's desk! Although it is likely that factual evidence will be available, a police officer meeting the *Oakley* criteria may give purely an opinion of how the collision occurred. Answer C is therefore incorrect.

Road Policing, para. 3.3.4

Answer 3.8

Answer **B** — A conviction for dangerous driving is covered by s. 36 of the Road Traffic Offenders Act 1988.

(1) Where this subsection applies to a person the court must order him to be disqualified until he passes the appropriate driving test...

(5) 'appropriate driving test' means—
   (a) an extended driving test, where a person is convicted of an offence involving obligatory disqualification or is disqualified under section 35 of this Act...

Disqualification is compulsory; therefore answers C and D are incorrect. As can be seen, this disqualification runs until an extended test has been passed; answer A is therefore incorrect.

Road Policing, para. 3.3.4

Answer 3.9

Answer **D** — A person is to be regarded as driving without due care and attention if (and only if) the way he or she drives falls below what would be expected of a competent and careful driver (s. 3ZA(2)). This element distinguishes dangerous driving from careless driving in that the dangerous driver falls *far* below the required standard, while the careless driver merely falls below the required standard and therefore answer B is incorrect.

Once the prosecution has proved that the defendant has departed from that standard, and that his or her actions were 'voluntary', the offence is complete. There is no requirement to prove any *knowledge* or *awareness* by the defendant that his or her driving fell below that standard (*R v Lawrence* [1982] AC 510). Answers A and C are therefore incorrect.

Road Policing, para. 3.3.5.1

Answer 3.10

Answer **A** — The Administrative Court has accepted that there will be a defence available to a charge of careless driving where the driver can show that for some reason they were distracted (*Plunkett* v *DPP* [2004] EWHC 1937). Answer D is therefore incorrect.

However, each case will be considered on its merits by the courts and certain factors, including the nature and extent of the distraction in question. Among these factors will be:

- how long the distraction was;
- the speed of the vehicle;
- any other hazards present.

This list is not exclusive, but since speed *may* be a factor for consideration by the court, answer C is incorrect.

The *Plunkett* case demonstrates that the court *may* consider distraction as a defence, even when the driver was not responding to an emergency situation. Answer B is therefore incorrect.

Road Policing, para. 3.3.5.1

Answer 3.11

Answer **C** — An offence is committed under s. 3 of the Road Traffic Act 1988 when a person drives a mechanically propelled vehicle on a road or public place, without due care and attention, or without due consideration for other persons using the road or public place.

Other persons using the road or public place can include pedestrians who are deliberately sprayed with water from a puddle, or passengers in a vehicle (*Pawley* v *Wharldall* [1966] 1 QB 373). Answers B and D are therefore incorrect.

It must be shown that another road user was *actually* inconvenienced by the defendant's driving; it is not enough that there was potential for inconvenience (see s. 3ZA(4)). Since the people in the bus shelter were not affected by WARE's actions, answer A is incorrect.

Road Policing, para. 3.3.5.1

Answer 3.12

Answer **D** — Breaching certain road traffic regulations will always be *potentially* relevant evidence of poor driving, but will not always be conclusive of the issue. Answer A is therefore incorrect.

Also, colliding with another vehicle has been held *not* to amount to sufficient evidence in itself of careless driving and therefore answer B is incorrect.

Finally, simply breaching the regulations at a pedestrian crossing is not of itself proof that the person's driving fell below the required standard (*Gibbons* v *Kahl* [1956] 1 QB 59). Answer C is therefore incorrect.

It should be noted that the fact that a traffic signal is showing a green light does *not* mean that a driver is entitled to assume that no other person or vehicle might be proceeding from another direction and it may be that, in the circumstances, a reasonably careful driver would have anticipated that a pedestrian or other road user might still move into his or her path (see *Goddard and Walker* v *Greenwood* [2002] EWCA Civ 1590). However, this case still does not support the point that a person may be prosecuted for a s. 3 offence, without further evidence.

Road Policing, para. 3.3.7.1

Answer 3.13

Answer **C** — Under s. 3A(1) of the Road Traffic Act 1988, if a person causes the death of another person by driving a mechanically propelled vehicle on a road or other public place without due care and attention, or without reasonable consideration for other persons using the road or place, and:

(a) he or she is, at the time when he or she is driving, unfit to drive through drink or drugs, or

(b) he or she has consumed so much alcohol that the proportion of it in his or her breath, blood or urine at that time exceeds the prescribed limit, or

(c) he or she is, within 18 hours after that time, required to provide a specimen in pursuance of s. 7 of this Act, but without reasonable excuse fails to provide it, or

(d) he or she is required by a constable to give his or her permission for a laboratory test of a specimen of blood taken from him or her under s. 7A of this Act, but without reasonable excuse fails to do so, he or she is guilty of an offence.

Section 3A(1)(d) was added by the Road Safety Act 2006 and by failing to give permission for the blood sample to be sent for a laboratory test, without reasonable excuse, RICHARDS commits this offence and therefore answer B is incorrect.

This is a *separate* requirement under s. 3A(1), therefore, it is immaterial whether or not the constable suspected RICHARDS had been drinking, or whether the request was made within 18 hours of the accident. Answers A and D are therefore incorrect.

Road Policing, para. 3.3.6

Answer 3.14

Answer **B** — Under s. 3A(1) of the Road Traffic Act 1988, if a person causes the death of another person by driving a mechanically propelled vehicle on a road or other public place without due care and attention, or without reasonable consideration for other persons using the road or place, and:

(a) he is, at the time when he is driving, unfit to drive through drink or drugs, or
(b) he has consumed so much alcohol that the proportion of it in his breath, blood or urine at that time exceeds the prescribed limit, or
(c) he is, within 18 hours after that time, required to provide a specimen in pursuance of section 7 of this Act, but without reasonable excuse fails to provide it, he is guilty of an offence.

In the first instance, a person must have driven without due care and attention, or without reasonable consideration for other persons using the road or place, which is why answer B is correct, and answer D is incorrect.

The offence may be committed by a person driving a mechanically propelled vehicle on a road or other public place, therefore answer C is incorrect.

Finally, the defendant may commit this offence if, at the time, he or she is unfit to drive through drink or drugs, or over the limit due to drink. Answer A is therefore incorrect.

Road Policing, para. 3.3.6

Answer 3.15

Answer **D** — Under s. 3ZB of the Road Traffic Act 1988, a person is guilty of an offence if he or she causes the death of another person by driving a motor vehicle on a road, and at the time the circumstances are such that he or she is committing an offence under:

(a) s. 87(1) of this Act (driving otherwise than in accordance with a licence), or
(b) s. 103(1)(b) of this Act (driving while disqualified), or
(c) s. 143 of this Act (using a motor vehicle while uninsured).

The fact that ADAMS has a full driving licence is irrelevant, because the offence may also be committed by a person in *any* of these circumstances. Answers A and C are therefore incorrect.

There is no requirement under this section to show that the driver actually drove without due care and attention (or dangerously or without reasonable consideration for other persons using the road). The offence is complete when a person causes the death of another, coupled with the required offence under s. 3ZB(a)–(c) and an uninsured, unlicensed or disqualified driver may commit this offence notwithstanding that the quality of his or her driving was otherwise excellent. (See *R* v *Williams* [2010] EWCA Crim 2552, where the deceased walked directly into the path of the uninsured defendant's car. The conviction was upheld despite the lack of any fault in the quality of the defendant's driving.) Answer B is therefore incorrect.

Note that this offence may only be committed by the driver of a motor vehicle (not a mechanically propelled vehicle) on a road.

Road Policing, para. 3.3.8

Answer 3.16

Answer **D** — Under s. 38(7) of the Road Traffic Act 1988, a failure on the part of a person to observe a provision of the Highway Code shall not of itself render that person liable to criminal proceedings of any kind. However, any such failure may be introduced into civil *or* criminal proceedings. Answer B is therefore incorrect.

The stopping distances shown in the Highway Code are not admissible in proving speeding cases in court, as they amount to hearsay (*R* v *Chadwick* [1975] Crim LR 105). Answer C is incorrect, because such evidence may not be introduced into *all* civil and criminal proceedings.

The failure to observe a provision of the Highway Code may be introduced to establish *or* negate any liability as to a person's driving, therefore, it may be introduced by the prosecution or the defence, and therefore answer A is incorrect.

Road Policing, para. 3.3.9

Answer 3.17

Answer **B** — Under s. 168(b) of the Road Traffic Act 1988, the rider of a cycle who is alleged to have committed an offence under s. 28 or s. 29 of this Act (dangerous or careless cycling), who refuses, on being so required by any person having reasonable grounds for so requiring, to give his or her name or address, or gives a false name or address, is guilty of an offence.

Since the rider must give these details to *any person having reasonable grounds for so requiring*, answer C is incorrect.

The offences to which this section applies include dangerous *and* careless cycling; therefore, answer D is incorrect.

Finally, there is no requirement for a person to be injured as a result of the driving and therefore answer A is incorrect.

Road Policing, para. 3.3.11

Answer 3.18

Answer **A** — Under s. 168 of the Road Traffic Act 1988, the driver of a mechanically propelled vehicle who is alleged to have committed an offence under s. 2 or s. 3 of the Act, who refuses, on being so required by any person having reasonable grounds for so requiring, to give his name or address, or gives a false name or address, is guilty of an offence. Since the offence applies to those who refuse *or* those who give false details, answer D is incorrect.

The section uses the word 'refuses', but makes no mention of a failure to provide the required details. Section 11 of the Road Traffic Act 1988 states:

(1) The following provisions apply for the interpretation of sections 3A to 10 of this Act.
(2) In those sections—'drug' includes any intoxicant other than alcohol, 'fail' includes refuse...

The interpretation of 'fail' in s. 11 of the Road Traffic Act 1988 only applies to ss. 3A to 10 of the Act, and not to s. 168, and although subs. (2) makes provision for a 'fail-ure' to include a 'refusal' (in relation to drink driving offences), the Act says nothing about a vice versa situation. Given that omission, together with the fact that the courts have held (albeit in an employment law case) that 'failure' is not synonymous with 'refusal' (see *Lowson v Percy Main & District Social Club and Institute Ltd* [1979] ICR 568), it would seem that a mere failure to provide the details required under s. 168 will not amount to the offence. Answers B and C are therefore incorrect.

Don't forget that the original offence is still committed and there is existing legisla-tion to take the offender to court to answer that charge.

Road Policing, para. 3.3.11

4 | Reportable Accidents

STUDY PREPARATION

The law relating to road traffic 'accidents' is primarily concerned with obligations on the drivers involved and the offences for failing to comply with those obligations. Throughout this chapter we will use the term 'road traffic collision', which is in line with current policing practice.

The most important bit of this subject is knowing what amounts to an 'accident' or 'collision'. You need to be able to recognise from the fact pattern of a question whether an 'accident' has happened. Then you need to know what obligations the law imposes and upon whom. You also need to know any offences which may apply, along with the attendant police powers.

QUESTIONS

Question 4.1

SULLIVAN and his friend HARRIS drove to the local shops. SULLIVAN was driving, although both had consumed 4 pints of cider. They parked outside a shop at the top of a hill and SULLIVAN went inside, leaving HARRIS in the passenger seat, saying 'I'll be back now'. For a joke HARRIS let off the handbrake and let the car roll downhill. HARRIS did not touch the steering wheel but unfortunately the car was travelling so fast that when he tried to apply the handbrake to stop it, it failed and the car collided with a pedestrian, severely injuring them. SULLIVAN saw this from the top of the hill and ran off, fearing being breathalysed, straight past the local police station.

> Who has a responsibility under s. 170 of the Road Traffic Act 1988 (duty of a driver to stop and exchange details) in these circumstances?

A HARRIS has the responsibility under s. 170, as the driver at the time of the collision.

B Both SULLIVAN and HARRIS have the responsibility under s. 170; both were drivers at the time of the collision.

C SULLIVAN committed offences of failing to stop and failing to report the collision, contrary to s. 170.

D SULLIVAN committed offences of failing to stop and failing to report the collision, contrary to s. 170, in addition to perverting the course of justice.

Question 4.2

While driving his car, DAWSON was involved in a road traffic collision with a motor cycle being ridden by WINTER. WINTER suffered cuts and grazes as a result. The drivers exchanged details and WINTER asked DAWSON for his insurance certificate. DAWSON did not have it with him, but gave WINTER the name of his insurance company and promised to show him the certificate the next day.

Has DAWSON complied with the requirements of s. 170 of the Road Traffic Act 1988 in these circumstances?

A Yes, he is not obliged to produce his insurance certificate to another driver, provided he gives the name of his insurance company.

B No, he must report the collision to the police as soon as reasonably practicable, and produce his insurance certificate within seven days.

C No, he must report the collision to the police as soon as reasonably practicable, and produce his insurance certificate at the same time.

D Yes, provided he produces his insurance certificate to WINTER within 24 hours.

Question 4.3

BENNETT was involved in a road traffic collision, while driving his employer's van. He drove into the rear of a car at a set of traffic lights. BENNETT was asked by the driver of the other vehicle for his name and address only. BENNETT gave his own name, but gave his employer's address as he was driving a works vehicle.

Has BENNETT complied with s. 170(2) of the Road Traffic Act 1988 (duty to stop and give details) in these circumstances?

A No, he should also have given the name of the owner of the vehicle to the other driver.

B No, he should also have given the name of the owner of the vehicle, and the registration number to the other driver.

C Yes, he has complied fully with the requirements of the Act in these circumstances.

D No, he should have given his own address to the other driver, not his employer's.

Question 4.4

McQUIRTER was involved in a road traffic collision where he aquaplaned on a wet road and hit a brick wall. He suffered whiplash injuries from the force of the spin and slight shock; his passenger, however, was uninjured. There were no other vehicles involved and the wall was undamaged. However, a bystander witnessed the incident. McQUIRTER drove straight home where he saw his neighbour, an off-duty police officer, in the garden and told her about the incident. Shortly afterwards, an on-duty police officer attended McQUIRTER's address as a result of a call from the witness. McQUIRTER told the officer he was just about to go to the police station and told the officer about the incident.

At what point, if any, did McQUIRTER comply with the requirements of s. 170 of the Road Traffic Act 1988?

A At no point, but he did not have to comply with s. 170.

B At no point, and he committed two separate offences in relation to s. 170.

C When he told a police officer; the fact she was off-duty is immaterial.

D When he told the on-duty police officer who arrived at his house.

Question 4.5

DERBYSHIRE was driving a motor vehicle on a road when she received a mobile phone call. DERBYSHIRE answered the call but did not have a hands-free kit and she pulled over to the side of the road, continuing the conversation. While on the phone, DERBYSHIRE realised she needed some information that was in a briefcase in the back of the car. She opened the driver's door, intending to get her briefcase. However, she was unaware the BEVAN was passing her vehicle at the time on a pedal cycle. DERBYSHIRE's actions caused BEVAN to collide with the car door and BEVAN was injured, falling off the cycle.

Because of her actions, does DERBYSHIRE attract any responsibility under s. 170 of the Road Traffic Act 1988 (duty of a driver to stop and exchange details) in these circumstances?

A Yes, provided the engine of DERBYSHIRE's vehicle was still running when she opened the door.

B No, DERBYSHIRE was not driving when the accident happened.

C Yes, provided it can be shown that DERBYSHIRE was at fault for the accident.
D Yes, whether or not the engine was still running, or whether or not she was at fault for the accident.

Question 4.6

MILLER drove a bus with 16 passenger seats and was employed by the local authority to drive children to school. The bus was approaching a set of traffic lights near the school at which there was a queue of vehicles. MILLER had lost concentration and had to brake sharply on the approach. This resulted in one of the school children falling over and banging their head. MILLER was told that one of the children was injured, but decided to carry on driving to the school, which was about 100 metres away.

Considering the driver's duty to stop, under s. 170(2) of the Road Traffic Act 1988, which of the following statements is correct in respect of MILLER's actions?

A The driver is required to stop at or near the scene and 100 metres away is not an unreasonable distance.
B The driver is required to stop at the scene and MILLER has failed to do so in these circumstances.
C The driver is required to stop at the scene; however, because damage has not been caused to another vehicle, MILLER's actions are not unreasonable in these circumstances.
D Because the injury was to a passenger in the bus, the bus could be considered to be the scene and MILLER's actions are not unreasonable in these circumstances.

Question 4.7

The police were called to an incident in a public car park on a Sunday evening. A group of young people were involved in racing each other. One of the vehicles had driven through a hedge and collided with a building adjacent to the car park and as a result, damage was caused to the building. The adjacent building was situated on private land.

Which of the following statements is correct in relation to 'property', as described in s. 170(1)(b)(iii) of the Road Traffic Act 1988?

A The property damaged was on private land and the requirements of s. 170 did not apply, because the car was not being driven on a road.
B Regardless of whether the property damaged was on private land, the requirements of s. 170 applied, because the vehicle was being driven on a road or public place.

C The property damaged was on private land and the requirements of s. 170 did not apply, regardless of whether the vehicle was being driven on a road or public place.

D Regardless of whether the damaged property was on private land, the requirements of s. 170 did not apply as the property was not fixed to, growing in or otherwise forming part of the land on which the collision occurred.

Question 4.8

CUTTER was involved in a collision in a multi-storey car park, which was open to the public at the time. CUTTER was driving out of a parking space in his van when he scraped the side of a parked car. CUTTER failed to stop after the collision; however, a witness noted his registration number. When he was traced by the police, CUTTER stated that he had not stopped as he was unaware of the collision.

Who would have responsibility for proving or disproving that CUTTER was unaware of the collision?

A The defence must show that on the balance of probabilities he was unaware of the collision.

B The prosecution must show that beyond reasonable doubt he would have been aware of the collision.

C The defence must show beyond reasonable doubt that he was unaware of the collision.

D The question is not relevant; there was no requirement to stop after the collision as it did not occur on a road.

Question 4.9

SAKI was involved in a road traffic collision, having driven into a stationary car in a rural area, late at night. SAKI tried to find the owner, but was unsuccessful. SAKI then found a police station nearby, but the station was closed. Finally, SAKI drove home, intending to report the collision in the morning.

Which of the following is correct in respect of SAKI's duty to report the collision under s. 170 of the Road Traffic Act 1988?

A SAKI has made reasonable efforts to report the collision; provided it is reported within 24 hours, s. 170 will have been complied with.

B Although SAKI has made efforts to report the collision, it must still be reported as soon as practicable, in person to a constable.

C Although SAKI has made efforts to report the collision, it must still be reported as soon as practicable, in person to a constable or at a police station.

D SAKI may report the collision by telephone, having made reasonable efforts to report it in person, provided this is done as soon as practicable.

Question 4.10

NEWENT was driving a car on the road. Due to a lack of concentration, NEWENT collided with a trailer, which had been left at the side of the road, unattached to a motor vehicle. Damage was caused to both NEWENT's car and the trailer.

Which of the following statements is correct in respect of NEWENT's duty to comply with the requirements of s. 170 of the Road Traffic Act 1988 (stopping and reporting a collision)?

A The trailer is not a vehicle, as it was not being drawn by a motor vehicle; therefore, s. 170 does not apply in these circumstances.

B The trailer is not a vehicle as it was not attached to a motor vehicle; therefore, s. 170 does not apply in these circumstances.

C The trailer is a vehicle; therefore, s. 170 does apply in these circumstances.

D The trailer is not a vehicle, but is property; therefore, s. 170 does apply in these circumstances.

Question 4.11

JIMENEZ was driving a Motorhome on the motorway and was towing a Smart car behind the Motorhome, which the family would use as a runaround when they reached their holiday destination. As JIMENEZ was driving, the tow hitch attaching the Smart car to the Motorhome broke and the car detached itself, falling away from the towing vehicle. The Smart car collided with another car which was driving behind JIMENEZ, causing damage to both vehicles.

Considering s. 170 of the Road Traffic Act 1988, which of the following statements is correct, in respect of 'reportable accidents'?

A The Smart car was not a mechanically propelled vehicle as it was being towed; therefore, a reportable accident has not occurred in these circumstances.

B The Smart car was not a mechanically propelled vehicle as it was not being 'driven' while it was being towed; therefore, a reportable accident has not occurred in these circumstances.

C The Smart car was neither a mechanically propelled vehicle nor a trailer while it was being towed; therefore, a reportable accident has not occurred in these circumstances.

D An accident has occurred owing to the presence of a mechanically propelled vehicle on a road; therefore, it is irrelevant whether the Smart car was being towed or not.

Question 4.12

HULL is employed as a care worker for the elderly. HULL had taken BROOKFIELD (aged 85 years) to a shopping centre and on the way home was involved in a road traffic accident. BROOKFIELD (seated in the front passenger seat) suffered shock and HULL suffered whiplash as a consequence of the accident. HULL was concerned about her position as a care worker and decided not to report the accident, hoping that BROOKFIELD would not tell anyone and no one would notice that she had suffered from shock. Two days later, BROOKFIELD's daughter found out about the incident and contacted the police. By then, however, BROOKFIELD had recovered from her shock.

Would HULL be guilty of an offence under s. 170(4) of the Road Traffic Act 1988 (failing to report) in these circumstances?

A Yes, the offence is complete.

B No, because the personal injuries were caused to people in HULL's car only.

C No, the shock suffered by BROOKFIELD is not classed as a personal injury.

D No, the shock suffered by BROOKFIELD was not a permanent or lasting injury.

Question 4.13

FORSYTHE was driving a motor vehicle on an isolated country road when he lost control on a bend and collided with a fence adjacent to the road. The fence was damaged and FORSYTHE suffered concussion from the accident. There was no one else around at the time and FORSYTHE decided to drive himself to hospital. After being discharged from hospital, FORSYTHE was considering whether or not to make enquiries to find the owner of the fence or, believing that there were no witnesses, wondering whether he could get away with not paying for the damage.

Which of the following statements is correct, in relation to offences either under s. 170(2) (failing to stop at the scene of an accident) or s. 170(3) (failing to report an accident) of the Road Traffic Act 1988?

A FORSYTHE could be guilty of an offence under s. 170(3), if he fails to report the matter to the police.
B The requirement to stop and report the accident may be negated by the fact that FORSYTHE had to go to hospital.
C FORSYTHE could be guilty of both offences if he fails to report the matter to the police, or fails to return to the scene to find the owner of the fence.
D FORSYTHE could be guilty of both offences if he fails to report the matter to the police, but the prosecution would have to decide which offence to proceed with; only one offence should be prosecuted under s. 170.

Question 4.14

SANDHURST was driving along a country lane which led to a popular beach. There were cars parked on either side of the lane and SANDHURST clipped the side of a vehicle, causing damage to it. There were people in the vicinity walking to the beach, none of whom appeared to be connected to the parked vehicle. SANDHURST was concerned about causing an obstruction to the lane and, after a few minutes, left a note under the windscreen wiper of the vehicle with a contact telephone number.

Which of the following statements is correct, in relation to SANDHURST's duties under s. 170(2) of the Road Traffic Act 1988 (requirement to stop after an accident)?
A SANDHURST was required to remain at the scene for such a time as would allow her to give her details to the owner of the vehicle.
B SANDHURST was required to remain at the scene for such a time as would allow anyone having a right or reason for doing so to ask for her details.
C SANDHURST was required to remain at the scene for such a time as would allow any person to ask for her details.
D SANDHURST was required to remain at the scene for such a time as would allow her to give her details to the owner of the vehicle, or alternatively, for her to make enquiries to find such a person.

Question 4.15

JORDAN was involved in a road traffic collision when he drove into a parked vehicle, causing damage to it. JORDAN sustained a head injury during the collision and was taken to the nearest hospital by BRUIN, a passenger in his vehicle at the time. JORDAN was detained at the hospital, eventually being released 12 hours after the collision.

4. Reportable Accidents

Which of the following statements is correct, in relation to s. 170(3) of the Road Traffic Act 1988 (duty to report an accident)?

A JORDAN must report the accident within 24 hours; however, s. 170(3) allows for a reasonable time in which to comply, when the *defendant* is unable to make the report.

B JORDAN has up to 24 hours to report the accident; therefore, he has another 12 hours in which to comply with s. 170(3).

C JORDAN must report the accident within 24 hours; it does not matter what the reason for the non-provision of the information is.

D JORDAN must report the accident within 24 hours; however, s. 170(3) allows for a reasonable time in which to comply, where the *police* are unavailable to take the report.

ANSWERS

Answer 4.1

Answer **C** — In *Cawthorn* v *DPP* [2000] RTR 45, the driver (*Cawthorn*) had left his vehicle on a road with its hazard warning lights on while he ran to a post box. While the driver was away from the vehicle, the passenger let off the handbrake and the vehicle had coasted downhill into a wall.

The court held that even though there may have been a break in the actual driving of the vehicle, the driver may still be under the obligations imposed by s. 170 if an accident occurs while he or she is away from it. The driver, therefore, still had a duty to report the accident, even given the fact that a passenger may have been directly responsible for the collision. Since this responsibility belonged to SULLIVAN, as the driver, answers A and B are incorrect.

Had SULLIVAN run straight into the police station he may have complied with his duty to report, but no doubt scored an 'own goal' with the breathalyser procedure!

The Court of Appeal has refused to accept that a driver who failed to stop and report an accident for fear of being breathalysed did not, without more, commit an offence of perverting the course of justice (*R* v *Clark* [2003] EWCA 991); therefore answer D is incorrect.

Road Policing, paras 3.4.2, 3.4.3, 3.1.6

Answer 4.2

Answer **C** — If a driver is involved in a collision where injury is caused to another person, he or she must, at the time of the collision, produce a certificate of insurance to a constable *or* any person having reasonable grounds for requiring it (s. 170(5) of the Road Traffic Act 1988). Answer A is therefore incorrect.

If the driver does not produce his or her insurance certificate as required, he or she *must* report the accident to the police *and* produce an insurance certificate as soon as practicable, and in any case within 24 hours (s. 170(6)).

Answer D is incorrect as once a driver fails to produce a certificate at the scene to the other driver, the requirement moves to reporting the collision and producing the certificate to the police.

Answer B is incorrect as the requirement is to report the collision *and* produce the insurance certificate as soon as practicable and within 24 hours. Under s. 170(7) of the 1988 Act, a person will escape prosecution for failing to produce insurance at the time of the collision, or later at the police station, if he or she produces it within seven days from the collision (usually as a result of the issue of an HORT/1). Therefore, although answer B may appear correct, the *first* process must be to report the collision and produce the certificate as soon as practicable.

Road Policing, paras 3.4.2, 3.4.3

Answer 4.3

Answer **C** — Under s. 170(2) of the Road Traffic Act 1988, the driver of a vehicle involved in a road traffic collision must stop and *if required to do so* by some person having reasonable grounds, give his or her name and address and also the name and address of the owner of the vehicle, and the registration mark of the vehicle.

Because the driver of the other vehicle did not ask for the name of the owner and the registration mark, BENNETT commits no offence by failing to give them. Answers A and B are therefore incorrect.

It has been held that, as the reason for the requirement to 'exchange details' is to allow future communications between parties, the address of the driver's solicitor would satisfy the requirements of s. 170(2) (*DPP* v *McCarthy* [1999] RTR 323). Answer D is therefore incorrect.

Road Policing, paras 3.4.2, 3.4.2.2

Answer 4.4

Answer **A** — Section 170 of the Road Traffic Act 1988 states:

(1) This section applies in a case where, owing to the presence of a mechanically propelled vehicle on a road or other public place, an accident occurs by which—
   (a) personal injury is caused to a person other than the driver of that mechanically propelled vehicle, or
   (b) damage is caused—
      (i)   to a vehicle other than that mechanically propelled vehicle or a trailer drawn by that mechanically propelled vehicle, or
      (ii) to an animal other than an animal in or on that mechanically propelled vehicle or a trailer drawn by that mechanically propelled vehicle, or
      (iii) to any other property constructed on, fixed to, growing in or otherwise forming part of the land on which the road or place in question is situated or land adjacent to such land…

Applying this principle, only the driver is injured; damage is not caused to another vehicle, roadside property or animal. In the circumstances of the scenario, s. 170 does not apply to McQUIRTER and he has done nothing wrong; therefore answers B, C and D are incorrect.

Note however that had subs. (1) applied in these circumstances, McQUIRTER's duty to stop and report is probably not discharged by waiting until the police call at his house and then telling them (see *Dawson* v *Winter* (1932) 49 TLR 128 *obiter*); neither is it discharged if the driver tells a friend who happens to be a police officer (*Mutton* v *Bates* [1984] RTR 256).

Road Policing, paras 3.4.2, 3.4.2.4

Answer 4.5

Answer **D** — It has been held that even though a driver may not have been to blame for a collision, he or she will still attract the duties imposed by s. 170 of the Road Traffic Act 1988 (*Harding* v *Price* [1948] 1 All ER 283). Answer C is therefore incorrect.

For the purposes of some road traffic offences, the person who takes out the vehicle remains the 'driver' of it until they have finished that journey. Therefore, even if the vehicle is stationary and has been for some time, a person may still be the 'driver' of it if they have not completed the journey (see *Jones* v *Prothero* [1952] 1 All ER 434, where the driver sitting in a parked car opened the offside door causing injury to a passing pedal cyclist).

A further example was seen in *Cawthorn* v *DPP* [2000] RTR 45, where the defendant stopped his car on a hill in order to post a letter and activated the hazard warning lights. While he was away from the vehicle, it started to roll down the hill and hit and damaged a wall. The roll was started by a passenger releasing the handbrake. The defendant left the scene and was subsequently convicted of failing to stop and exchange details and failing to report an accident. The Divisional Court said that, although there had been a break in the driving, the appellant was still making his journey as evidenced by the use of the hazard warning lights. The intervening act by the passenger did not make that passenger the driver.

Both *Jones* and *Cawthorn* relate to the obligations of a 'driver' under s. 170 of the Road Traffic Act 1988 and confirm that a person in DERBYSHIRE's circumstances *could* still have been driving when the accident occurred, and could have been so whether the engine of the vehicle was running or not. Answers A and B are therefore incorrect.

Road Policing, paras 3.4.2, 3.1.6

Answer 4.6

Answer **B** — The requirement to stop under s. 170(2) of the Road Traffic Act 1988 means to stop safely and remain *at the scene* for such a time as would allow anyone having a right or reason for doing so to ask for information from the driver (*Lee* v *Knapp* [1967] 2 QB 442). Whether or not the vehicle stops at the appropriate point is a question of fact; where a driver choose to drive on for 80 yards before stopping and returning to the scene of the accident, the Divisional Court was not prepared to interfere with a decision finding that this constituted a failure to stop as required (*McDermott* v *DPP* [1997] RTR 474). The offence is complete as soon as the failure to stop occurs. Answer A is therefore incorrect.

Where a bus driver braked hard, causing injury to one of his passengers, the Divisional Court held that he had a duty to stop at the place and the time that the passenger was caused to be injured. It was not open to the driver to claim that the bus itself was the scene of the accident. The fact that the driver failed to stop immediately meant that he was guilty of an offence under s. 170(4) (*Hallinan* v *DPP* [1998] Crim LR 754)—this is regardless of whether any other vehicles are involved and therefore answers C and D are incorrect.

Road Policing, paras 3.4.2, 3.4.2.1

Answer 4.7

Answer **B** — Under s. 170(1)(b)(iii) of the Road Traffic Act 1988, if owing to the presence of a mechanically propelled vehicle on a road or other public place, an accident occurs by which damage is caused to any other property constructed on, fixed to, growing in or otherwise forming part of the land on which the road or place in question is situated or land adjacent to such land, there will be a requirement on the driver to stop and report an accident.

Since the requirements apply when damage is caused to property which is 'adjacent' to land, answer D is incorrect.

Section 170(1)(b)(iii) makes no distinction between private land or public land adjacent to the road or public place where the collision occurred. Provided damage was caused to the land, the general requirements under s. 170 apply and therefore answers A and C are incorrect.

Road Policing, para. 3.4.2

Answer 4.8

Answer **A** — The case of *Cutter* v *Eagle Star Insurance Co. Ltd* [1998] 4 All ER 417 changed the requirements under s. 170 of the Road Traffic Act 1988. Prior to this case, a collision was not 'reportable' unless it occurred on a road. The section has now been extended to include 'public places'. Since the car park was open to any member of the public, it was a public place and covered by s. 170. Answer D is therefore incorrect.

When a driver alleges he or she was unaware that a collision had taken place, it is for the defence to show *on the balance of probabilities* that this was the case (*Selby* v *Chief Constable of Avon and Somerset* [1988] RTR 216). Answers B and C are therefore incorrect.

Road Policing, paras 3.4.2, 3.1.10

Answer 4.9

Answer **C** — Under s. 170(2) of the Road Traffic Act 1988, the driver of a mechanically propelled vehicle involved in an accident must stop and, if required to do so by any person having reasonable grounds for so requiring, give his or her name and address and also the name and address of the owner and the identification marks of the vehicle.

If for any reason the driver of the mechanically propelled vehicle does not give his or her name and address under subs. (2), he or she must report the accident (s. 170(3)).

Under s. 170(6), to comply with this duty, the driver:

(a) must do so at a police station or to a constable, and
(b) must do so as soon as is reasonably practicable and, in any case, within twenty-four hours of the occurrence of the accident.

Section 170(6)(a) allows for the collision to be reported *either* at a police station *or* to a constable. Therefore, if the collision is reported at a police station, the provisions of s. 170(6) will be met even if the person receiving the report is a police staff member— which reflects the reality of modern policing, where most station enquiry offices are staffed by police staff members and not police officers. Alternatively, the collision can be reported to a police officer (either at a police station or anywhere else). Answer B is therefore incorrect.

This must also be done *in person*; telephoning (and presumably sending a fax or email to) a police station is not enough (*Wisdom* v *McDonald* [1983] RTR 186). Answer D is therefore incorrect.

The driver is not given 24 hours to report the collision—in most circumstances there is no reason for a collision not to be reported as soon as practicable because of the availability of police officers 24 hours a day. Therefore, even though the person in the question has tried to contact the police, there is still a requirement to report the accident as soon as practicable. Answer A is therefore incorrect.

Road Policing, para. 3.4.2.4

Answer 4.10

Answer **C** — The duties to stop and report accidents under s. 170 of the Road Traffic Act 1988 apply where, owing to the presence of a mechanically propelled vehicle on a road or other public place, an accident occurs by which personal injury is caused to a person other than the driver of that mechanically propelled vehicle, or damage is caused:

- to a vehicle other than that mechanically propelled vehicle or a trailer drawn by that mechanically propelled vehicle, or
- to an animal other than an animal in or on that mechanically propelled vehicle or a trailer drawn by that mechanically propelled vehicle, or
- to any other property constructed on, fixed to, growing in or otherwise forming part of the land on which the road or place in question is situated or land adjacent to such land.

In the first instance, the trailer cannot be 'property'; therefore, answer D is incorrect.

A 'trailer' is defined under s. 185(1) of the Act as a vehicle drawn by a motor vehicle. However, the definition under this section applies to circumstances when the trailer is being drawn by a motor vehicle (the 'offending vehicle') and damage is caused to something other than that trailer. The definition under s. 185(1) is irrelevant for the purposes of this question.

The next thing to establish is whether the trailer is a 'vehicle' in its own right, because s. 170 applies when damage is caused to a vehicle other than that mechanically propelled vehicle or a trailer drawn by that mechanically propelled vehicle. 'Vehicle' is not defined in the Act; the *Oxford English Dictionary* defines a 'vehicle' as a 'carriage or conveyance of any kind used on land'. In addition, the courts have ruled that virtually anything is capable of amounting to a vehicle under the right circumstances, even a chicken shed on wheels (see *Garner* v *Burr* [1951] 1 KB 31) or a hut (*Horn* v *Dobson* [1933] JC 1). In *Ellis* v *Nott-Bower* (1896) 60 JP 760, the court held that damage caused under the circumstances set out at s. 170(1)(b) applies to any vehicle (such as bicycles) and not just one which is mechanically propelled.

It follows, therefore, that a trailer parked at the side of the road will be a vehicle, even though it is not being drawn by, or is not attached to, a motor vehicle, and if damage is caused to it during a reportable accident, s. 170 will apply. Answers A and B are therefore incorrect.

Road Policing, paras 3.4.2, 3.1.3

Answer 4.11

Answer **D** — When a motor vehicle is towing another motor vehicle, the latter still falls within the category of motor vehicle, but can also be regarded as a 'trailer' (*Milstead v Sexton* [1964] Crim LR 474) and it is irrelevant whether the towed vehicle is being 'driven' at the time. Answers A, B and C are therefore incorrect.

However, the issue of whether the Smart car was a motor vehicle, a mechanically propelled vehicle or a trailer is irrelevant. The duties to stop and report accidents under s. 170 of the Road Traffic Act 1988 apply where, owing to the presence of a mechanically propelled vehicle on a road or other public place, an accident occurs by which personal injury is caused to a person other than the driver of that mechanically propelled vehicle, or damage is caused:

- to a vehicle other than that mechanically propelled vehicle or a trailer drawn by that mechanically propelled vehicle, or
- to an animal other than an animal in or on that mechanically propelled vehicle or a trailer drawn by that mechanically propelled vehicle, or
- to any other property constructed on, fixed to, growing in or otherwise forming part of the land on which the road or place in question is situated or land adjacent to such land.

The accident in these circumstances occurred owing to the presence of a mechanically propelled vehicle on a road, the Motorhome, and damage was caused to another vehicle. The presence of the Motorhome on the road, towing the Smart car, was the cause of the accident and it would be no different, for example, if a roof box had fallen off the Motorhome and damaged the vehicle behind it—damage would still have occurred to another vehicle, owing to the presence of the Motorhome on a road.

Road Policing, para. 3.4.2

Answer 4.12

Answer **A** — If the driver of the vehicle is the only person injured then the accident will not be reportable; it will, however, be reportable if the passenger in the vehicle is injured. Answer B is therefore incorrect.

Injury under s. 170 has been held to include shock and, given the developments in the area of assaults, it would appear that psychological harm may well amount to an 'injury' for these purposes. Answer C is therefore incorrect.

It is immaterial whether the injury was 'permanent or lasting' and for that reason answer D is incorrect.

Road Policing, paras 3.4.2, 3.4.2.3

Answer 4.13

Answer **A** — Under s. 170(2) of the Road Traffic Act 1988, the driver of a mechanically propelled vehicle involved in an accident must stop and, if required to do so by any person having reasonable grounds for so requiring, give his or her name and address and also the name and address of the owner and the identification marks of the vehicle.

If for any reason the driver of the mechanically propelled vehicle does not give his or her name and address under subs. (2), he or she must report the accident (s. 170(3)).

Under s. 170(6), to comply with this duty, the driver:

(a) must do so at a police station or to a constable, and
(b) must do so as soon as is reasonably practicable and, in any case, within twenty-four hours of the occurrence of the accident.

Section 170 imposes a clear obligation on the driver of a vehicle involved in an accident resulting in damage or injury to report the accident to the police. That requirement is not negated either by police attendance at the accident or by the driver being taken to hospital—*DPP v Hay* [2005] EWHC 1395.

'Stop' under s. 170(2) means to stop safely and remain at the scene for such a time as would allow anyone having a right or reason for doing so to ask for information from the driver (*Lee v Knapp* [1967] 2 QB 442); it does not require the driver to make enquiries of his or her own to try and find such a person (see *Mutton v Bates* [1984] RTR 256).

Therefore, while FORSYTHE clearly had an obligation to do something, he was not required to remain at the scene (which would have been unreasonable considering his injury), or even return there after being discharged from hospital. Answers B and C are therefore incorrect.

Answer D is incorrect for the same reasons, but it is also incorrect because of *Roper* v *Sullivan* [1978] RTR 181, where it was decided that if a driver fails to stop *and* fails to report an accident, he or she commits two offences.

Road Policing, paras 3.4.2, 3.4.2.1, 3.4.2.4, 3.4.3

Answer 4.14

Answer **B** — Section 170(2) of the Road Traffic Act 1988 states that:

the driver of the mechanically propelled vehicle must stop and, if required to do so by any person having reasonable grounds for so requiring, give his name and address and also the name and address of the owner and the identification marks of the vehicle.

'Stop' under s. 170(2) means to stop safely and remain at the scene for such a time as would allow anyone having a right or reason for doing so to ask for information from the driver (*Lee* v *Knapp* [1967] 2 QB 442). The requirement under s. 170(2) is not so narrow that the driver must remain at the scene to only provide details to the *owner* of the vehicle (answer A is therefore incorrect); conversely, the requirement is not so wide that the driver must remain to provide details to *any person*. Answer C is therefore incorrect.

Section 170(2) does *not* require the driver to make enquiries of his or her own to try and find such a person (see *Mutton* v *Bates* [1984] RTR 256) and for that reason answer D is incorrect.

Note that this duty also appears to require the driver to stay with his or her vehicle for a reasonable time (see *Ward* v *Rawson* [1978] RTR 498), but it does not require the driver to remain there indefinitely (*Norling* v *Woolacott* [1964] SASR 377).

Road Policing, para. 3.4.2.1

Answer 4.15

Answer **C** — Under s. 170(3) of the Road Traffic Act 1988, if there are no other persons in the vicinity to whom the information may be given, then the matter must be reported to a police officer or at a police station as soon as is reasonably practicable and, in any case, within 24 hours of the occurrence of the accident.

Section 170(3) does not allow for a reasonable time in which to comply, when the defendant is unable to make the report, or where the police are unavailable to take the report; therefore, answers A and D are incorrect.

The report must be made as soon as reasonably practicable (which will be a question of fact for the court to decide in each circumstance) and in any case within 24 hours of the occurrence of the incident. This requirement does *not* give the driver up to 24 hours to report the accident; that report must be made as soon as is reasonably practicable. Answer B is therefore incorrect.

It is possible that, given the requirement that the report must be made as soon as reasonably practicable, the person in this scenario might have a defence for not doing so. However, the section is prescriptive in that if the driver does *not* give his or her name and address, it does not matter what the reason for the non-provision of the information is, even if it is not practicable, or possible, to do so within that time limit (see *Bulman* v *Lakin* [1981] RTR 1).

Road Policing, para. 3.4.2.4

5 | Drink, Drugs and Driving

STUDY PREPARATION

This is a big one. The areas of law and procedure covered in this chapter are extensive. You will need to know the elements of each of the main drink driving offences first. Entwined with those offences is a range of police powers such as the powers to require breath samples. Recent changes to the Road Traffic Act 1988 allow police officers to administer three preliminary tests—a breath test, a test indicating whether a person is unfit to drive due to drink or drugs, and a test to detect the presence of drugs in a person's body. Failure or refusal to comply with such requirements can lead to further offences and further powers.

It is sometimes helpful to divide this subject area into roadside, police station and hospital procedures.

The evidential issues are also important and there is a great deal of established case law to clarify this area of the legislation.

QUESTIONS

Question 5.1

Constable HASKELL was on patrol in the evening when she came across an unoccupied vehicle, which had its engine running, and its driver's door open. The officer found RAINER asleep in a garden adjacent to the vehicle, sitting with his back against a tree. From the smell of intoxicants, Constable HASKELL formed the opinion that RAINER was drunk. The officer woke RAINER and administered a breath test, which proved positive.

Would Constable HASKELL's suspicion that RAINER had driven the vehicle be sufficient to convict RAINER of driving while over the prescribed limit under s. 5(1) of the Road Traffic Act 1988?

A No, it would provide sufficient evidence to arrest him, but not to convict RAINER.

B Yes, because RAINER failed a breath test, Constable HASKELL's suspicion would be sufficient.

C No, but it would be sufficient to convict RAINER of an offence under s. 4 of the Act.

D Yes, if RAINER is proved to be owner of the vehicle, Constable HASKELL's suspicion due to his close proximity to the vehicle would be sufficient.

Question 5.2

Constable BOTAN was walking past a public car park when PALMER called him over. PALMER pointed out HODGES, who was driving around the car park on a quad bike and being cheered on by a group of teenagers. PALMER had seen HODGES drinking cans of lager earlier and was concerned for the safety of people using the car park. Constable BOTAN managed to stop the vehicle and on speaking to HODGES, formed the opinion that he was drunk.

Given that the quad bike was a mechanically propelled vehicle (and not a motor vehicle), has HODGES committed an offence under either s. 4(1) (unfit to drive through drink or drugs) or s. 5(1) (driving while over the prescribed limit) of the Road Traffic Act 1988?

A Yes, under s. 4(1), as HODGES was driving a mechanically propelled vehicle in a public place.

B Yes, under either section, as HODGES was driving a mechanically propelled vehicle in a public place.

C No, HODGES was not driving a motor vehicle on a road.

D No, HODGES was not driving a motor vehicle or a mechanically propelled vehicle on a road.

Question 5.3

Constable LANGLEY was following a vehicle being driven by FORSYTHE. The officer observed the vehicle being driven erratically, swerving across the road. Constable LANGLEY lost sight of the vehicle, but following a computer check, attended FORSYTHE's home address. On arrival, Constable LANGLEY saw FORSYTHE asleep inside the vehicle, which was inside a detached garage, a building adjacent to FORSYTHE's house. The garage door was open.

Given that the officer may have formed a reasonable suspicion that FORSYTHE was drunk, did Constable LANGLEY have the power to enter the garage or the vehicle, under s. 4 of the Road Traffic Act 1988?

A No, because the vehicle was inside a detached garage, which is not a dwelling for the purposes of s. 4.

B Yes, because the vehicle was inside a garage, which is a dwelling for the purposes of s. 4.

C Yes, but only the garage, as a vehicle is not a 'premises' for the purposes of s. 4.

D Yes, both the garage and the vehicle are 'premises' for the purposes of s. 4.

Question 5.4

Constable DERECK attended the Fox and Hounds Public House as a result of a call from the licensee, BELL. BELL had seen MEARS enter the premises from the car park in a drunken condition with some friends. They had bought two rounds of drinks when it had been brought to BELL's attention that MEARS had driven to the premises. Constable DERECK spoke to MEARS who admitted he had driven to the premises, but stated that he had only drunk two pints, which had been bought since he'd arrived. BELL was adamant that MEARS had been drunk when he'd arrived and that he was too intoxicated for someone who had only drunk two pints.

Considering the offence under s. 4 of the Road Traffic Act 1988, which of the following statements is correct, in relation to the evidence BELL has provided so far?

A BELL could give an opinion of MEARS's impairment and his ability to drive a vehicle on a road, which would provide sufficient evidence for Constable DERECK to arrest him for this offence.

B BELL's suspicion that MEARS had been drunk when he'd arrived would provide sufficient evidence for Constable DERECK to arrest him for this offence.

C BELL's opinion of MEARS's impairment would not be sufficient; Constable DERECK must formulate a separate reasonable suspicion of the defendant's condition before arresting him.

D BELL's opinion of MEARS's impairment would only provide sufficient evidence for Constable DERECK to arrest him for this offence if BELL was an expert on such matters.

Question 5.5

Constable SATO stopped HENSON who was driving a motor vehicle on a road at night. Constable SATO noticed that HENSON smelled of intoxicants and requested a sample of breath. The screening test proved negative; however, as HENSON was returning to her car, Constable SATO noticed that she was staggering, which gave the officer reason to believe that she was unfit to drive through drink, despite the negative screening test. Constable SATO then arrested HENSON under s. 4 of the Road Traffic Act 1988 (unfit to drive through drink or drugs).

Did Constable SATO act correctly in these circumstances?

A Yes, the officer was entitled to arrest HENSON in these circumstances alone.

B No, Constable SATO should have required HENSON to provide a further sample of breath before making this decision.

C No, Constable SATO could not have formed a reasonable suspicion that HENSON was unfit to drive through drink, as the screening test was negative.

D No, the arrest would only have been lawful if Constable SATO had suspected HENSON was unfit to drive through drugs.

Question 5.6

BEDFORD is appealing against a conviction for driving a motor vehicle on a road, while over the prescribed limit. The circumstances were that BEDFORD was on a night out and was bought several alcoholic drinks by friends. BEDFORD claims that she had told her friends to buy her soft drinks and she was unaware that the drinks she had consumed contained alcohol.

Which of the following statements is correct, regarding the responsibility BEDFORD had in relation to the proportion of alcohol in her body?

A BEDFORD had some positive duty to enquire whether the drinks contained alcohol before consuming them.

B BEDFORD had an absolute duty to enquire whether the drinks contained alcohol before consuming them.

C BEDFORD had no particular duty to enquire whether the drinks contained alcohol before consuming them.

D If BEDFORD's claim is correct, her friends had an absolute duty to inform her that the drinks contained alcohol before she consumed them.

Question 5.7

SHELLEY was charged with an offence of being in charge of his motor vehicle on a road, while over the prescribed limit, having been found asleep at the wheel of the vehicle one night. At his court hearing, SHELLEY claimed that he would not have driven the vehicle while he was still unfit to do so.

Who is responsible for proving or disproving SHELLEY's claim, that he was unlikely to drive the vehicle while unfit to do so?

A SHELLEY must demonstrate an arguable case that there was no likelihood of his driving while unfit to do so.

B The prosecution must demonstrate beyond reasonable doubt that there was a likelihood of SHELLEY driving while unfit to do so.

C SHELLEY must demonstrate on the balance of probabilities that there was no likelihood of his driving while unfit to do so.

D The prosecution must demonstrate on the balance of probabilities that there was a likelihood of SHELLEY driving while unfit to do so.

Question 5.8

Constable WARE attended a road in the city centre, due to a report from a CCTV operator that a vehicle had been seen being driven on a road with two deflated tyres. On arrival, Constable WARE saw BEDFORD sitting in the driver's seat of a vehicle, which had two deflated tyres and was stationary at the side of the road. A radio call confirmed that the CCTV operator had seen BEDFORD driving that vehicle prior to the officer's arrival.

Would Constable WARE be entitled to breathalyse BEDFORD without further suspicion that the driver had consumed alcohol, using powers under s. 6(4)(b) of the Road Traffic Act 1988 (committing a traffic offence while a vehicle is in motion)?

A No, the vehicle was no longer in motion when Constable WARE arrived at the scene.

B Yes, Constable WARE had reason to suspect that BEDFORD had committed an offence while the vehicle was in motion.

C No, driving with deflated tyres is covered by the Road Vehicles (Construction and Use) Regulations 1986; therefore, the power under this section does not apply.

D Yes, the power under this section applies to any offence committed while a vehicle was in motion.

Question 5.9

While on patrol in plain clothes, Constable GUNNEY came across an accident involving two vehicles. Nobody was injured as a result of the accident. The officer called for uniformed officers to attend the scene to deal with the accident. While waiting, Constable GUNNEY noticed that VILLIS, the driver of one of the vehicles, smelled strongly of intoxicants. The uniformed officers took a considerable time to attend the scene, and Constable GUNNEY was considering whether to breathalyse VILLIS, prior to their arrival.

Which of the following statements is correct, in relation to Constable GUNNEY's decision?

A An officer making a requirement for any breath test must be in uniform; therefore, Constable GUNNEY is not able to make the request.

B An officer making a requirement for a breath test following an accident need not be in uniform; therefore, Constable GUNNEY is able to make the request.

C An officer administering a breath test in any circumstances need not be in uniform; therefore, Constable GUNNEY is able to conduct the test.

D An officer making a requirement for a breath test following an accident need not be in uniform, but only if the accident involved personal injury; therefore, Constable GUNNEY is not able to make the request.

Question 5.10

WHEELAN attended a police station to report a crime and spoke to Constable BLOOM. As they were speaking, the officer suspected that WHEELAN may have been drinking and asked whether she had been. WHEELAN stated she had and the officer asked whether or not she had driven to the station. Again, WHEELAN stated she had. Constable BLOOM requested a sample of breath from WHEELAN, which proved to be positive. WHEELAN was charged with the offence, but pleaded not guilty in court, stating that Constable BLOOM should have cautioned her prior to administering the breath test as their conversation constituted an interview.

Is the court likely to accept WHEELAN's defence in these circumstances?

A Yes, as the conversation occurred prior to the breath test, Constable BLOOM had formed the suspicion that WHEELAN had committed an offence and a caution was required.

B No, Constable BLOOM only formed the suspicion an offence had been committed after the breath test was administered, therefore a caution was not required.

C Yes, the questions asked by Constable BLOOM were preliminary to a breath test and designed to establish whether an offence had taken place, therefore a caution was required.

D Yes, Constable BLOOM knew that WHEELAN had been drinking, therefore the question as to whether she had driven there constituted an interview and a caution was required.

Question 5.11

Constable COURT was conducting her first breath test procedure, having stopped KAY, who was driving with a defective light. During the test, Constable COURT failed to hold down a button on the breath test device for the recommended amount of time. However, the reading still showed a positive breath result and Constable COURT arrested KAY.

Has Constable COURT acted correctly in these circumstances?

A Yes, Constable COURT has acted correctly in the circumstances and the arrest is lawful.

B No, the arrest is unlawful, as Constable COURT made a mistake with the procedure.

C No, the arrest is unlawful, but this would not affect the result of the case if KAY provided a positive sample at the station.

D No, the arrest is unlawful, and KAY should have been made to take the test again.

Question 5.12

Constable WU has stopped MULHOLLAND as she was driving her car erratically. The officer could not smell intoxicants on her breath, but she was unsteady on her feet, and she was acting very strangely. Constable WU suspected that she may have taken a drug and that the drug had impaired her driving.

Which is true in relation to a preliminary drug test that Constable WU may conduct?

A Constable WU would not have to be in uniform, unlike breath tests in similar circumstances.

B Constable WU could only take the sample at the place where the requirement was made.

C Constable WU could only carry out the test if she has been specially authorised by her Chief Constable.

D Constable WU may, if suitable to the circumstances, take the sample at a police station.

Question 5.13

Constable PENG is trained to conduct preliminary impairment tests. He was called to assist another officer who had stopped a motor vehicle, which was being driven erratically by WENGER. The officer had administered a breath test, which was negative; however, WENGER's behaviour led the officer to believe that he was under the influence of either drink or drugs. On his arrival, Constable PENG gave instructions to WENGER as part of the test, but WENGER was not able to complete the test because of his condition.

Would the officer be able to arrest WENGER now, for failure to complete the impairment test?

A Yes, provided the officer suspects the presence of alcohol or drugs.

B No, as he has not refused to take the impairment test.

C Yes, regardless of whether the officer suspects the presence of alcohol or drugs.

D No, the officer would have to arrest him under s. 4 of the Act.

Question 5.14

Constable TAYLOR was called to a collision in a shopping centre car park, which was open to the public. SINGH had reversed his car into the path of a dumper truck being driven by WALSH. WALSH was working on an adjacent building site and the dumper truck he was driving was not manufactured for use on roads.

From whom, if anyone, may Constable TAYLOR require a breath test, in these circumstances?

A SINGH only, provided she suspects he has alcohol in his body.

B Neither driver, as the accident did not occur on a road.

C Both drivers, as they have been involved in an accident.

D SINGH only, whether or not she suspects he has alcohol in his body.

Question 5.15

Constable ZACHARIA was on mobile patrol and stopped WILSON, who was driving a motor vehicle on a road. Constable ZACHARIA could smell intoxicants on WILSON's breath and requested a preliminary breath test. WILSON refused to supply the test and ran away from Constable ZACHARIA. The officer gave chase and caught WILSON nearby. The officer arrested WILSON for failing to cooperate with the test and called for assistance. Other officers arrived at the scene and one of them had a hand-held evidential breath test device. WILSON agreed to provide an evidential specimen and the result was positive.

Has Constable ZACHARIA acted correctly in these circumstances?

A No, WILSON should have been arrested and taken to the station for failing to cooperate with the first test and an evidential specimen should have been requested there.

B Yes, the officer has acted correctly in these circumstances.

C No, WILSON should have been arrested and returned to where the first request was made and an evidential specimen should have been requested there.

D No, WILSON should not have been arrested for failing to cooperate with the pre-liminary test; Constable ZACHARIA should have proceeded straight to the request for an evidential specimen.

Question 5.16

Constable CAREY was investigating an incident that occurred outside a public house one night. HALL had been found lying in a gutter with blood coming from a head wound. Witnesses had seen PRIOR driving away from the scene, but could not say how HALL had sustained the injury. Constable CAREY attended PRIOR's address and saw a vehicle parked outside matching the description of the one that had driven away from the scene. PRIOR was at home but refused to open the door. Suspecting that an accident involving injury had taken place, Constable CAREY entered the premises by force and administered a breath test, which was positive. The officer then arrested PRIOR and asked for an evidential breath test at the house.

Has Constable CAREY acted correctly in these circumstances?

A No, there was no power of entry as Constable CAREY did not know for certain that an accident involving injury had taken place.

B Yes, Constable CAREY had a reasonable belief that an accident involving injury had taken place and was entitled to remain on the premises to request both specimens.

C Yes, Constable CAREY had a reasonable suspicion that an accident involving injury had taken place and was entitled to remain on the premises to request both specimens.

D No, there is only a power to enter by force and remain on a premises to request a preliminary breath test, not an evidential specimen.

Question 5.17

BALL drove his car into a garden wall and, without stopping, made his way home. He was uninjured, alone in the car and no other people were involved. Constable DAWE arrived at the scene and, following a Police National Computer (PNC) check, attended BALL's home address. Constable DAWE found BALL in the front garden of his house and asked him for a sample of breath, as the officer suspected he had been involved in a road traffic accident. BALL refused and was arrested by the officer. BALL refused to go with Constable DAWE and told him to leave his property.

Does Constable DAWE have the power to continue with his arrest now that he has become a trespasser?

A Yes, BALL was arrested before Constable DAWE became a trespasser.

B Yes, Constable DAWE had a power to enter premises, as BALL had been involved in an accident.

C No, the arrest was unlawful, as Constable DAWE was trespassing as soon as he entered the garden.

D No, Constable DAWE has now become a trespasser and must leave the property.

Question 5.18

Constable WEAR was on mobile patrol and saw BALE driving through a red traffic light. The officer stopped BALE and requested a preliminary breath sample, which proved to be positive. Constable WEAR arrested BALE and then requested two further samples of breath, using a hand-held evidential breath test device. BALE provided two samples; however, the device produced zero readings. Because the preliminary sample had proved positive, Constable WEAR suspected that the hand-held device may be defective. Constable WEAR arrested BALE on suspicion of driving with excess alcohol, based on the preliminary breath sample.

Can BALE be asked to provide two further evidential samples of breath at the police station?

A No, BALE has provided two samples and must now be asked to provide a sample of blood or urine.

B No, a constable may only make this request if there was no device available at the scene. BALE should now be asked to provide a sample of blood or urine.

C Yes, but only if it can be shown that it was impracticable to use a device at the scene.

D Yes, the police can request a further two samples of breath at the station under these circumstances alone.

Question 5.19

Constable CAMPBELL stopped CAMERON, who was driving a motor vehicle on a road. The officer suspected that CAMERON had been drinking and requested a sample of breath. The sample proved positive; however, it transpired that CAMERON had consumed a non-alcoholic drink approximately ten minutes before the request was made. Constable CAMPBELL had forgotten to ask whether CAMERON had consumed anything in the previous 20 minutes, prior to administering the test.

Would the validity of the breath test have been compromised in these circumstances?

A Yes, it is mandatory that the officer asks whether anything has been consumed in the 20 minutes prior to the breath test.

B No, provided the officer did not know, or had no reason to suspect that any substance had been consumed in the 20 minutes prior to the breath test.

C No, it is mandatory that the officer asks whether any alcohol has been consumed in the previous 20 minutes, but CAMERON had consumed a non-alcoholic drink.

D No, a test would only be compromised in these circumstances if the officer had actually known that a substance had been consumed in the 20 minutes prior to the breath test.

Question 5.20

GRANT was arrested and taken to a police station following a positive preliminary breath test. GRANT provided a further two specimens of breath, the readings being 47 and 45 microgrammes of alcohol in 100 millilitres of breath respectively. GRANT elected to replace these samples and it was decided that the defendant should provide a urine sample.

Which of the following statements is correct in relation to the provision of the urine sample, under s. 7(5) of the Road Traffic Act 1988?

A GRANT must provide two separate samples within an hour of being requested to do so.

B GRANT must provide two samples from the same act of urinating, within an hour of being requested to do so.

C GRANT must provide two separate samples within an hour of providing the second breath sample.

D GRANT must provide two samples, which may or may not be from the same act of urinating, within an hour of providing the second breath sample.

Question 5.21

RADCLIFFE was taken to hospital from a custody office, having been in police detention following a positive breath test. RADCLIFFE had suffered a suspected heart attack while about to provide samples for the station breath test procedure. Following tests, it was decided that RADCLIFFE had most likely suffered an anxiety attack, but would need to remain on a ward in hospital for observation. The arresting officer, Constable SAMPSON, spoke to the medical practitioner in charge of the ward about the breath test procedure. Constable SAMPSON was told that obtaining a sample of blood may be detrimental to RADCLIFFE's medical health. The officer decided to contact the custody officer for advice about how to proceed.

Considering s. 7 of the Road Traffic Act 1988, which of the following statements is correct, in respect of the options open to Constable SAMPSON?

A A Force Medical Examiner (FME) should be called to the hospital to take a sample of urine from RADCLIFFE.

B An FME should take the urine sample, but if one is not available, a medical practitioner not in immediate charge of RADCLIFFE's case should take it.

C A sample of urine may not be requested in these circumstances; such a sample may only be requested at a police station.

D A sample of urine may be requested in these circumstances and it may be taken by a police officer.

Question 5.22

Constable COLE attended a road traffic collision involving a car which had struck a wall. There were two occupants in the vehicle: PEARSON, the owner, and his friend, STUART. Constable COLE could smell intoxicants on both persons, but neither admitted being the driver of the vehicle at the time of the collision. PEARSON and STUART provided screening samples of breath, which were both positive. They were arrested and taken to the police station.

From whom, if either, could a specimen of breath for analysis be requested, under s. 7 of the Road Traffic Act 1988 (provision of specimens for analysis)?

A Both, provided it is believed one of them was driving.

B PEARSON only, as the owner of the vehicle.

C Both, regardless of who was suspected to be the driver.

D Neither, Constable COLE should not have breathalysed both persons.

Question 5.23

Sergeant DEMPSEY was conducting the station breath test procedure for PARFITT and was aware that the defendant had been in possession of a mouth spray and tablets for angina at the time of arrest. Sergeant DEMPSEY decided that PARFITT's illness might impair the breath test procedure and that a specimen of blood should be taken instead of breath. Before the test, the officer asked PARFITT if there were any medical reasons why blood should not be taken and the defendant replied that there were none. However, in court proceedings, PARFITT claimed that the blood sample had been taken unlawfully, as Sergeant DEMPSEY had not taken medical advice before making the decision.

Which of the following statements is correct, in relation to Sergeant DEMPSEY's decision?

A Because PARFITT was taking medication for angina, Sergeant DEMPSEY should have consulted a medical practitioner before deciding that the specimen to be provided would be blood.

B Even though Sergeant DEMPSEY asked whether there were any medical reasons for not taking a blood sample, she was not entitled to rely on PARFITT's answer unless medical advice was first sought.

C Because Sergeant DEMPSEY had reasonable cause to believe that medical reasons existed for not providing a sample of breath, she should have sought medical advice before deciding that the specimen to be provided would be blood.

D Even though Sergeant DEMPSEY had reasonable cause to believe that medical reasons existed for not providing a sample of breath, there was no need to seek medical advice before deciding that the specimen to be provided would be blood.

Question 5.24

FOSTER was arrested under s. 4 of the Road Traffic Act 1988 and was taken to the police station. FOSTER provided one specimen of breath, but then the machine malfunctioned. The custody officer, Sergeant CANNON, considered transferring FOSTER to another police station to complete the station procedure.

Would Sergeant CANNON be able to transfer FOSTER to another station, in these circumstances?

A Yes, FOSTER may be transferred and may be required to supply two further specimens of breath.

B No, FOSTER must now be asked to provide a sample of blood or urine at the current station, to replace the specimen of breath.

C Yes, FOSTER may be transferred and may only be required to supply one specimen of breath.

D No, a person may only be transferred to another station if there is no one available to conduct the station procedure.

Question 5.25

Constable HAYES conducted the station breath test procedure for BOBIN. The lowest reading was 49 microgrammes of alcohol in 100 millilitres of breath and BOBIN elected to replace the samples. Constable HAYES decided that BOBIN should provide a specimen of blood. However, BOBIN failed to provide a specimen and was charged with the offence. BOBIN pleaded not guilty in court, citing that Constable HAYES had failed to issue a warning under s. 7(7) of the Road Traffic Act 1988 (failure to provide the specimen may render a person liable to prosecution).

If Constable HAYES did fail to issue a warning, would BOBIN's defence be successful?

A No, the warning was not required in these circumstances.

B Yes, the warning should have been given by the person conducting the procedure.

C Yes, the warning should have been given by a constable, not necessarily the person conducting the procedure.

D No, the warning under s. 7(7) only relates to the provision of specimens of breath.

Question 5.26

Constable BERKIN was conducting the station breath test procedure for CAREY. The lowest reading was 48 microgrammes of alcohol in 100 millilitres of breath and CAREY elected to replace the samples. Constable BERKIN decided that CAREY should provide a specimen of blood, but she stated it was against her religion to provide blood, and that on medical grounds she would prefer to provide urine. Constable BERKIN did not believe the medical grounds were valid and asked VORIN, a registered health care professional, to attend the station to take the sample.

Is VORIN authorised to make the decision that CAREY should continue to provide a specimen of blood under s. 7(4) of the Road Traffic Act 1988, in these circumstances?

A No, only a medical practitioner can make this decision in these circumstances.
B Yes, provided a medical practitioner has been consulted first.
C Yes, provided a medical practitioner has not declared that there is a medical reason preventing CAREY from providing the specimen.
D No, the decision as to whether the specimen should be blood or urine is entirely Constable BERKIN's.

Question 5.27

Constable DAMON was on mobile patrol and stopped a vehicle being driven by SHALKE. Constable DAMON suspected that SHALKE had been drinking and requested a preliminary breath test and the test proved positive. Constable DAMON arrested SHALKE and requested two further samples of breath, using a hand-held evidential breath test device. SHALKE provided the samples and the lowest reading was 49 microgrammes of alcohol in 100 millilitres of breath. Constable DAMON informed SHALKE that the breath sample could be replaced by a sample of blood or urine and SHALKE requested this course of action.

What action should Constable DAMON take now?
A SHALKE may now be arrested and taken to a police station for a blood or urine sample to be obtained.
B SHALKE should now be taken to a police station to obtain two further samples of breath.
C SHALKE may be asked to attend a police station voluntarily, but if SHALKE refuses, the lowest reading should be used and there is no power of arrest.
D SHALKE must now be arrested and taken to a police station for a blood or urine sample to be obtained.

Question 5.28

KHAN has provided two specimens of breath during the station breath test procedure, the readings being 49 and 50 microgrammes of alcohol in 100 millilitres of breath respectively. Sergeant WILSON informed KHAN that he could replace the samples with blood or urine. KHAN stated that he would prefer not to give blood, as he had a fear of needles. Sergeant WILSON has been informed that a medical practitioner is available by telephone only and will not attend immediately.

What action should Sergeant WILSON now take in respect of KHAN?
A Speak to the medical practitioner on the telephone and proceed as advised by him or her.

B Request a sample of blood if necessary; a fear of needles is not a medical reason for not giving blood.
C Take a sample of urine from KHAN, as the choice is his as to which sample may be taken.
D Wait until the medical practitioner arrives and proceed as advised by him or her; such advice may not be taken by telephone.

Question 5.29

Sergeant DONELLY was conducting the station breath test procedure for BEECH, who had provided one sample of breath. However, BEECH stated that he was tired, and fell asleep before providing a second sample. Sergeant DONELLY tried to wake BEECH, without success, and in the end placed him in a cell. BEECH was later charged with driving with excess alcohol, based on the reading provided, which was 150 microgrammes of alcohol in 100 millilitres of breath.

Has Sergeant DONELLY acted correctly in these circumstances?
A Yes, Sergeant DONELLY has acted correctly in these circumstances as BEECH has driven with excess alcohol.
B No, BEECH should have been charged with failing to provide a sample, but his drunken condition may provide a defence.
C No, BEECH should have been given the opportunity to provide a sample of blood or urine when he was sober enough.
D No, BEECH should have been charged with failing to provide a sample and would have no defence arising from his drunken condition.

Question 5.30

BAUER was in police detention after providing a positive preliminary breath test. During the station procedure, BAUER provided two specimens of breath, the readings being 49 and 48 microgrammes of alcohol in 100 millilitres of breath respectively. BAUER elected to replace these samples and it was decided that the defendant should provide a blood sample. However, BAUER later refused to provide a blood sample and the custody officer is deciding what offence to charge the defendant with.

Which of the following statements is correct, in respect of the decision the custody officer should make?
A BAUER should be charged with exceeding the prescribed limit and the breath test reading may be used as evidence.

B BAUER should be charged with failing to provide a specimen of blood and the breath test reading may be used as evidence.

C BAUER may be charged with either offence; however, the breath test reading may only be used as evidence if the charge is exceeding the prescribed limit.

D BAUER should be charged with failing to provide a specimen of blood; however, the breath test reading may not be used as evidence.

Question 5.31

LONSDALE was stopped by Constable McMAHON for driving through a red traffic light. He requested a preliminary breath test, but LONSDALE stated that he could not provide a sample, claiming to suffer from bronchitis. Constable McMAHON arrested LONSDALE for failing to provide a specimen; however, during the booking in procedure, the officer did tell the custody officer LONSDALE's excuse at the scene. During the station procedure, LONSDALE made no effort to provide a sample and nor did he mention his condition. He was charged with failing to provide a specimen of breath but pleaded not guilty, claiming that the custody officer had reasonable cause to believe that a specimen of breath should not be required for medical reasons and should have consulted a medical practitioner.

Considering the offence under s. 7(6) of the Road Traffic Act 1988, would LONSDALE have a reasonable excuse for failing to provide a specimen?

A Yes, Constable McMAHON should have informed the custody officer of LONSDALE's alleged medical condition.

B No, the offence is complete in these circumstances alone.

C Yes, the custody officer should have made enquiries of LONSDALE as to whether he had a medical condition.

D Yes, LONSDALE was not required to declare the reasonable excuse at the time, but it may be raised subsequently.

Question 5.32

ASKEW was involved in a road traffic collision during which she received head injuries, and was taken to hospital. The officer dealing with the accident, Constable LEE, was told by witnesses that ASKEW's driving was erratic immediately prior to the collision. Constable LEE attended the hospital to interview ASKEW and require her to provide a sample of breath. On his arrival, Constable LEE was told that ASKEW was unconscious due to her injuries. Constable LEE considered that a sample of blood should be taken from ASKEW without her permission.

5. Drink, Drugs and Driving

Who would be able to take such a sample from ASKEW, under s. 7A of the Road Traffic Act 1988?

A A police medical practitioner or the medical practitioner in charge of the patient.

B A police medical practitioner or any other medical practitioner, but not the one in charge of the patient.

C A police medical practitioner only.

D A police medical practitioner, the medical practitioner in charge of the patient or a registered health care professional.

Question 5.33

WEBBER was at a hospital, having been involved in a road traffic accident. Having consulted with the medical practitioner in immediate charge of WEBBER's case, Constable O'SHEA required WEBBER to provide a specimen of breath, but she refused. Constable O'SHEA arrested WEBBER for failing to provide a specimen. After further consultation with the medical practitioner, Constable O'SHEA asked WEBBER to supply a specimen of blood.

Has Constable O'SHEA complied with the requirements of s. 9 of the Road Traffic Act 1988?

A No, because WEBBER was under arrest, the request for blood should have been made at a police station.

B No, Constable O'SHEA should not have arrested WEBBER while she was still a patient at the hospital.

C Yes, as the medical practitioner has agreed to both specimens being requested, Constable O'SHEA has complied with the Act.

D Yes, but there was no need to ask permission on the second occasion, as permission had already been granted.

Question 5.34

PELLOW was involved in a road traffic collision with another vehicle driven by CASE. As they were exchanging details, CASE noticed that PELLOW smelled strongly of intoxicants. CASE asked PELLOW to remain at the scene for the police. PELLOW refused, stating she had an out-patient's appointment at the local hospital. After PELLOW left, CASE contacted the police and gave details of her vehicle. Constable GRADY attended the local hospital intending to breathalyse PELLOW. The officer found her in the out-patient's department—she had been seen by a medical practitioner and had been discharged, to return for another appointment the following week.

Which of the following statements is correct, in relation to PELLOW's status as a 'patient' when she was seen by Constable GRADY, in respect of s. 9 of the Road Traffic Act 1988?

A PELLOW was an out-patient at the hospital; therefore she was not a 'patient' according to s. 9.

B PELLOW was still a 'patient', as she had to return to the hospital for further treatment.

C PELLOW was still a 'patient' as she was within the precincts of the hospital.

D PELLOW was not a 'patient' as she had been discharged.

Question 5.35

PEARCE has been charged with an offence of driving with excess alcohol (under s. 5 of the Road Traffic Act 1988) and is still in custody. Sergeant REVERS is considering whether or not to detain PEARCE at the custody office, because the lowest reading of the sample provided by PEARCE was 130 microgrammes of alcohol in 100 millilitres of breath.

What matters should Sergeant REVERS take into consideration, before detaining PEARCE under s. 10(1) of the Road Traffic Act 1988?

A Sergeant REVERS has a statutory power to confiscate PEARCE's car keys under this subsection, to prevent her from committing an offence under s. 5 or s. 4 of the Act.

B Sergeant REVERS has a statutory power to detain PEARCE until she has provided a negative screening test, to prevent her from committing an offence under s. 5 or s. 4 of the Act.

C PEARCE may be detained, provided Sergeant REVERS has reasonable grounds to believe she will commit an offence under s. 5 or s. 4 if she were to drive a motor vehicle on a road.

D PEARCE may be detained, provided Sergeant REVERS has reasonable grounds to believe she will commit an offence under s. 5 or s. 4 if she were to drive a mechanically propelled vehicle on a road.

Question 5.36

NEWMAN is in custody and is suspected of being unfit to drive through taking drugs. NEWMAN has provided a specimen of blood, which the custody officer, Sergeant

BURKE, intends to submit for analysis. NEWMAN will not be charged until the results of the analysis are known and, therefore, Sergeant BURKE intends to release him on bail for the period. However, NEWMAN has stated his intention to drive when released. Sergeant BURKE suspects that NEWMAN would still be unfit if he were to drive a motor vehicle on a road.

What does s. 10 of the Road Traffic Act 1988 say, in relation to the advice Sergeant BURKE should seek, before detaining NEWMAN further until he is fit to drive a motor vehicle on a road?

A Sergeant BURKE may make this decision herself; she does not need to seek advice from anyone.

B Sergeant BURKE may seek advice from a medical practitioner, and must act on any advice given.

C Sergeant BURKE may not detain NEWMAN under this section, as he has not been charged or reported for an offence.

D Sergeant BURKE must seek advice from a medical practitioner, and must act on any advice given.

Question 5.37

Constable TREEN was dealing with a road traffic collision and one of the drivers, BENSKIN, was taken to hospital with a leg injury, which was not serious. While at the hospital, Constable TREEN received permission from the medical practitioner to request a breath sample from BENSKIN. The preliminary breath test was positive and BENSKIN provided two evidential specimens, which were also positive. Following initial treatment, the medical practitioner discharged BENSKIN; however, Constable TREEN believed that BENSKIN was likely to drive a motor vehicle on a road while unfit to do so.

Given that Constable TREEN's belief was reasonable, did the officer have authority to detain BENSKIN under s. 10 of the Road Traffic Act 1988, to prevent the defendant from driving a motor vehicle on a road while unfit to do so?

A No, Constable TREEN would only have had the power to arrest BENSKIN if it was necessary, under s. 24 of the Police and Criminal Evidence Act 1984.

B Yes, provided it would not be prejudicial to BENSKIN's proper care and treatment as a patient.

C No, the power to detain people under s. 10 only applies to people who have been arrested and detained at a police station.

D No, the power to detain people under s. 10 only applies to people who have been required to provide a blood sample under s. 7 of the Act.

ANSWERS

Answer 5.1

Answer **A** — Under s. 6(3) of the Road Traffic Act 1988, if a constable reasonably suspects that the person has been driving, attempting to drive or is in charge of a motor vehicle on a road or other public place while having alcohol or a drug in his body or while unfit to drive because of a drug, and the person still has alcohol or a drug in his body or is still under the influence of a drug, he or she may require a person to cooperate with any one or more preliminary tests administered to the person by that constable or another constable.

However, although reasonable suspicion may be sufficient to require a breath sample, it would not be enough to rely on mere suspicion that the defendant had been driving prior to the administration of the test, and the officer would have to prove that the defendant had been driving before he or she could be convicted of an offence under either s. 4 or s. 5 of the Act, even if the person has failed a breath test (see *R (On the application of Huntley)* v *DPP* [2004] EWHC 870 (Admin)). Answers B and C are therefore incorrect.

This is true whether or not the suspicion was reasonably held by the officer, even if it could be shown that the suspect was the owner of the car and was found nearby (although this would be strong circumstantial evidence and would benefit the case if other evidence were uncovered, such as witness substantiation). Answer D is therefore incorrect.

Road Policing, para. 3.5.2

Answer 5.2

Answer **A** — Under s. 5(1)(a) of the Road Traffic Act 1988, a person who drives or attempts to drive a motor vehicle on a road or other public place after consuming so much alcohol that the proportion of it in his breath, blood or urine exceeds the prescribed limit is guilty of an offence. There can be no offence, therefore, under s. 5, and answer B is incorrect.

However, under s. 4(1) of the Act, a person who, when driving or attempting to drive a *mechanically propelled vehicle* on a road or *other public place,* is unfit to drive through drink or drugs is guilty of an offence. There *can* be an offence, therefore, under s. 4, and answers C and D are incorrect.

Road Policing, paras 3.5.2, 3.5.3

Answer 5.3

Answer **D** — The power of entry in connection with an offence under s. 4 is found in s. 17(1)(c)(iiia) of the Police and Criminal Evidence Act 1984, which states:

> Subject to the following provisions of this section, and without prejudice to any other enactment, a constable may enter and search any premises for the purpose of...
>> (iiia) section 4 (driving etc. when under influence of drink or drugs) or s. 163 (failure to stop when required to do so by constable in uniform) of the Road Traffic Act 1988.

Since the power is given to enter a 'premises', as opposed to a 'dwelling', answers A and B are therefore both incorrect.

'Premises' is not defined, but would include a vehicle; answer C is therefore incorrect.

Note that the power of entry under this section is only exercisable if the constable has reasonable grounds for believing that the person whom he is seeking is on the premises (s. 17(2)(a)).

Road Policing, para. 3.5.2

Answer 5.4

Answer **B** — This question deals with whether a 'reasonable suspicion' would provide sufficient evidence to arrest a person and prove an offence under s. 4 of the Road Traffic Act 1988, when that evidence is provided by a 'lay' witness. In *R v Lanfear* [1968] 2 QB 77, it was held that while evidence of impairment must be produced by the prosecution, that evidence *may* be provided by a 'lay' witness, who would not need to be an expert on such matters (see also *R v Davies* [1962] 3 All ER 97). Answers C and D are therefore incorrect.

However, that witness *may* not be required to give expert testimony or to *comment on the defendant's ability to drive*. Answer A is therefore incorrect.

Road Policing, paras 3.5.2, 3.5.2.2

Answer 5.5

Answer **A** — The circumstances in this question are similar to those in *DPP v Robertson* [2002] EWHC 542 (Admin). In that case, the officers had breathalysed the defendant who produced a negative result. However, on talking to the officers further, the defendant slurred his speech when giving the name of his solicitor. The officers then arrested the defendant under s. 4 and took him to a police station where he provided an evidential sample of breath which was over the prescribed limit.

The magistrates held that the defendant had been unlawfully arrested and the prosecutor appealed on a number of grounds. However, the Administrative Court held that it was quite conceivable to have a case where, notwithstanding that a driver had given a negative screening breath test, he or she was seen moments later staggering in a way that gave rise to a suspicion of unfitness. In such a case the law (s. 4) clearly gave a constable a power to arrest if what he or she had witnessed amounted to reasonable cause to suspect that the person was impaired, regardless of whether the impairment was due to drink or drugs. Answers C and D are therefore incorrect.

There would be no requirement for the police to require a further breath sample from the driver in these circumstances; therefore, answer B is incorrect.

Road Policing, para. 3.5.2.2

Answer 5.6

Answer **A** — The Divisional Court has held that there is some positive duty on a person to enquire whether a drink contains alcohol before drinking it if that person intends to drive afterwards (see *Robinson* v *DPP* [2003] EWHC 2718 (Admin)).

Answers B, C and D are therefore incorrect.

Road Policing, para. 3.5.3

Answer 5.7

Answer **A** — Section 5(2) of the Road Traffic Act 1988 provides a defence for a person charged with an offence under s. 5(1)(b) (in charge of a motor vehicle while over the prescribed limit), provided there was no likelihood of him or her driving the vehicle while unfit.

The situation was examined in the Divisional Court, in the case of *Sheldrake* v *DPP* [2003] 2 All ER 497. The defendant claimed that the application of s. 5(2) was contrary to Art. 6(2) of the European Convention on Human Rights (presumption of innocence). The court held that s. 5(2) did not breach Art. 6(2), and that a person charged with an offence under s. 5(1)(b) must demonstrate from the evidence an arguable case that there was no likelihood of him driving while unfit to do so. Answer C is therefore incorrect.

The prosecution do have a responsibility under s. 5(2) to show beyond reasonable doubt that there was a likelihood of the defendant driving, but *only if* the defendant has first presented a successful argument as referred to previously. Since the initial responsibility lies with the defendant, answers B and D are incorrect.

The case came before the House of Lords as *Attorney General's Reference (No. 4 of 2002) Sheldrake* v *DPP* [2004] UKHL 43. There it was held that, although s. 5(2) did in fact infringe the presumption of innocence under Art. 6, the burden placed on the defendant was reasonable because it was in pursuance of a legitimate aim.

The likelihood of the defendant's driving was so closely linked to his or her own knowledge at the relevant time that it made it much more appropriate for the defendant to prove—on the balance of probabilities—that he or she would not have been likely to drive (as opposed to the prosecution being required to prove the opposite beyond reasonable doubt).

Road Policing, para. 3.5.3.1

Answer 5.8

Answer **B** — Section 6 of the Road Traffic Act 1988 states that if any of subss. (2) to (5) applies, a constable may require a person to cooperate with any one or more preliminary tests administered to the person by that constable or another constable. Under s. 6(4), a constable may require a person to cooperate with such a test, if the constable reasonably suspects that the person:

(a) is or has been driving, attempting to drive or in charge of a motor vehicle on a road or other public place, and
(b) has committed a traffic offence while the vehicle was in motion.

This section applies to a combination of the past and present, e.g. someone who it is reasonably suspected is or *has been* driving, attempting to drive or in charge of a motor vehicle on a road or other public place, and who is reasonably suspected to *have* committed a traffic offence while the vehicle was in motion. Answer A is therefore incorrect.

'Traffic offence' includes an offence under *any provision* of the Road Traffic Act 1988 (other than Part V—driving instruction), the Road Traffic Offenders Act 1988 (other than Part III—the fixed penalty system), the Road Traffic Regulation Act 1984 and Part II of the Public Passenger Vehicles Act 1981. The offence of driving a vehicle so that the tyre is not so inflated as to make it fit for the use to which the motor vehicle or trailer is being put is covered by reg. 27 of the Road Vehicles (Construction and Use) Regulations 1986 (SI 1986/1078), but this offence is *prosecuted* under s. 41A of the Road Traffic Act 1988; therefore, the power to require a breath test under s. 6(4) applies in these circumstances and answer C is incorrect.

Finally, the power under s. 6(4) does not apply to any offence committed while the vehicle was in motion. There are omissions as can be seen previously. Answer D is therefore incorrect.

Road Policing, paras 3.5.4, 3.9.4.2, 3.9.4.11

Answer 5.9

Answer **B** — Section 6 of the Road Traffic Act 1988 allows a constable to require a person to cooperate with one or more of the preliminary tests under certain circumstances. Requests can be made under s. 6(2)–(4) where a constable reasonably suspects that the person:

- is driving, attempting to drive or is in charge of a motor vehicle on a road or other public place and has alcohol or a drug in his or her body or is under the influence of a drug (s. 6(2)), or
- has been driving, attempting to drive or in charge of a motor vehicle on a road or other public place while having alcohol or a drug in his or her body or while unfit to drive because of a drug, and still has alcohol or a drug in his or her body or is still under the influence of a drug (s. 6(3)), or
- is or has been driving, attempting to drive or in charge of a motor vehicle on a road or other public place, and has committed a traffic offence while the vehicle was in motion (s. 6(4)).

For requests made under these sections, the police officer *making the requirement* does not have to be in uniform and therefore answer A is incorrect. However, the officer *administering* a preliminary test does (s. 6(7)). Answer C is incorrect for this reason.

A constable may also require a person to cooperate with one or more of the preliminary tests if an accident occurs owing to the presence of a motor vehicle on a road or other public place, and a constable reasonably believes that the person was driving, attempting to drive or in charge of the vehicle at the time of the accident (s. 6(5)). There is no need for the officer making the requirement or administering the test to be in uniform under this section, *whether the accident involves injury or not*. Answer D is therefore incorrect.

Road Policing, paras 3.5.4, 3.5.4.3

Answer 5.10

Answer **B** — The facts in the question are similar to the case of *Ridehalgh* v *DPP* [2005] RTR 26. In this case, the defendant (a police officer) argued that the questions asked prior to the breath test procedure constituted an interview and as he had not been cautioned, Code C, paras 10.1 and 11.1(A) of the Codes of Practice had been breached. It was held that no interview had taken place and that there had been no breach of Code C. It was held that the questions regarding driving and whether he had been drinking first were merely preliminary and had been made with the intention of finding the possibility of whether an offence had been committed. On appeal, the Divisional Court held that a necessary precondition of the giving of a caution was that there had to be grounds for the suspicion of a criminal offence and that the magistrates were correct. The police officers merely suspected that the defendant had been drinking alcohol; they had no indication as to how much alcohol had been consumed, or whether he had actually driven. The ruling followed an earlier, similar decision in the case of *Whelehan* v *DPP* [1995] RTR 177. Answers A, C and D are therefore incorrect.

Road Policing, para. 3.5.4.1

Answer 5.11

Answer **A** — It has been held that where a constable innocently fails to follow the manufacturer's instructions, it will not render the test nor any subsequent arrest unlawful (*DPP* v *Kay* [1999] RTR 109). Answer B is therefore incorrect. Answer C is also incorrect, as the arrest was not unlawful.

In addition to the case of *Kay*, it was decided in *DPP* v *Carey* [1970] AC 1072, that failing to comply with the manufacturer's instructions on the use of an approved device will mean that the person *has not provided* a preliminary breath test and *may* be asked to provide another; refusing to do so will be an offence. Answer D is incorrect as the case is not the authority for the view that a person *must* be made to take another test. Since the purpose of the test is to indicate whether there is a *likelihood* of an offence being committed, an arrest in these circumstances is appropriate, as the test did show a positive result.

Road Policing, para. 3.5.4.2

Answer 5.12

Answer **D** — Section 6C of the Road Traffic Act 1988 states:

(1) A preliminary drug test is a procedure by which a specimen of sweat or saliva is—
    (a) obtained, and

(b) used for the purpose of obtaining, by means of a device of a type approved by the Secretary of State, an indication whether the person to whom the test is administered has a drug in his body.

(2) A preliminary drug test may be administered—

(a) at or near the place where the requirement to co-operate with the test is imposed, or

(b) if the constable who imposes the requirement thinks it expedient, at a police station specified by him...

As the test can be carried out at a police station, answer B is incorrect.

All the procedures under s. 6, i.e. preliminary breath test, preliminary impairment test and preliminary drug test must be administered by a constable only if they are in uniform (s. 6(7)). Answer A is therefore incorrect.

A preliminary impairment test under s. 6B is a completely different procedure from the other two and involves an appropriately trained and authorised police officer observing the person performing specified tasks. This special authorisation does not extend to s. 6C; therefore answer C is incorrect.

Road Policing, para. 3.5.4.2

Answer 5.13

Answer **A** — Under s. 6B of the Road Traffic Act 1988, an appropriately trained officer has the power to require the driver of a motor vehicle on a road or public place to submit to a preliminary impairment test, to observe the driver's behaviour. Such observations may be used as evidence in any subsequent court cases—but will not provide absolute proof of a person's guilt.

A person who fails to cooperate with a preliminary impairment test commits an offence under s. 6(6) of the Act. A person does not cooperate unless his or her cooperation is sufficient to allow the test to be carried out (s. 11(3)). In the question, the driver's behaviour meant that the test could not be carried out, even though he did not refuse to take it. Answer B is therefore incorrect.

A constable may arrest a person who has failed to cooperate with a test under this section, *provided* the constable reasonably suspects that the person has alcohol or drugs in his or her body, or is under the influence of drugs (s. 6D(2)). Answers C and D are therefore incorrect.

Road Policing, paras 3.5.4.2, 3.5.4.4, 3.5.4.5

Answer 5.14

Answer **D** — The power to conduct a breath test under s. 6(5) of the Road Traffic Act 1988 applies where an accident has occurred owing to the presence of a motor vehicle on a road or public place. Since WALSH was driving a mechanically propelled vehicle and not a motor vehicle, there is no power to request a breath test from him. Answer C is therefore incorrect. As s. 6 applies to accidents that occur in a public place as well as on a road, answer B is also incorrect.

There is no need for the officer making the enquiry to suspect or believe that the driver has been drinking, nor that he has committed an offence in order to require a breath test following an accident. Answer A is therefore incorrect.

Road Policing, para. 3.5.4.3

Answer 5.15

Answer **B** — Under s. 6D(2) of the Road Traffic Act 1988, a constable may arrest without warrant any person who fails to cooperate with a preliminary test in pursuance with a requirement imposed under s. 6 of the Act and the constable reasonably suspects that the person has alcohol or a drug in his or her body or is under the influence of a drug (the officer suspected that WILSON had been drinking and therefore has complied with this section).

Section 7 of the Road Traffic Act 1988 (the obtaining of evidential samples) permits the police to carry out an evidential breath test not only at a police station, but also at a hospital, or at or near a place (such as the roadside) where a preliminary breath test has been administered. Section 6D(2A) states that a person arrested under s. 6D(2) may, instead of being taken to a police station, be detained at or near the place where the preliminary test was, or would have been, administered, with a view to imposing on him or her there a requirement under s. 7. Answers A and C are therefore incorrect.

The power to request an evidential test at the scene under s. 7 does not negate the powers of arrest already in place under s. 6D(2). Therefore, there was nothing preventing the officer from arresting the suspect for a failure to cooperate with the initial request and proceeding with the request for an evidential sample at or near the scene. Answer D is therefore incorrect.

Road Policing, para. 3.5.4.5

Answer 5.16

Answer **A** — Under s. 6E(1)(a) of the Road Traffic Act 1988, a constable may enter any place using reasonable force for the purpose of requesting a preliminary breath test following an accident involving injury. Before the power is used, there are four criteria that must apply. The officer must:

- know that an accident has taken place (mere suspicion is not enough);
- have reasonable cause to believe that the person had been driving or attempting to drive, or had been in charge of the vehicle (mere suspicion is not enough);
- have reasonable cause to suspect that the accident involved injury to another person (here suspicion is enough); and
- have reasonable cause to suspect that the person he or she is seeking is in the place to be entered (again suspicion is enough).

Since Constable CAREY did not know for certain that an accident had taken place, there was no power to enter the premises. Answers B and C are therefore incorrect.

Where a constable imposes a requirement to cooperate with a preliminary breath test at any place, he or she is entitled to remain at or near the place in order to impose on the person an evidential specimen under s. 7 (s. 7(2C)). Answer D is therefore incorrect.

Road Policing, paras 3.5.4.6, 3.5.4.7

Answer 5.17

Answer **A** — Generally, where an officer is trespassing on a defendant's property, he or she is not entitled to require a breath test (*R* v *Fox* [1986] AC 281). Also, if officers are trespassing, any subsequent arrest made by them is unlawful (*Clowser* v *Chaplin* [1981] RTR 317). However, any requirement for a sample of breath properly made and any subsequent arrest remains lawful until the officer becomes a trespasser.

A police officer, like any other citizen, has an implied licence to go on to certain parts of property (which might include a garden), unless and until that licence is withdrawn. It is when the licence is withdrawn that the officer may become a trespasser. Therefore, if a police officer is on the defendant's property and has not been told to leave, any requirement for a breath test and subsequent arrest is lawful (*Pamplin* v *Fraser* [1981] RTR 494). This would still be the case even if the licence were withdrawn later. Answer D is therefore incorrect.

In the scenario given, the officer was not a trespasser until the defendant told him to leave the garden. Answer C is therefore incorrect.

Constable DAWE has no statutory power to enter the premises under s. 6E of the Road Traffic Act 1988, as this section only affords a power of entry following an accident involving injury to any person other than the driver. Answer B is incorrect as the scenario did not involve an injury.

Road Policing, para. 3.5.4.7

Answer 5.18

Answer **D** — Section 7 of the Road Traffic Act 1988 (the obtaining of evidential samples) permits the police to carry out an evidential breath test not only at a police station, but also at a hospital, or at or near a place (such as the roadside) where a preliminary breath test has been administered. Section 7(2D) of the Road Traffic Act 1988 states that if a requirement is made under s. 7(1)(a) at a place other than a police station, such a requirement may subsequently be made at a police station if (but only if):

(a) a device or a reliable device was not available at that place or it was for any other reason impracticable to use such a device, or
(b) the constable who made the previous requirement had reasonable cause to believe that the device used there has not produced a reliable indication of the proportion of alcohol in the breath of the person concerned.

Since the request can be made either if a device is not available or it was impracticable to use the device or the device was defective, answers B and C are incorrect.

A requirement may be made for a sample of blood or urine, under s. 7(3) of the Act. Section 7(3)(bb) states that a requirement may be made for such a sample if a device has been used at the police station or elsewhere, but the constable who required the specimens of breath has reasonable cause to believe that the device has not produced a reliable indication of the proportion of alcohol in the breath of the person concerned. In theory, therefore, the defendant in the scenario could have been asked to provide a blood or urine sample at the station, or evidential breath samples. However, it is not mandatory to request a sample of blood or urine in these circumstances, therefore answer A is incorrect.

Road Policing, para. 3.5.5.1

Answer 5.19

Answer **B** — It is common for device manufacturers to issue guidelines that require a 20-minute period free from consumption of alcohol or other substances prior to the administration of the test. In *DPP* v *Carey* [1970] AC 1072, the House of Lords ruled that if an officer has no knowledge or reason to suspect consumption of any substances within the relevant 20-minute period, the test remains valid even if it later transpires that some substance was actually consumed during that 20-minute period.

The 20-minute rule is guidance and not part of legislation, therefore, answers A and C are incorrect. This is true whether the person has consumed alcohol or any other substance.

The ruling in *Carey* demonstrates that the test could be compromised if the officer administers the breath test and either knows *or* has reason to suspect a substance has been consumed in the 20 minutes prior to the test. This is less prescriptive than the answer given in D, which is why the answer is incorrect.

Road Policing, para. 3.5.5.1

Answer 5.20

Answer **A** — Urine samples must be provided within an hour *from the time the request is made* (s. 7(5)). Answers C and D are therefore incorrect.

The defendant must provide two distinct samples (as opposed to two samples taken during the same act of urinating) (*Prosser* v *Dickeson* [1982] RTR 96). Answers B and D are incorrect for this reason also.

Note that the defendant must be given the opportunity to provide the urine within the one-hour period (see *Robertson* v *DPP* [2004] EWHC 517).

Road Policing, para. 3.5.5.1

Answer 5.21

Answer **D** — Under s. 7(3) of the Road Traffic Act 1988, a requirement to provide a specimen of blood or urine can only be made at a police station or at a hospital. Answer C is therefore incorrect.

Urine samples do not need to be taken by a medical practitioner. The samples will be admissible as long as they are provided within the time set out under s. 7(5) and may be taken by a police officer. Answers A and B are therefore incorrect.

Road Policing, para. 3.5.5.1

Answer 5.22

Answer **A** — It was held in the case of *Pearson* v *Metropolitan Police Commissioner* [1988] RTR 276 that the requirement under s. 7 may be made of more than one person (in this instance three people were involved), in respect of the same vehicle. Answers B and D are therefore incorrect. However, it must be believed that one of them was driving the vehicle, and for that reason answer C is incorrect.

Road Policing, para. 3.5.5.2

Answer 5.23

Answer **D** — In *Kinsella* v *DPP* [2002] EWHC 545 (Admin), the Divisional Court held that, just because the defendant had a mouth spray (for angina) and tablets at the time of arrest, that did not of itself impose an obligation on the relevant police officer to consult a medical practitioner before deciding that any specimen to be provided would be blood. In that case the officer had asked the defendant if there were any medical reasons why blood should not be taken and he had said that there were not. Answer A is therefore incorrect.

Also, where an officer specifically asks whether there are any medical reasons for not taking a blood sample, he or she is entitled to rely on the answer given unless it is obvious that such reasons exist (see *Jubb* v *DPP* [2002] EWHC 2317 (Admin)). Answer B is therefore incorrect.

For the officer making the requirement to have 'reasonable cause to believe' that medical reasons exist, there is no need to seek medical advice first (see *Dempsey* v *Catton* [1986] RTR 194), which is why answer D is correct, and answer C is incorrect.

Road Policing, para. 3.5.5.3

Answer 5.24

Answer **A** — If the machine being used at one station is unreliable, by virtue of the fact that it will not calibrate the reading correctly, it will be 'unavailable'. In this case, the driver may be taken to another station, where another machine is available, even if the driver has already provided two specimens on the inaccurate machine (*Denny* v *DPP* [1990] RTR 417). Answer B is incorrect for this reason.

When a person is transferred in such a way, the procedure will start again and the defendant may be required to provide two further specimens (logically, the sample from the first station could not be used as the machine has malfunctioned). Answer C is therefore incorrect.

A person *may* be transferred to another station if there is no trained officer to operate the machine (see *Chief Constable of Avon and Somerset* v *Kelliher* [1986] Crim LR 635). However, this is not the only circumstance in which a person can be transferred and answer D is therefore incorrect.

Road Policing, para. 3.5.5.4

Answer 5.25

Answer **A** — Under s. 7(7) of the Road Traffic Act 1988, when a constable is requesting the provision of a specimen under s. 7(3), a warning must be given that a failure to provide the specimen may render a person liable to prosecution. This warning is generally critical to a successful prosecution for failing to provide a specimen.

However, the warning is not needed when a driver elects to give an alternative specimen under s. 8 (i.e. choice made by the driver to replace the samples provided)—see *Hayes* v *DPP* [1993] Crim LR 966 and also *DPP* v *Jackson; Stanley* v *DPP* [1999] 1 AC 406. Answers B and C are therefore incorrect.

Answer D is incorrect because the warning relates to *any* specimen requested under s. 7 (breath, blood or urine), even though it is not required in relation to a specimen required under s. 8.

Answer B is incorrect for a further reason—in *Bobin* v *DPP* [1999] RTR 375, it was held that as long as the information set out previously is provided by a police officer, it does not matter which police officer. Therefore, the warning under s. 7(7) might be given by, for instance, the arresting officer or by the custody officer who makes the requirement for the relevant specimen.

Road Policing, paras 3.5.5.6, 3.5.5.7

Answer 5.26

Answer **C** — Section 7(4) of the Road Traffic Act 1988 states that the constable making the request can decide whether the sample to be provided should be blood or urine. However, this is subject to s. 7(4A) of the Act, which was amended to allow the sample to be taken by a registered health care professional. Under this section, where a constable decides for the purposes of subs. (4) to require the provision of a specimen of blood, the defendant will not be required to provide such a specimen if:

(a) the medical practitioner who is asked to take the specimen is of the opinion that, for medical reasons, it cannot or should not be taken; or

(b) the registered health care professional who is asked to take it is of that opinion and there is no contrary opinion from a medical practitioner.

This means that the opinion of the health care professional will be sufficient to authorise the taking of a blood sample provided that there is no contrary opinion from a medical practitioner. Answer A is therefore incorrect.

However, this does not mean that the health care professional's opinion has to be confirmed by, or routinely referred to, a medical practitioner (this would defeat the whole purpose of the changed legislation). Answer B is therefore incorrect.

Although s. 7(4) provides the constable with the authority to make the decision as to whether the specimen should be blood or urine, this is subject to s. 7(4A). The statutory discretion given to the officer by s. 7(4), although wide, has to be exercised reasonably—see *Joseph* v *DPP* [2003] EWHC 3078 (Admin). In *Joseph*, the driver told the officer that he was a Rastafarian and therefore could not give blood. The officer's insistence that the driver give blood anyway, even though there was no reason not to take urine instead, was held to be so unreasonable as to make it unlawful. Answer D is therefore incorrect.

Road Policing, para. 3.5.5.7

Answer 5.27

Answer **A** — Section 8(2) of the Road Traffic Act 1988 states that if the specimen of breath with the lower proportion of alcohol contains no more than 50 microgrammes of alcohol in 100 millilitres of breath, the person who provided it may claim that it should be replaced by such specimen as may be required under s. 7(4) (blood or urine) and if he or she then provides such a specimen, neither specimen of breath shall be used.

The police are permitted to carry out an evidential breath test not only at a police station, but also at a hospital, or at or near a place (such as the roadside) where a preliminary breath test has been administered. Section 8(2A) of the 1988 Act states that if the person who makes the claim under subs. (2) was required to provide specimens of breath under s. 7 of this Act at or near a place mentioned in subs. (2)(c) of that section (at the scene), a constable *may* arrest him or her without warrant. Since the arrest under s. 8(2A) is not mandatory, answer D is incorrect.

Answer C is incorrect because the suspect should not be given the choice as to whether he or she wishes to attend the police station once he or she has made the decision to replace the sample of breath. The power of arrest is provided to allow the constable to continue with the procedure at a police station because, naturally, a blood or urine sample may not be obtained at the scene of arrest.

Finally, once the suspect has provided two samples of breath at the scene, he or she has satisfied the requirements under s. 7 of the Act. There is no power to require the suspect to provide any further evidential samples of breath. Answer B is therefore incorrect.

Road Policing, para. 3.5.5.11

Answer 5.28

Answer **A** — When the person has provided two samples, and the lower reading is below 50 microgrammes of alcohol in 100 millilitres of breath, the person who has provided the sample may replace the breath sample with either a specimen of blood or urine (s. 8(1) and (2) of the Road Traffic Act 1988). Although the defendant is given the choice as to whether he or she wishes to replace his or her sample, the choice as to which sample will be provided will be that of the officer. Answer C is therefore incorrect.

As with s. 7 of the 1988 Act, the possibility of medical reasons for not providing blood *must* be considered. An alleged fear of needles by the driver is a relevant consideration when making this decision (*DPP* v *Jackson; Stanley* v *DPP* [1999] 1 AC 406 and also *Johnson* v *West Yorkshire Metropolitan Police* [1986] RTR 167). Answer B is therefore incorrect.

The medical advice may be given to the officer over the telephone if appropriate (*Andrews* v *DPP* [1992] RTR 1). Answer D is therefore incorrect.

Note the extended power given to registered health care professionals to take blood.

Road Policing, paras 3.5.5.11, 3.5.5.12

Answer 5.29

Answer **D** — Sergeant DONELLY has not acted correctly in these circumstances. Where a driver provides one specimen only, and fails without a reasonable excuse to provide the second sample, he or she has committed the offence of 'failing to provide' a sample (*Cracknell* v *Willis* [1988] AC 450). Answers A and C are incorrect for this reason.

'Mental impairment' may provide a reasonable excuse for failing to provide a sample. However, being drunk or under stress is not in itself enough to provide a 'reasonable excuse' for failing to provide a specimen (*DPP* v *Falzarano* [2001] RTR 14). This is confirmed by the case of *DPP* v *Beech* [1992] Crim LR 64, where it was decided that where the defendant's mental capacity to understand the warning was impaired by his or her drunkenness, this was not a 'reasonable' excuse. Answer B is therefore incorrect.

Road Policing, para. 3.5.5.12

Answer 5.30

Answer **A** — If a driver elects to substitute a breath specimen (which gave a reading of no more than 50 microgrammes) with one of blood/urine under s. 8 of the Road Traffic Act 1988, and subsequently fails or refuses to do so, they do not commit the offence under s. 7(6) (failing to provide a sample). The custody officer reverts to the original breath specimen and charges the defendant with an offence under s. 5(1), using the breath test reading as evidence.

Answers B, C and D are therefore incorrect.

Road Policing, para. 3.5.5.12

Answer 5.31

Answer **B** — A case similar to this one was heard by the Administrative Court in *DPP v Lonsdale* [2001] EWHC Admin 95. In this case, the driver alleged at the roadside that he suffered from bronchitis and therefore could not provide a breath sample. The arresting officer did not tell the custody officer of this alleged condition, but neither did the motorist himself. As a result, the court held that no objective observer could say that the custody officer had 'reasonable cause to believe that for medical reasons a specimen of breath should not be required' and therefore the defendant should have been convicted for failing to provide a specimen. Answers A and C are therefore incorrect.

In *DPP v Furby* [2000] RTR 181, it was held that if a police officer required a motorist to provide a breath specimen at the police station and the motorist made no effort at all to blow into the machine, they could not subsequently argue that they had a reasonable excuse for failing to do so. Any such reasons should be raised promptly and where a driver clearly declined the option of replacing the breath specimen with a blood or urine sample, he was not permitted to claim later that a phobia of needles had caused him to decline the opportunity (*R (On the application of Ijaz)* v DPP [2004] EWHC 2635 (Admin)). Answer D is therefore incorrect.

Road Policing, para. 3.5.5.12

Answer 5.32

Answer **B** — The power under s. 7A of the Road Traffic Act 1988 allows a sample of blood to be taken from a person without his or her consent, at a hospital. It may be taken if the driver has been 'involved' in an accident and is incapable of giving consent because he or she is incapacitated due to medical reasons.

Section 7A(2)(a) states that a request under this section shall not be made to a medical practitioner 'who for the time being has any responsibility for the clinical care of the person concerned'. Note, however, that the medical practitioner in charge of the patient must still be consulted under s. 9 of the Act, as he or she will still be concerned with the physical well-being of the patient. This means that both medical practitioners must be consulted—one under s. 7A and one under s. 9. Answers A and D are incorrect as the question referred to who could take a sample under s. 7A.

Section 7A(2)(b) states that the request must be made to a police medical practitioner unless this is not reasonably practicable, in which case the request may be made to any other medical practitioner (other than the one clinically responsible for the patient). Answer C is therefore incorrect.

The Road Traffic Act has been altered to enable registered health care professionals to take a sample of blood under s. 8 of the Act (station procedure), but not to take samples at a hospital, therefore answer D is incorrect.

Road Policing, para. 3.5.6

Answer 5.33

Answer **B** — While a person is at a hospital as a patient, he or she shall not be required to cooperate with a preliminary test or to provide a specimen under s. 7 of the Road Traffic Act 1988, unless the medical practitioner in immediate charge of his or her case agrees. Section 7 applies to both breath samples and samples of blood/urine.

However, if a patient provides a positive reading or fails to provide a sample at a hospital, he or she cannot be arrested while still a 'patient' (s. 6(5)). Answer B is therefore correct and answer C is incorrect as, even though the officer sought permission to take the second sample, the arrest that preceded it was unlawful.

Since the arrest was unlawful, answer A is incorrect, as the patient should not have been taken to a police station in these circumstances. However, if the person had been arrested after ceasing to be a patient, she could have been taken to the station to provide a sample (see *Webber v DPP* [1998] RTR 111).

Answer D is incorrect as permission must be sought from a medical practitioner for each sample that is required under s. 9(1).

Road Policing, para. 3.5.6

Answer 5.34

Answer **D** — Under s. 9 of the Road Traffic Act 1988:

(1) While a person is at a hospital as a patient, he or she shall not be required to co-operate with a preliminary test or to provide a specimen of breath for a breath test or to provide a specimen under section 7 of this Act unless the medical practitioner in immediate charge of his/her case has been notified of the proposal to make the requirement; and—
(a) if the requirement is then made it shall be for co-operation with a test administered, or for the provision of a specimen, at the hospital, but
(b) if the medical practitioner objects on the ground specified in subsection (2) below, the requirement shall not be made.

A 'hospital' will include an institution providing medical treatment for in-patients or out-patients (s. 11(2) of the Road Traffic Act 1988). Answer A is therefore incorrect.

If a person has been treated and then discharged from the hospital, he or she ceases to be a 'patient' for these purposes, even if he or she has to return at a future date for further, related treatment (e.g. to have stitches removed). Therefore, even though PELLOW was still within the precincts of the hospital, she had been discharged and was no longer a 'patient'. Answers B and C are therefore incorrect.

Road Policing, para. 3.5.6

Answer 5.35

Answer **D** — Section 10(1) of the Road Traffic Act 1988 states that a person required to provide a specimen of breath, blood or urine may afterwards be detained at a police station (or if the specimen was provided otherwise than at a police station, arrested and taken to and detained at a police station) if the constable has reasonable grounds for believing that, were the person to drive or attempt to drive a *mechanically propelled* vehicle on a road, he or she would commit an offence under s. 4 or s. 5 of the Act. Answer C is therefore incorrect.

Although the provision of a negative screening test would be a good indication that the person would not commit an offence under s. 4 or s. 5, there is no specific power to demand such a sample. Answer B is therefore incorrect. Similarly, there is no statutory power to retain a person's car keys to prevent them from driving (although this is common practice) and therefore answer A is incorrect.

Road Policing, para. 3.5.7

Answer 5.36

Answer **D** — Section 10 of the Road Traffic Act 1988 allows for the detention of a person who has provided a specimen of breath, blood or urine, until it appears to a constable that were the person to drive a mechanically propelled vehicle on a road, he or she would not be committing an offence. The power does not apply if it appears to a constable that there is no likelihood of the person driving such a vehicle on a road. There is no mention of a person having been charged or reported for an offence, merely that they have been required to provide the relevant sample. Answer C is therefore incorrect.

Under s. 10(3), a constable *must* consult a medical practitioner on any question arising under this section whether a person's ability to drive properly is or might be impaired through drugs. The constable must act on such advice. This is mandatory; therefore, both answers A and B are incorrect.

Road Policing, para. 3.5.7

Answer 5.37

Answer **B** — Section 10 of the Road Traffic Act 1988 states:

(1) Subject to subsections (2) and (3) below, a person required under section 7 or 7A to provide a specimen of breath, blood or urine may afterwards be detained at a police station (or, if the specimen was provided otherwise than at a police station, arrested and taken to and detained at a police station) if a constable has reasonable grounds for believing that, were that person then driving or attempting to drive a mechanically propelled vehicle on a road, he would commit an offence under section 4 or 5 of this Act.

Therefore, subs. (1) allows for a person to be arrested and taken to a police station if the specimen under s. 7 was obtained otherwise than at a police station. Answers A and C are incorrect.

Section 10(1) refers to occasions where a person was required to provide a specimen of breath, blood or urine under s. 7 or s. 7A (and not just blood), therefore answer D is incorrect.

Note that under s. 10(2), a person may not be detained if it ought reasonably to appear to the constable that there is no likelihood of his driving or attempting to drive a mechanically propelled vehicle while his ability to drive properly is impaired or while the proportion of alcohol in his breath, blood or urine exceeds the prescribed limit.

Also, a person who is at a hospital as a patient shall not be arrested and taken from there to a police station in pursuance of this section if it would be prejudicial to his proper care and treatment as a patient (s. 10(2A)).

Road Policing, para. 3.5.7

6 | Insurance

STUDY PREPARATION

Insurance matters are straightforward and, after the detail of the previous chapter, are also relatively brief.

It is important to understand the requirements for compulsory insurance and the main related offences—including causing and permitting.

The duties on drivers and owners in relation to production of insurance documents are also important when studying this area.

QUESTIONS

Question 6.1

PERRY has just bought a new vehicle and has applied for a new certificate of insurance from an insurance company. PERRY completed the application on the Internet and was informed at the end of the process that the certificate of insurance would be made available online in approximately two hours, due to the number of applications being administered. The message also informed PERRY that a copy of the certificate of insurance would be sent by email within 24 hours, and a hard copy would be delivered by post within two days.

At which point, according to s. 147 of the Road Traffic Act 1988, was PERRY insured to drive the new vehicle?

A When the online application process was completed.

B When the certificate of insurance was made available online.

C Only when the certificate of insurance was emailed to PERRY.

D Only when PERRY received the certificate of insurance by post.

Question 6.2

NEWBURY persuaded DAVIS to lend him his car to take his mother shopping. DAVIS agreed to do so, but on condition that NEWBURY arranged his own insurance. While driving DAVIS's car, NEWBURY was involved in an accident, and it was discovered that he had no insurance and that DAVIS's insurance did not cover him to drive either.

Would DAVIS be guilty of 'permitting' an offence by NEWBURY of driving without insurance?

A Yes, because permitting without insurance is an offence of strict liability on every occasion.

B No, because he told NEWBURY to insure the car before driving it, and has therefore discharged any liability for this offence.

C Yes, because even though he told NEWBURY to insure the car, he should have seen evidence that he had done so.

D Yes, because even though he told NEWBURY to insure the car, he should have checked with him that he had done so.

Question 6.3

MARCEAUX was a French national who was staying in this country for three months with her friend, FULTON, who was a UK national. MARCEAUX was a full licence holder in France and had a motor vehicle in that country which was insured there, but she did not bring it to this country. FULTON allowed MARCEAUX to drive her home from the pub one night, as she'd had too much to drink. They were stopped by the police while MARCEAUX was driving. FULTON stated that she thought MARCEAUX might be insured through her own policy in France; MARCEAUX herself was not sure if this was the case. Both persons were later prosecuted for using a vehicle without insurance.

Considering the requirements of s. 143(1) of the Road Traffic Act 1988, in respect of which defendant, if either, would the prosecution have to prove knowledge of the fact that MARCEAUX was uninsured?

A In respect of MARCEAUX only, as the driver of the vehicle.

B In respect of neither; there is no requirement to prove guilty knowledge in these circumstances.

C In respect of FULTON only, as the owner of the vehicle.

D In respect of FULTON and MARCEAUX, as the owner and driver of the vehicle.

Question 6.4

DOUGLAS was stopped while driving GARCIA's motor vehicle on a road. He was asked to produce his driving documents, including his insurance certificate. It transpired that GARCIA's certificate of insurance had expired, and DOUGLAS did not have a policy of his own to cover his use of the vehicle. DOUGLAS claimed that he was employed by GARCIA and that he was using the vehicle in the course of employment.

If both persons were to be prosecuted, with whom does the burden of proof lie, in relation to DOUGLAS's claim to be employed by GARCIA?

A In relation to both persons, the prosecution.

B In relation to DOUGLAS, the defence; in relation to GARCIA, the prosecution.

C In relation to DOUGLAS, the prosecution; in relation to GARCIA, the defence.

D In relation to both persons, the defence.

Question 6.5

QURESHI drove a car which was registered in her own company's name and the car was being repaired in a garage owned by AHEARNE. MILTON, who had recently started employment there, telephoned QURESHI to say the vehicle was ready for collection; however, QURESHI was in a meeting and asked if the vehicle could be brought to her office. AHEARNE was not around; therefore, MILTON decided to drive the vehicle to QURESHI. On the way MILTON was involved in a road traffic accident. It transpired that AHEARNE's insurance policy was restricted to 'named persons acting in the course of the insured's business' and MILTON had not been added to the policy. QURESHI's policy was restricted to 'any person acting in the course of the insured's business'. MILTON was prosecuted for driving without insurance, but AHEARNE gave evidence in court that there was no company policy to return vehicles after they had been repaired, that MILTON had not been acting in the course of his employment when he drove the vehicle and, had he been present, he would not have authorised MILTON's use of the vehicle.

The court has accepted that AHEARNE's statement is true; however, is there any other way that MILTON could avoid being found guilty of this offence?

A Yes, if MILTON could show that he reasonably believed he was covered by AHEARNE's policy to drive in the course of 'the insured's business'.

B Yes, AHEARNE could claim that cover in respect of 'the insured's business' extended to other colleagues, even though they were not yet named on the policy.

C No, MILTON may not avoid prosecution for this offence; once it was established that he was not acting in the course of his employment, he was not insured by either insurance policy.

D Yes, QURESHI could claim that MILTON was acting in the course of her business and therefore was employed by *her* insurance policy.

Question 6.6

BROWN was involved in a road traffic collision while driving his employer's delivery van in the course of his work. The collision occurred about two miles from his normal delivery route. At the time, BROWN was helping a friend by giving him a lift. The insurance policy for the van allows its use in connection with business only and it is company policy not to carry passengers in vehicles. BROWN does not have an insurance policy of his own and the journey was not authorised by his company.

Would the insurance policy for the van cover BROWN's use of the vehicle at the time of the collision?

A Yes, BROWN's use of the vehicle would be covered in these circumstances.

B No, because the van was being used in a manner not authorised by BROWN'S employer.

C No, as BROWN has made a detour from his normal route, his use of the vehicle would not be covered.

D No, as the van was not being used for business purposes at the time.

Question 6.7

GRIFFITHS owned a small van, which was insured for social, domestic and pleasure purposes only. His friend, LONGMAN, was moving house and GRIFFITHS helped him by moving furniture in the van, to LONGMAN's new house. Because this entailed several trips, LONGMAN reimbursed GRIFFITHS's petrol costs.

Would GRIFFITHS be covered by his insurance policy for the use of the van in these circumstances?

A No, the use of the van would amount to a business arrangement, regardless of whether money was paid to GRIFFITHS.

B No, because money was paid to GRIFFITHS and the van was being used for purposes other than social, domestic or pleasure.

C No, either because money was paid to GRIFFITHS, or because the van was being used for purposes other than social, domestic or pleasure.

D Yes, this will not amount to a business arrangement, regardless of whether payment was paid to GRIFFITHS.

Question 6.8

SAGGERS owned a 2.0 litre Rover motor vehicle and one day the crankshaft on the vehicle failed, causing catastrophic damage to the engine. SAGGERS bought a similar Rover which was being sold for parts, which had a 2.5 litre engine that could be reconditioned and fitted to SAGGERS's car. SAGGERS paid a friend to fit the engine and then took out a new insurance policy on the vehicle; however, he failed to tell the insurance company about the increased engine capacity, despite being asked directly whether any modifications had been made to the vehicle. A week later, SAGGERS was involved in a road traffic collision, in which he was to blame, and which resulted in the Rover suffering serious damage. When the vehicle was examined by the loss adjustor, it was discovered that the engine had been modified and the insurance company declared the policy void.

Considering the requirements of s. 143(1) of the Road Traffic Act 1988, would SAGGERS's vehicle have been insured at the time of the accident?

A No, SAGGERS's false representation to the insurance company would make the policy invalid.

B Yes, unless it can be shown that SAGGERS intended to gain an advantage by making false representations to the insurance company.

C No, SAGGERS's modification to the vehicle without informing the insurance company means that the policy may be declared void retrospectively.

D Yes, the policy may not be declared void retrospectively: despite SAGGERS's false representation to the insurance company, the policy was valid at the time of the accident.

Question 6.9

Constable FENTON is a Neighbourhood Officer, who arranged to take a group of school children to the police station to take part in a community meeting. Constable FENTON had arranged for a minibus owned by the police to pick up the children; however, the vehicle broke down before arriving at the school. Fortunately, the officer owned a people carrier and offered to take the children to the police station in it. However, Constable FENTON's vehicle was only insured for social, domestic and pleasure purposes.

Would Constable FENTON's vehicle qualify for an exemption from the requirement for insurance, as outlined in s. 144 of the Road Traffic Act 1988?

A Yes, this exemption applies to on-duty officers using their vehicles for police purposes.

B No, Constable FENTON's vehicle would need to be insured for journeys to and from work.

C Yes, Constable FENTON's vehicle was being used for police purposes.

D No, the exemption would only apply if the vehicle was being used for operational purposes, such as the prevention or detection of crime.

Question 6.10

HOLDING was travelling as a passenger in his son's car. HOLDING's son was involved in a road traffic collision, when he collided with a stationary car. As a result, HOLDING sustained spinal injuries, which meant that he had to give up work. It was later discovered that HOLDING's son had no insurance for his car, therefore HOLDING made a claim to the Motor Insurers' Bureau (MIB) for damages as a result of the accident.

In which of the following circumstances could the MIB deny liability for the injuries caused to HOLDING?

A If it could be shown that he either knew or ought to have known that his son was not insured.

B Only if it could be shown that he actually knew that his son was not insured.

C Because HOLDING himself was not responsible for the collision, the claim cannot be refused.

D Because HOLDING's son was not involved in a criminal act, the claim cannot be refused.

ANSWERS

Answer 6.1

Answer **B** — Under s. 143(1)(a) of the Road Traffic Act 1988, a person must not use a motor vehicle on a road or other public place unless there is in force in relation to the use of the vehicle by that person such a policy of insurance or such a security in respect of third party risks as complies with the requirements of this Part of this Act.

Compliance with s. 143(1) requires a certificate of insurance to be 'delivered' to the owner/user of the vehicle. Anyone using, or causing or permitting to be used, a motor vehicle on a road or other public place before the delivery of such a certificate, commits this offence (s. 147(1)).

Delivery may now also take place electronically—so a certificate of insurance transmitted from the insurer to the insured by email or made available for access on a website is sufficient (s. 147(1A)(a) and (b)). Answer D is incorrect for this reason.

Therefore, in this particular question, delivery had not been made when the person completed the application process online, as they were told the certificate would be made available two hours after completion. Answer A is therefore incorrect. However, it was made when the certificate was made available online, before it was emailed to PERRY, and so answer C is incorrect.

Road Policing, para. 3.6.2

Answer 6.2

Answer **B** — Permitting the use of a vehicle by another without insurance is an offence under s. 143 of the Road Traffic Act 1988, and generally the offence is one of strict liability; however, *Newbury* (in the following paragraph) demonstrates that there will be exceptions to this rule and therefore answer A is incorrect.

If a person allows another to use his or her vehicle on the express condition that the other person insures it first, the lender cannot be guilty of 'permitting' (*Newbury v Davis* [1974] RTR 367). There is no mention of having to check the person's certificate before allowing him or her to drive, or making a secondary check that he or she has done so and presumably stating the condition will suffice. Answers C and D are therefore incorrect.

Road Policing, para. 3.6.2.1

Answer 6.3

Answer **B** — Generally, the offence under s. 143(1) of the Road Traffic Act 1988 is one of strict liability, that is, you need not prove any intent or guilty knowledge by the defendant in order to convict, especially in these circumstances (*Tapsell* v *Maslen* [1967] Crim LR 53).

Answers A, C and D are therefore incorrect.

Road Policing, para. 3.6.2.1

Answer 6.4

Answer **B** — Section 143(3) of the Road Traffic Act 1988 provides a statutory defence for an employee, if he or she is using the employer's vehicle without insurance, provided he or she was not the owner of the vehicle, it was used in the course of his or her employment and he or she did not know or have any reason to believe that the vehicle was not insured. The burden of proof lies with the employee and the issue will be judged on the balance of probabilities (*R* v *Carr-Briant* [1943] KB 607). Answers A and C are therefore incorrect.

Where an owner is suspected of committing an offence of using, causing or permitting the use of a motor vehicle on a road without insurance, the burden of proof lies with the prosecution to show the driver was acting in the course of his or her employment. The driver's statement that he or she was doing so will not in itself be sufficient to convict the owner of the offence of using (*Jones* v *DPP* [1999] RTR 1). Answers C and D are therefore incorrect.

Road Policing, para. 3.6.2.2

Answer 6.5

Answer **C** — Section 143(3) of the Road Traffic Act 1988 provides a statutory defence for an employee, if he or she is using the employer's vehicle without insurance, provided he or she was not the owner of the vehicle, it was used in the course of his or her employment and he or she did not know or have any reason to believe that the vehicle was not insured. The burden of proof lies with the employee and the issue will be judged on the balance of probabilities (*R* v *Carr-Briant* [1943] KB 607). However, if it is established that the person was not acting in the course of his or her employment (which it has been in this case), the person's belief that he or she was covered by the employer's insurance is no defence. Answer A is therefore incorrect.

If a policy refers to 'agents' or 'employees', you will need to establish whether or not the relevant person fits into those categories. Garage proprietors returning vehicles to the owner after repairing them are not in the vehicle owner's employment (*Lyons* v *May* [1948] 2 All ER 1062). Answer D is therefore incorrect.

Finally, insurance cover in respect of 'the insured's business' does not extend to other businesses of friends or colleagues (see *Passmore* v *Vulcan etc. Insurance Co.* (1935) 154 LT 258) and therefore answer B is incorrect.

Road Policing, paras 3.6.2.2, 3.6.2.3

Answer 6.6

Answer **A** — A vehicle may be insured for business purposes, and normally, if an employee deviates from the ordinary course of his or her duties, the policy will be invalidated. However, it was decided in the case of *Ballance* v *Brown* [1955] Crim LR 384 that taking a two-mile detour to give someone a lift will not necessarily invalidate the employer's insurance. Answers C and D are therefore incorrect. In a further case that emphasises this point, *Marsh* v *Moores* [1949] 2 KB 208, it was held that an employee driving an employer's vehicle in an unauthorised manner will not negate the effect of the insurance policy. Answer B is therefore incorrect.

Road Policing, para. 3.6.2.3

Answer 6.7

Answer **D** — Lending a vehicle to a friend in return for payment reimbursing petrol costs has been held *not* to contravene s. 143 of the Road Traffic Act 1988, even when the vehicle was insured only for social, domestic and pleasure purposes (see *Lee* v *Poole* [1954] Crim LR 942). Answers B and C are incorrect for this reason. In the same case, it was held that using the vehicle to help a friend to move house will still amount to using the vehicle for social, domestic and pleasure purposes, therefore answer A is also incorrect.

Road Policing, para. 3.6.2.3

Answer 6.8

Answer **D** — Section 148(1) of the Road Traffic Act 1988 makes the effects of some restrictions in a policy void in relation to s. 143. This means that, if a policy purports to restrict the extent of its cover by reference to any of these features, breach of them by the insured person will *not* affect the validity of that policy for the purposes of s. 143. Those features will include, under s. 148(2)(f), 'the horsepower or cylinder capacity or value of the vehicle'.

It was held in *Durrant* v *MacLaren* [1956] 2 Lloyd's Rep 70 that an insurance policy obtained by false representations will be valid for the purposes of s. 143; therefore, SAGGERS's vehicle was covered by his insurance at the time of the accident despite the false representations to the insurance company and regardless of whether he intended to gain an advantage. Answers A and B are therefore incorrect.

Also, while the insurance company was entitled to declare the policy void, the vehicle remains insured until the contract has been 'avoided' (ended) by the insurer (see *Durrant*) and answer C is therefore incorrect.

Road Policing, paras 3.6.2.3, 3.6.2.4

Answer 6.9

Answer **C** — Section 144 of the Road Traffic Act 1988 sets out occasions where vehicles will be exempt from the requirement for having insurance. Such occasions include police authority vehicles and vehicles being used for police purposes. Since the officer in the scenario would be using the vehicle for police purposes, the vehicle would be exempt and no additional insurance would be required. Answer B is therefore incorrect.

The exemption will include an off-duty police officer using his or her own vehicle for police purposes (*Jones* v *Chief Constable of Bedfordshire* [1987] RTR 332). However, the exemption is not restricted to *on-duty* officers using their vehicles for police purposes and for this reason answer A is incorrect.

There is nothing in the Act which states that the vehicle must be used for operational purposes, such as the prevention or detection of crime. Answer D is therefore incorrect.

Road Policing, para. 3.6.2.5

Answer 6.10

Answer **A** — The Motor Insurers' Bureau (MIB) will generally deny liability for any damages or loss to passengers who either knew or ought to have known that the driver was uninsured (see *Akers* v *Motor Insurance Bureau* [2003] EWCA Civ 18). Answer B is incorrect, as the claim could fail if the MIB thought the passenger ought to have known that his son was uninsured. This would be the case whether or not the passenger was not responsible for the collision, therefore answer C is incorrect. Also, it is irrelevant in this particular case that the driver was not involved in a criminal act. This may be a reason for refusing a claim in some circumstances, but the claim in the scenario could be refused for the reasons listed previously. Answer D is therefore incorrect.

Road Policing, para. 3.6.3

7 Protection of Drivers, Riders and Passengers

STUDY PREPARATION

Safety measures cover a range of statutory provisions, including the requirements for seat belts, crash helmets and speed restrictions.

Once again this is a pretty straightforward area.

QUESTIONS

Question 7.1

Constable TILLEY stopped RORY who was 17 years of age, had recently passed his driving test and was driving a motor vehicle on a road. At the time, RORY's sister, KIA aged 13, was a front seat passenger and was not wearing a seat belt. RORY explained that he had told KIA to wear the seat belt, but they had had an argument and she had refused.

Which of the following statements is correct, as to whether either RORY or KIA would commit the substantive offence, under the Road Traffic Act 1988, of failing to wear a seat belt?

A As the driver of the vehicle, only RORY would commit the offence.

B Both persons would commit the offence in these circumstances.

C As the person not wearing the seat belt, only KIA would commit the offence.

D As the person not wearing the seat belt, only KIA would commit the offence, but she would have a defence because of her age.

Question 7.2

Constable FARRELL has stopped BALE while driving a motor vehicle on a road, for failing to wear a seat belt. BALE claimed an exemption to wearing a seat belt for medical reasons. Constable FARRELL has decided to issue BALE with an HORT/1 to produce a driving licence, certificate of insurance and test certificate, together with proof of the exemption from wearing a seat belt.

What are BALE's responsibilities to produce documents in these circumstances?

A BALE must be in possession of a certificate of exemption and produce it on request, immediately, and produce the other documents at a police station within seven days.

B BALE must produce a certificate of exemption on request, or at a police station within seven days, with the other documents.

C BALE must produce a certificate of exemption within a reasonable time, or at a police station within seven days, with the other documents.

D BALE need only produce a driving licence, certificate of insurance and test certificate at a police station within seven days; the exemption from wearing a seat belt should be indicated on the driving licence.

Question 7.3

WEBSTER works for a delivery company and visits ten shops in a shopping precinct, in a small goods vehicle. WEBSTER delivers fresh fruit, vegetables and flowers to various shops in the morning from a market situated half a mile from the precinct. The shops were situated just under 100 metres apart. One Saturday morning, WEBSTER took his son, aged 14, to help him. That day, they drove to the shops from the market without their seat belts fastened and then delivered the goods, again while not wearing seat belts.

Which of the following statements is correct in relation to whether WEBSTER or his son would qualify for the exemption from wearing seat belts, under s. 14(2)(b)(i) of the Road Traffic Act 1988?

A Only WEBSTER would qualify for the exemption, his son cannot qualify because of his age.

B Both would qualify for the exemption as they were on a journey to deliver goods.

C They would only qualify for the exemption when they were in the shopping precinct; they committed an offence while driving there.

D They would not qualify for the exemption at any time in these circumstances.

Question 7.4

ANDERSON was driving a motor vehicle on a road. There was a child sat in the rear passenger seat, aged 2. The car was old, and was not fitted with seat belts to the rear. ANDERSON was wearing a seat belt, but the child in the rear was not.

Has ANDERSON committed an offence in relation to the child's failure to wear a seat belt?

A Yes, because the child is under the age of 3.

B Yes, regardless of the age of the child.

C No, because seat belts were not fitted to the rear of the vehicle.

D Yes, because the child is under the age of 14.

Question 7.5

AMIR was driving in a family car which was fitted with air bags protecting both the driver and the front seat passenger. Accompanying AMIR in the car was a young child who was sat in a rear-facing car seat.

What regulations are in place under s. 15(1A) of the Road Traffic Act 1988, to ensure the safety of the young child in the passenger seat?

A The air bag must be de-activated, if the child is under 3 years of age.

B The child must not be placed in this seat if it is fitted with an air bag.

C The air bag must be de-activated, if the child is under 2 years of age.

D The air bag must be de-activated, regardless of the age of the child.

Question 7.6

MAREK and FIELDS went out one Sunday, riding their motor cycles on roads. MAREK was riding a three-wheeler motor cycle, while FIELDS was riding a motor bicycle with a side-car combination. FIELDS's son EDDIE, aged 15, was sitting in the side-car throughout the whole journey.

Who of the persons listed, if any, would be required to wear appropriate protective headgear while riding the motor cycles on the road, according to s. 16(4) of the Road Traffic Act 1988?

A None, because of the type of motor cycles they were riding.

B FIELDS only, because of the type of motor cycle he was riding.

C MAREK and FIELDS only, because of the type of motor cycles they were riding.

D All three; MAREK and FIELDS because of the type of motor cycles they were riding and EDDIE because of his age.

Question 7.7

Constable FURNHAM saw ASHBY sitting astride a motor cycle, pushing it with his feet along the road and steering it. ASHBY was being assisted by FILER, who was pushing the motor cycle from behind. At the time he was seen by Constable FURNHAM, ASHBY was not wearing a helmet.

Would ASHBY be exempt from the requirements of s. 16(4) of the Road Traffic Act 1988 (driving or riding a motor cycle in contravention of regulations relating to motor cycle helmets)?

A No, both ASHBY and FILER were 'driving' the motor cycle.

B Yes, ASHBY was not in control of the propulsion of the motor cycle.

C Yes, ASHBY and FILER were pushing a motor cycle; therefore it was not being ridden.

D No, ASHBY was riding the motor cycle in these circumstances.

Question 7.8

HEALEY, aged 22, has a full licence to ride motor cycles. One day, HEALEY gave WORTH, aged 15, a ride on a motor cycle as a pillion passenger. They were stopped while riding on the road by Constable MALLOY and at the time, WORTH was not wearing a helmet.

Who, if either, would commit an offence in these circumstances (because of WORTH's failure to wear a helmet)?

A Both, because of WORTH's age.

B WORTH only, because of his age.

C Both, regardless of WORTH's age.

D HEALEY only, because of WORTH's age.

Question 7.9

HAMILTON is the holder of a full licence to ride motor cycles. One day, HAMILTON gave STEWART a ride on a motor cycle as a pillion passenger. As a joke, STEWART sat astride the motor cycle, behind HAMILTON, facing the rear. HAMILTON was fully aware of what STEWART was doing. They were stopped by Constable CHOI while riding on the road.

Who, if either, would commit an offence in these circumstances (because of STEWART's seating position), under s. 23 of the Road Traffic Act 1988?

A Both HAMILTON and STEWART commit the full offence because STEWART was not sitting properly astride the motor cycle.

B HAMILTON commits the full offence because STEWART was not sitting properly astride the motor cycle. STEWART is guilty of aiding and abetting HAMILTON.

C Neither; there is no requirement for a pillion passenger to face the front, provided they are sitting astride the motor cycle.

D STEWART commits the full offence of not sitting properly astride the motor cycle. HAMILTON is guilty of aiding and abetting STEWART.

Question 7.10

Constable BASTABLE was conducting a speeding operation on a main road, using a hand-held speed detection camera. The officer was positioned on a long stretch of road, which led to a bend and was pointing the camera towards the bend. BETTS was travelling in a vehicle in the opposite direction, away from the officer. Upon negotiating the bend, BETTS attempted to warn other drivers approaching Constable BASTABLE by flashing the headlights of the vehicle. BETTS was seen by another police officer who was driving a police vehicle towards Constable BASTABLE.

Would BETTS's actions amount to an offence of obstructing a police constable in the execution of their duty, in these circumstances?

A Yes, merely giving such a warning can amount to an offence.

B Yes, provided it can be shown that the other drivers were exceeding the speed limit.

C No, warning drivers in such a way does not amount to an offence.

D Yes, provided it can be shown that the other drivers were exceeding the speed limit or were likely to do so.

Question 7.11

STEPHENS was driving in a car at 40 mph along a road, and was stopped by Constable CRANE. The officer believed that the road was a 'restricted road', and therefore, that STEPHENS was speeding.

Which of the following statements is correct in respect of 'restricted roads' and other roads, as defined in s. 82 of the Road Traffic Regulation Act 1984?

A If a road has a system of street lighting of more than 200 yards apart, it may have signs indicating the speed limit.

B If a road has a system of street lighting not more than 200 yards apart, it will always be restricted to 30 mph.
C If a road has a system of street lighting not more than 200 yards apart, it must have signs indicating the speed limit is 30 mph.
D If a road has a system of street lighting of more than 200 yards apart, it must have signs indicating the speed limit.

Question 7.12

OLSEN is appearing in Crown Court, having been charged with causing death by dangerous driving. OLSEN was driving along an unfamiliar country road and failed to negotiate a sharp right-hand bend. OLSEN's car collided with a stone wall and the front seat passenger, CROWLEY, was killed outright. OLSEN is pleading not guilty to the offence, claiming that there were no warning signs or chevrons on the approach to the sharp bend. OLSEN's defence will be that the liability for the accident lay with the local authority, as it had failed in its statutory duty to maintain the highway, under s. 41 of the Highways Act 1980.

Which of the following statements is correct in relation to OLSEN's claim?
A The local authority has committed an offence under this section and could be liable.
B The local authority has not committed an offence, but it has a common law duty to promote road safety and has failed in this case.
C The local authority has not committed an offence; drivers bear their own responsibility to protect themselves and their passengers and OLSEN is liable.
D The local authority has not committed an offence, but the absence of road signs may provide OLSEN with a defence in these circumstances.

Question 7.13

Constable MACINTYRE was a Roads Policing Officer and was driving a police vehicle fitted with specialist speed measuring equipment along a restricted road. The road normally had a set speed limit of 50 mph; however, road works were being conducted at the location and a temporary speed restriction was in place, reducing the speed limit to 30 mph. Constable MACINTYRE stopped GRETTON, who had been travelling at 49 mph and reported her for exceeding the speed limit.

Is Constable MACINTYRE required to give GRETTON a notice of intended prosecution (NIP), in these circumstances?

A Yes, a NIP is required for this offence on a restricted road, even when there is a temporary speed restriction in place.

B No, a NIP is not required for this offence on a restricted road, when there is a temporary speed restriction in place.

C Yes, a NIP is required for all speeding offences, regardless of where they are committed.

D No, a NIP is not required for speeding offences committed on restricted roads or motorways.

Question 7.14

EMMERICH works in the Fire and Rescue Service and is on a training course to learn how to drive fire tenders. EMMERICH has been given instructions by the instructor to drive at speeds above the statutory speed limits.

Would EMMERICH be exempt from the laws in relation to speed limits in these circumstances, under s. 87 of the Road Traffic Regulation Act 1984?

A No, the exemption does not apply to such vehicles being used on training courses.

B Yes, provided EMMERICH has been previously trained in driving at high speeds.

C Yes, the exemption applies to EMMERICH regardless of any previous training received.

D Yes, provided EMMERICH does not exceed any speed limit by more than 30 mph.

Question 7.15

Constable WOODS and Constable HUSSEIN were on duty in a marked police vehicle, which was not equipped with specialist speed measuring equipment. They were driving along a restricted road, which had a speed limit of 30 mph. They followed DICKSON, who was driving at 40 mph in his car, for about a mile. The officers stopped DICKSON and spoke to him.

Would the officers be able to give evidence of DICKSON's speed, in order to prosecute him for the offence of speeding?

A No, their evidence does not amount to corroboration, and would not be accepted in court.

B Yes, provided it can be shown that they saw the vehicle at exactly the same time.

C Yes, the evidence that they both saw the vehicle speeding is sufficient alone to prosecute.

D Yes, corroboration is not required, as the offence took place on a restricted road.

Question 7.16

Constable NOBLE was a Roads Policing Officer on patrol in a marked police vehicle single crewed. The officer was trialling the latest speed measuring equipment, which was fitted to the vehicle, but was yet to be approved for operational use by the Association of Chief Police Officers (ACPO). The intention was that Constable NOBLE would record vehicle speeds for testing purposes, not to prosecute drivers; however, the officer was driving on a road with a speed limit of 40 mph behind MONCRIEFF, who was travelling at 70 mph. Constable NOBLE stopped and reported MONCRIEFF for the offence, due to the vehicle's excessive speed.

If MONCRIEFF were to be prosecuted for speeding, could the prosecution rely on the reading provided by the device being tested?

A Yes, the opinion of the police officer could be supported by reference to the reading on the device, even though it is not approved by ACPO.

B No, the officer's evidence and a calibration certificate of the speed detection device are required in all cases.

C No, a person prosecuted for exceeding the speed limit cannot be convicted solely on the evidence of one witness.

D No, the court will only accept the evidence provided by a device approved by ACPO.

ANSWERS

Answer 7.1

Answer **A** — Section 14(3) of the Road Traffic Act 1988 states that a person who drives or rides in a motor vehicle in contravention of regulations under this section is guilty of an offence; but notwithstanding any enactment or rule of law, no person other than the person actually committing the contravention is guilty of an offence by reason of the contravention. However, s. 14(6) states that this rule does not apply to children under the age of 14 (in other words, a child under the age of 14 does *not* commit the offence by virtue of not wearing a seat belt). The child would not, therefore, require a defence and for this reason answers B, C and D are incorrect.

Under s. 15 of the Act, when a child under the age of 14 is not wearing a seat belt, the *driver* is responsible for the passenger's offence and the passenger is exempt, which is why answer A is correct.

Note that in theory it would be possible for the child to be guilty of aiding and abetting the driver by not wearing a seat belt, but this is untested and the question asks for the reader to identify the substantive offence under the Road Traffic Act 1988.

Road Policing, para. 3.7.2

Answer 7.2

Answer **B** — A person may be exempt from wearing a seat belt, provided they have been issued with a medical certificate, signed by a doctor, stating that the wearing of a seat belt by that person is inadvisable on medical grounds. Answer D is incorrect as a separate certificate is required.

If the certificate is to be used in evidence in answer to a charge under s. 14(3) of the Road Traffic Act 1988, the certificate must be produced to a constable *either* on request, *or* within seven days at a police station. Answers A and C are therefore incorrect.

Road Policing, para. 3.7.2.1

Answer 7.3

Answer **D** — Section 14(2)(b)(i) of the Road Traffic Act 1988 provides a general exemption in relation to the wearing of seat belts by drivers and the passengers in motor vehicles constructed or adapted for carrying goods while on a journey related to the transport of such goods. However, the exemption only applies to journeys that do not exceed the prescribed distance, which is 50 metres (see reg. 6(1)(b) of the Motor Vehicles (Wearing of Seat Belts) Regulations 1993). This means that neither WEBSTER nor his son could claim the exemption at any time in these circumstances and answers A, B and C are therefore incorrect.

There is no mention of a person's age in s. 14(2)(b)(i); therefore, in theory, WEBSTER's son *could* qualify for the exemption if the journeys were shorter. Answer A is also incorrect for this reason.

Road Policing, para. 3.7.2.1

Answer 7.4

Answer **A** — Under s. 15(3) of the Road Traffic Act 1988, where:

(a) a child under the age of three years is in the rear of a motor vehicle, or
(b) a child of over that age but under the age of fourteen years is in the rear of a motor vehicle and any seat belt is fitted in the rear of that vehicle,
a person must not without reasonable excuse drive the vehicle on a road unless the child is wearing a seat belt in conformity with regulations.

Therefore, because of s. 15(3)(a), if the child is under 3 years of age, regardless of whether seat belts are fitted to the rear of the vehicle, an offence is committed by ANDERSON. Answer C is therefore incorrect.

If the child had been over 3 years of age, but under 14, he or she would have been covered by s. 15(3)(b) and no offence would be committed because there were no seat belts fitted to the rear of the vehicle. Answers B and D are therefore incorrect.

Road Policing, para. 3.7.2.2

Answer 7.5

Answer **D** — Under s. 15(1A) of the Road Traffic Act 1988, where:

(a) a child is in the front of a motor vehicle other than a bus,
(b) the child is in a rear-facing child restraint device, and
(c) the passenger seat where the child is placed is protected by a front air bag, a person must not without reasonable excuse drive the vehicle on a road unless the airbag is deactivated.

Therefore, even though there is legislation protecting the child, he or she may be placed in the front passenger seat in these circumstances, provided the air bag is deactivated (and answer B is therefore incorrect).

There is no mention of the age of the child; therefore answers A and C are incorrect. Of course, only very young children are likely to be placed in rear-facing seats, therefore the age and size of the child will be self-regulating.

Road Policing, para. 3.7.2.2

Answer 7.6

Answer **B** — Under s. 16 of the Road Traffic Act 1988, the Secretary of State may make regulations relating to the wearing of protective headgear by people riding motor cycles. The relevant regulations are the Motor Cycles (Protective Helmets) Regulations 1998 (SI 1998/1807) as amended.

The Regulations require every person driving or riding on a motor *bicycle* on a road to wear protective headgear (reg. 4). Section 16 of the Road Traffic Act 1988 s. 16 states:

> (4) A person who drives or rides on a motor cycle in contravention of regulations under this section is guilty of an offence...

The Regulations do not apply to all motor cycles; they only apply to motor bicycles. The rider of a three-wheeler motor cycle is not required to wear protective headgear, therefore, answers C and D are incorrect.

The rider of a two-wheeled motor cycle is required to wear protective headgear, whether it has a side-car attached or not (answer A is therefore incorrect). However, the Regulations apply to a person driving or riding *on a motor bicycle* and not to a person sitting in a side-car, regardless of their age. Answer D is incorrect for this reason also.

Road Policing, para. 3.7.3

Answer 7.7

Answer **D** — Section 16(4) of the Road Traffic Act 1988 states that a person who drives or rides on a motor cycle in contravention of regulations under this section is guilty of an offence.

The term 'driving' takes in many forms and in the case of *Crank* v *Brooks* [1980] RTR 441, the court decided that where a person straddled a motor cycle and pedalled it along with their feet, he or she would require a helmet (and, therefore, would not be exempt). Answer C is therefore incorrect.

It has also been decided that if a person used the vehicle's controls in order to direct its movement (*Burgoyne* v *Phillips* [1983] RTR 49), he or she would be driving. Therefore, a person may be in charge of the direction of the vehicle, but not the propulsion and he or she would still be driving. Answer B is incorrect for this reason.

Finally, pushing a car along while steering it has been held not to be driving so far as the law in England and Wales is concerned (*R* v *MacDonagh* [1974] 2 All ER 257). If these principles were applied to motor cycles, it is unlikely that FILER was driving/riding and therefore answer A is incorrect.

Road Policing, paras 3.7.3, 3.1.7

Answer 7.8

Answer **A** — Section 16(4) of the Road Traffic Act 1988 makes it an offence to ride on a motor cycle without a crash helmet. 'Ride on' includes being a pillion passenger.

If the pillion passenger is under 16, the offence is committed by both the rider and the passenger. If the pillion passenger is 16 or over, he or she alone is responsible.

This is in contrast to seat belt legislation, where young passengers are not responsible for their own actions. As the person in the question was 15, both he and the driver commit the offence. Answers B, C and D are therefore incorrect.

Road Policing, paras 3.7.3, 3.7.3.1

Answer 7.9

Answer **C** — Section 23 of the Road Traffic Act 1988 states:

(1) Not more than one person in addition to the driver may be carried on a motor bicycle.

(2) No person in addition to the driver may be carried on a motor bicycle otherwise than sitting astride the motor cycle and on a proper seat securely fixed to the motor cycle behind the driver's seat.

(3) If a person is carried on a motor cycle in contravention of this section, the driver of the motor cycle is guilty of an offence.

There is no specific requirement for the passenger to face the *front* (under subs. (2))—though this is presumably because it did not occur to the legislators that anyone would be daft enough to face the other way! Answers A, B and D are incorrect for this reason.

Under this section it is the *driver* who commits the offence (s. 23(3)), and the passenger can be convicted of aiding and abetting. Therefore, if an offence had been present, answers A and D would have been incorrect for this reason also.

It should be noted that a person travelling as a passenger astride a motor cycle but facing the rear *may* commit an offence of aiding and abetting the driver to drive dangerously, but this is not specifically legislated for.

Road Policing, para. 3.7.3.1

Answer 7.10

Answer **D** — The practice of warning other motorists of the presence of a police speed detection operation can amount to an offence of obstructing a police constable in the execution of their duty (see *DPP* v *Glendinning* [2005] EWHC 2333 (Admin) and *Betts* v *Stevens* [1910] 1 KB 1). Answer C is therefore incorrect.

In such cases, it is critical that it is shown that those warned were either exceeding the speed limit or were likely to do so (answer B is therefore incorrect). However, in the absence of such evidence, merely giving a warning to drivers who were observing the speed limit at the time will not amount to this offence (see *Bastable* v *Little* [1907] 1 KB 59). Answer A is therefore incorrect.

Note that the signal emitted by a hand-held radar speed gun has been deemed *not* to amount to a 'communication' for the purposes of the Wireless Telegraphy Act 1949 and a person intercepting such signals cannot be prosecuted under that legislation (*R* v *Crown Court of Knightsbridge, ex parte Foot* [1999] RTR 21).

Road Policing, para. 3.7.4, 3.7.4.6

Answer 7.11

Answer **D** — Under s. 82(1)(a) of the Road Traffic Regulation Act 1984, a 'restricted road' is one which has a system of street lamps not more than 200 yards apart (such as most side streets in towns or cities). On these roads, the speed limit is generally 30 mph. It follows that, generally, if a road has a system of street lamps *more* than 200 yards apart, it will *not* be a restricted road and the speed limit is normally higher than 30 mph.

Under s. 85(5), if a road is a 'restricted' road because of the physical features described previously, it *need not* have signs indicating that the speed limit is 30 mph and therefore answer C is incorrect.

If the street lamps on a road are *more* than 200 yards apart, the road *must* have signs indicating the speed limit (s. 85(4)). This is not optional and therefore answer A is incorrect.

The traffic authority can use the power under s. 82(2)(b) to impose 'restricted' status (and therefore a speed limit of 30 mph) on a road even though the road does not have a system of lighting as set out in s. 82(1)(a) (see *DPP* v *Evans* [2004] EWHC 2785).

Conversely, s. 82(2)(a) allows the traffic authority to declare that a road which is a restricted road (because of the features described previously) shall *cease* to be a restricted road. This means that where a road has a system of street lighting not more than 200 yards apart, it will *not* always be restricted to 30 mph (if the traffic authority so directs). Answer B is therefore incorrect.

Road Policing, para. 3.7.4.1

Answer 7.12

Answer **C** — The primary responsibility for maintaining highways rests with the highways authority for the relevant area. This includes a general statutory duty to maintain the highway itself (see s. 41 of the Highways Act 1980), which includes a duty, so far as reasonably practicable, to ensure that safe passage along the highway is not endangered by snow or ice (s. 41(1A)).

However, failure by a local authority to erect signs does not amount to a breach of the general statutory duty to maintain highways nor the general duty to promote road safety. As the House of Lords has put it, 'drivers have to take care for themselves and drive at a safe speed irrespective of whether or not there was a warning sign; they were not entitled to suppose that the need for care on their journeys would be highlighted so as to protect them from their own negligence' (*Gorringe* v *Calderdale MBC* [2004] UKHL 15).

Answers A, B and D are therefore incorrect.

Road Policing, paras 3.7.4.2, 3.8.2

Answer 7.13

Answer **B** — Section 88 of the Road Traffic Regulation Act 1984 provides for both maximum and minimum temporary speed limits to be imposed on certain roads.

Traffic authorities may impose temporary speed *restrictions* in connection with road works or similar operations near to the road which present a danger to the public or serious damage to the highway (see ss. 14–16 of the 1984 Act). These restrictions cannot generally exceed 18 months without approval from the Secretary of State.

As speed *restrictions* rather than speed limits, offences under this heading do not require notices of intended prosecution (*Platten* v *Gowing* [1983] Crim LR 184). Answers A and C are incorrect.

Answer D is incorrect as a NIP *would* normally be required for a speeding offence committed on a restricted road (or a motorway).

Note that when prosecuting for speed restrictions in these circumstances, corroboration is also not required.

Road Policing, para. 3.7.4.3

Answer 7.14

Answer **A** — Section 87(1) of the Road Traffic Regulation Act 1984 provides that speed limits will not apply to vehicles being used for fire and rescue authority, ambulance or police purposes, if the observance of that provision would be likely to hinder the use of the vehicle for the purpose for which it is being used on that occasion.

Section 87(2)(b) provides an exemption to members of the Serious Organised Crime Agency (SOCA), when the vehicle is being used for training purposes. However, s. 87(2)(b) is specific in that it only applies to members of SOCA. The exemption therefore does not apply to people serving in the Fire and Rescue Service when being trained, regardless of any previous training they have received, or how far they drive above the speed limit. Answers B, C and D are therefore incorrect.

Road Policing, para. 3.7.4.5

Answer 7.15

Answer **B** — When a prosecution takes place under s. 89(2) of the Road Traffic Regulation Act 1984 (exceeding a speed *limit*), a person may not be convicted solely on the evidence of one person for exceeding the speed limit. In other words, corroboration is required (unless the offence took place on a motorway). Corroboration is required when the offence takes place on a restricted road. Answer D is therefore incorrect.

Corroboration is normally provided by specialist speed measuring equipment in a police vehicle (such as *Vascar*); however, two police officers may provide sufficient evidence in a case of speeding, but the court will decide how much weight to give to such evidence. It is important to show that the officers saw the vehicle at exactly the same time (*Brighty* v *Pearson* [1938] 4 All ER 127). Answers A and C are incorrect for this reason.

Road Policing, para. 3.7.4.6

Answer 7.16

Answer **A** — Section 89(2) of the Road Traffic Regulation Act 1984 requires that a person prosecuted for driving a motor vehicle at a speed exceeding the limit shall not be convicted solely on the evidence of one witness to the effect that, in his or her opinion, the defendant was exceeding the speed limit. However, corroboration *may* be provided by the equipment in a police vehicle such as LTI 20/20 or Provida or similar speed measuring equipment (see *Nicholas* v *Penny* [1950] 2 KB 466). Answer C is therefore incorrect.

While it may be preferable, it is not necessary in all cases to prove the accuracy of the equipment being used (see *Darby* v *DPP* [1995] RTR 294). Answer B is therefore incorrect.

In *Connell* v *DPP* [2011] EWHC 158 (Admin), the opinion of the police officer was supported by reference to the reading on a Police Pilot device even though the device is an unapproved prescribed device. The magistrates' court allowed the police officer's evidence to be admitted and the Administrative Court upheld the magistrates' court ruling. Answer D is therefore incorrect.

Note that the requirements for corroboration do not apply to general speeding offences on motorways.

Road Policing, para. 3.7.4.6

8 | Highways and Safety Measures

STUDY PREPARATION

The areas covered by this chapter are wide and varied, ranging from the disposal of abandoned vehicles to powers to seize and retain vehicles under the Police Reform Act 2002.

Many of the police powers covered are particularly useful in practical situations and therefore will be of interest to those who train and test police officers.

QUESTIONS

Question 8.1

MARSHALL is the manager of a retail food outlet, which has recently opened on the High Street of a small town. MARSHALL called the police to the premises to deal with local business owners, who were distributing leaflets outside the store, encouraging people to shop in their own shops instead. When Constable BURTON arrived at the scene, the protesters were peaceful, but were standing outside the store's entrance. MARSHALL claimed that they were causing an obstruction and insisted that Constable BURTON arrest them.

Which of the following statements is correct, in relation to whether Constable BURTON could act on MARSHALL's request?

A Handing out leaflets would not amount to an obstruction; therefore, Constable BURTON has no powers to act on MARSHALL's request.

B Constable BURTON *could* act on MARSHALL's request, provided the people had created an actual obstruction.

C Constable BURTON *could* act on MARSHALL's request, provided the people had created a potential obstruction.

D *Any* assembly on the highway is unlawful and could amount to an obstruction; therefore, Constable BURTON *could* act on MARSHALL's request.

Question 8.2

TOGHILL owns a restaurant, which is managed by STEAD, who placed several tables and chairs on the wide pavement outside the restaurant to attract customers in the summer. STEAD was reported for causing an unnecessary obstruction, and when the case appeared before the magistrates was ordered to remove the obstruction. STEAD refused to do so because of the extra revenue the tables and chairs attracted.

As the owner of the restaurant, could TOGHILL be held liable for the further offence of failing to remove an obstruction, under s. 137ZA of the Highways Act 1980?

A Yes, but only if TOGHILL either consented to the continued obstruction, assisted in it or was neglectful.

B Yes, TOGHILL has absolute liability, as the owner of the restaurant.

C No, only the manager is liable for the obstruction itself and for failing to remove it.

D Yes, but only if TOGHILL either consented to the obstruction, or was neglectful.

Question 8.3

A committee has been formed by a group of local shop owners, who are concerned with incidents of violence that have occurred regularly over the past three months. The shops are located in a pedestrianised area. Access for shop workers is restricted to a lane at the rear of the premises and recently four employees have been the victims of robberies, while walking to their cars in the early evening. The committee invited officers from the local authority and the police to a meeting, to discuss blocking off the lane with Alleygates, to protect their employees.

The Highways Act 1980 allows for highways to be stopped up or diverted where it is expedient to do so. Could such an order be granted in these circumstances?

A No, this power is restricted to areas adjacent to educational premises.

B Yes, the highway authority can make this decision, provided it has consulted with the police authority for the area.

C No, this power is restricted to residential areas, or areas adjacent to educational premises.

D Yes, and the highway authority can make this decision without consultation.

Question 8.4

NEWMAN and DUNN lived on a housing estate and were continually disturbed by local youths on motor cycles on a field behind their houses. The only access to the field was via a bridleway, which was used by horse riders and ramblers. The motorcyclists used the bridleway to get onto the field, usually in the evenings. In an attempt to try to stop the motorcyclists, NEWMAN and DUNN tied a length of rope across the bridleway at waist height, hoping that it would unseat the riders. They were not particularly bothered if the riders were injured or their vehicles damaged, they were merely trying to prevent access to the field and stop the disturbance they created.

Considering the location of the obstruction created by NEWMAN and DUNN, could they have committed an offence under s. 22A of the Road Traffic Act 1988 (causing danger to other road users)?

A   No, an offence under this section can only be committed on a road.

B   Yes, a bridleway is a road for the purposes of s. 192(1) of the Act.

C   Yes, an offence under this section can be committed on a road or public place.

D   No, the location is irrelevant; an offence is committed under this section when a person causes anything to be *on* a road in circumstances that would lead to danger.

Question 8.5

ADAMS and WALKER were walking home on the pavement alongside a busy dual carriageway which had a speed limit of 40 mph. It was late at night and they were in a drunken condition. They came across a wheelie bin outside someone's house and decided to roll it into the road and then push it down the hill to see how fast it would go. The bin ended up in the middle of the road, rolling towards oncoming traffic, causing a potential danger to motorists. The incident was captured on CCTV and the pair were located and identified by the police a short while later.

Considering s. 22A of the Road Traffic Act 1988 (causing danger to other road users), what further evidence, if any, would be required in relation to ADAMS's and WALKER's intent, in order to prove the offence?

A   No evidence is required relating to their intent; the offence was complete when ADAMS and WALKER caused a danger to other road users.

B   That ADAMS and WALKER intended to create a danger to other road users.

C   That they intended to cause the wheelie bin to be on the road; and that it would be obvious to a reasonable person that to do so would be dangerous.

D That ADAMS and WALKER intended to create a danger to other road users, or were reckless as to whether such a danger would be caused.

Question 8.6

GRANT bought some fireworks, and one evening he discharged some rockets while standing on the pavement outside his house.

Has GRANT committed an offence by discharging the fireworks in these circumstances?

A No, as the fireworks were not discharged in the road.

B Yes, provided a danger was caused to people using the road.

C Yes, provided people using the road were injured, interrupted or endangered.

D Yes, the offence is committed by simply discharging the fireworks.
Note: This does not take account of s. 28 of the Town Police Clauses Act 1847 (wantonly discharging fireworks).

Question 8.7

AHMED used a 3.5 tonne van to deliver furniture. AHMED was delivering to a house situated in a street, which had a grass verge in the centre of the road dividing two carriageways. There were no parking spaces outside the delivery address; therefore, AHMED parked the vehicle on the grass verge until a space became available.

Has AHMED committed an offence contrary to s. 19 of the Road Traffic Act 1988 (parking commercial vehicles on verges)?

A No, because of the vehicle's weight.

B Yes, as the vehicle was parked on land in the centre of the road.

C Yes, provided the vehicle was causing a danger.

D No, as the vehicle was not parked on a verge at the side of a road.

Question 8.8

MAGUIRE owns a large flat bed trailer, which he frequently leaves outside his house, which is situated on a hill. MAGUIRE left the trailer outside the house one evening, but forgot to set the braking mechanism. As a consequence, the trailer rolled down-hill, colliding with another vehicle.

Would MAGUIRE commit an offence under s. 22 of the Road Traffic Act 1988 (dangerous vehicles) in these circumstances?

A No, the trailer was not attached to a motor vehicle.
B No, this offence only applies to the condition of a vehicle.
C Yes, the offence is complete in these circumstances.
D No, this offence only applies to stationary vehicles.

Question 8.9

KWASHI applied for a disabled badge to be issued under the Chronically Sick and Disabled Persons Act 1970, due to a confirmed disability. KWASHI had not previously been issued with such a badge. However, following checks, the local authority discovered that KWASHI had been issued with two fixed penalty notices in the previous six months, for parking on double yellow lines.

Would the local authority be entitled to refuse to issue KWASHI with a badge because of the parking offences?

A No, the offences did not relate to the misuse of a disabled badge.
B Yes, the offences were committed in the 12 months prior to the application being made.
C No, KWASHI only committed two relevant offences prior to the application being made.
D Yes, KWASHI committed at least one relevant offence prior to the application being made.

Question 8.10

QUINN went shopping on a Sunday afternoon and, to avoid paying car park charges, she parked her car in a private car park of a business premises. There was no barrier at the car park entrance, although there was a sign stating that the car park was private property. QUINN thought it would be ok to park there, believing that no one would be in work on a Sunday. When QUINN returned to her car, she found that another vehicle had been parked directly in front of hers, blocking her car in completely. QUINN tried knocking at the door of the premises and could see lights on inside; however, she was made to wait there for over an hour until the owner of the vehicle, TRENT, came outside.

Would TRENT commit an offence in these circumstances, under s. 54 of the Protection of Freedoms Act 2012 (immobilising vehicles)?

A Yes, TRENT has restricted the movement of QUINN's vehicle.
B No, TRENT may claim a lawful authority for his actions, because QUINN has parked unlawfully on private property.

C No, TRENT has not restricted the movement of the vehicle by attaching an immobilising device to it.

D Yes, provided TRENT has prevented or inhibited the removal of the vehicle for monetary gain or the equivalent.

Question 8.11

HARRIS was in a multi-storey car park attached to a shopping centre. The car park was operated by a private company, which owned the shopping centre, but was open to the general public at the time. The car park was covered by CCTV and the night security guard saw HARRIS climb onto the bonnet of a car and then run over the roof, jumping off the vehicle from the boot. He did this to several vehicles in the car park. The night security guard called the police and when they arrived, HARRIS was walking away from the car park.

Has HARRIS committed the offence of tampering with vehicles, under s. 25 of the Road Traffic Act 1988, in these circumstances?

A No, because the vehicles were not on a road.

B No, because the car park was not owned by the local authority.

C Yes, because the vehicles were in a public place.

D No, because he did not interfere with the brake or mechanism of the vehicles.

Question 8.12

SHAW was playing on roller blades in a leisure centre car park. The car park was owned and maintained by the local authority, but was open to the general public. The car park was built on a flat area, but the exit was on a steep hill. On several occasions, SHAW caught hold of passing vehicles, which were going down the hill. SHAW let go of the vehicles before they reached the road, but was able to accelerate to high speeds while holding onto the cars in the car park. The leisure centre manager complained to the police.

Has SHAW committed an offence under s. 26(1) of the Road Traffic Act 1988 in these circumstances?

A Yes, because SHAW was on a road or in a local authority car park.

B No, because SHAW did not get onto a vehicle.

C Yes, because SHAW was on a road or in a public place.

D No, because SHAW was not on a road.

Question 8.13

DOUGLAS lived near some woodland, which was accessible from the road. One day, he drove to the woodland in his van and abandoned a settee and two chairs in a clearing in the woods.

Has DOUGLAS committed an offence under the Refuse Disposal (Amenity) Act 1978 (disposing of property on land)?

A No, the offence relates to abandoning a motor vehicle only.

B Yes, he has committed an offence in these circumstances.

C No, he has not abandoned anything on a highway or land forming part of a highway.

D No, the offence relates to abandoning a motor vehicle or part of a motor vehicle only.

Question 8.14

Section 3(1) of the Refuse Disposal (Amenity) Act 1978 imposes a duty on local authorities to remove motor vehicles that have been abandoned in their area, in certain circumstances. Before it can remove a vehicle under this section, a local authority must affix a notice to the vehicle advising the owner of its intention.

What is the period of notice that must be given by the local authority in England, to the owner of a vehicle which appears to have been abandoned and ought to be destroyed?

A 7 days.

B 28 days.

C 24 hours.

D 21 days.

Question 8.15

FAULKNER owns a distribution warehouse situated near a Premiership football ground. The warehouse receives deliveries seven days a week and at all hours of the day. FAULKNER is frustrated because every time the football club plays at home, ROSE parks a van in the warehouse car park (which is private property) to sell burgers. This causes disruption at the warehouse because ROSE's van causes an obstruction to drivers attempting to make deliveries. FAULKNER has approached ROSE several times to ask him to leave the premises; however, ROSE makes a significant profit on these occasions and has refused to do so. One Saturday afternoon,

FAULKNER called the police to deal with the problem and Constable HANSEN attended. FAULKNER asked Constable HANSEN to remove ROSE's vehicle from the premises.

Did Constable HANSEN have the power to remove ROSE's vehicle, as requested by FAULKNER?

A Yes, providing ROSE's vehicle was causing an unnecessary obstruction.

B No, it is unlikely that ROSE's vehicle created a danger.

C Yes, providing ROSE's vehicle was causing a major obstruction.

D No, Constable HANSEN did not have the power to remove a vehicle which was not on a road or other public place.

Question 8.16

PETERS owned a trials motor cycle, which was not intended for use on roads. Near PETERS's house is an area of common land and he took his motor cycle there one day. PETERS had just started up his motor cycle and had ridden onto the land, approximately 10 yards from the road, when he was stopped by Constable MENDEZ.

Has PETERS committed an offence of driving on land other than a road, in these circumstances?

A No, as he was not driving a motor vehicle.

B Yes, as he has driven on common land other than a road.

C No, he has driven within 15 yards of the road.

D Yes, as he has driven on common land within 15 yards of the road.

Question 8.17

DEERE retired from work and went on a touring holiday to Europe for six months. DEERE's teenage son, JEFFREY, was allowed to use the family car while DEERE was away. In the first month, the car was seized from JEFFREY for using it while causing harassment. Several times during the following months, the relevant authority wrote to DEERE, the registered owner, serving notice that the vehicle had been seized. Upon returning from holiday, DEERE discovered that JEFFREY had ignored all correspondence from the authority and that as no reply had been received, the vehicle had been sold at a car auction.

Would DEERE have the right to claim the proceeds from the sale of the vehicle?

A No, the proceeds may be kept by the authority, as DEERE failed to comply with the seizure notice.

B Yes, DEERE can claim the net proceeds from the sale in these circumstances alone.

C No, unless it can be shown that the authority did not take reasonable steps to contact DEERE before the vehicle was sold.

D Yes, provided it can be shown that DEERE was not aware that the vehicle would be driven in such a manner by JEFFREY.

Question 8.18

PEARCE is a designated police community support officer (PCSO) working on a housing estate. He has received a number of complaints from residents about HOGAN riding his motor cycle in a park nearby. Last week, PEARCE stopped HOGAN while he was riding his motor cycle and issued him with a warning under s. 59 of the Police Reform Act 2002, as he had narrowly missed colliding with some children playing football. PEARCE has today received a further complaint about HOGAN, who again rode his motor cycle in the park, nearly injuring a child. PEARCE attended HOGAN's home address and saw the motor cycle on the road outside.

Does PEARCE have the power to seize HOGAN's motor cycle, under s. 59(3)(b) of the Police Reform Act 2002, in these circumstances?

A No, a PCSO's power is restricted to stopping vehicles.

B Yes, he has the power to seize and remove the vehicle in these circumstances.

C Yes, provided he is accompanied by a police officer in uniform.

D No, as the motor cycle is no longer being used.

Question 8.19

SHAH has hired PRICE to do some building work at his house. PRICE has hired a skip from BARRY for a period of three weeks. After a week, neighbours complain to the police that the skip is unlit during the night and is causing a danger to motorists.

Who has committed an offence in relation to the skip in these circumstances?

A SHAH only.

B PRICE only.

C PRICE and BARRY only.

D BARRY only.

Question 8.20

KAHL was approaching a zebra crossing on his motor cycle when GIBBONEY stepped on to the crossing at the last moment. KAHL did not see GIBBONEY and drove over the crossing, nearly hitting him. GIBBONEY took down the registration number of KAHL's motor cycle.

In relation to KAHL's failure to stop at the pedestrian crossing, which of the following statements is true?

A He is guilty of driving without due care and attention in these circumstances alone, which is an absolute offence.

B He is guilty of failing to stop at the crossing and driving without due care and attention.

C He is guilty of failing to stop at the crossing in these circumstances alone, which is an absolute offence.

D He is guilty of driving without due care and attention in these circumstances alone.

Question 8.21

TROTT was working as a school crossing patrol outside a school at 7.50 am. BOYCE was riding on the road on his pedal cycle, when TROTT stood in the road to allow some people to cross. As none of the people were school children, BOYCE did not stop his cycle. TROTT was wearing her uniform and exhibiting her sign at the time of the incident.

Has BOYCE committed an offence in these circumstances?

A No, because of the time of day.

B Yes, an offence has been committed.

C No, because the people crossing were not children.

D No, because he was not driving a motor vehicle.

Question 8.22

The Fire and Rescue Service have been called to a large fire at a warehouse premises. Their entrance is blocked by a motor vehicle that is locked, but has the engine running.

What action may the fire and rescue personnel take to move the vehicle?

A They may enter the vehicle if possible, but may not use force to enter the vehicle unless the owner would have consented had they known the circumstances.

B They may enter the vehicle using force if necessary, but they may not drive it without the owner's consent.

C They may enter the vehicle using force if necessary and actually drive the vehicle without the owner's consent.

D They may enter the vehicle using force if necessary and actually drive the vehicle without the owner's consent and have it statutorily removed.

ANSWERS

Answer 8.1

Answer **B** — Section 28 of the Town Police Clauses Act 1847 states:

Every person who in any street, to the obstruction, annoyance, or danger of the residents or passengers,... wilfully interrupts any public crossing, or wilfully causes any obstruction in any public footpath or other public thoroughfare...

What amounts to an obstruction is a question of fact for the magistrate(s) to decide in each case (*Wade* v *Grange* [1977] RTR 417). In arriving at that decision they will have regard to, amongst other things: 'the length of time the obstruction continued, the place where it occurred, the purpose for which it was done and whether it caused an *actual* as opposed to a potential obstruction' (Lord Parker CJ in *Nagy* v *Weston* [1965] 1 WLR 280). Answer C is therefore incorrect.

In *DPP* v *Jones* [1999] 2 AC 240, Lord Irvine gave examples of lawful use of the highway as including the handing out of leaflets (see *Hirst and Agu* v *Chief Constable of West Yorkshire* (1987) 85 Cr App R 143) and making sketches and collecting for charity. Answer A is incorrect, as this type of behaviour *could* amount to an obstruction.

Their lordships in this case had also been asked to consider the lawful use of the highway in the light of Art. 11 of the European Convention on Human Rights, the article that protects a right of peaceful assembly generally. Lord Irvine stated that to view *any* assembly on the highway as being *prima facie* unlawful (as the Divisional Court had done) would not be compatible with Art. 11. Answer D is therefore incorrect.

Road Policing, para. 3.8.2

Answer 8.2

Answer **A** — An offence of obstruction is committed under s. 137 of the Highways Act 1980, if a person without lawful authority or excuse, in any way wilfully obstructs the free passage along a highway. If a person convicted of this offence fails to remove an obstruction, the magistrates' court can make an order requiring them to do so. Failing to comply with such an order is a further criminal offence under s. 137ZA of the Act.

As a result of the Highways (Obstruction by Body Corporate) Act 2004, a director, manager or other officer of a company can be guilty of either of these offences (answer

C is therefore incorrect). In order for such a person to be guilty of the offence, it must be proved that the offence was committed with the consent or connivance of the officer, or that it was attributable to their neglect. Answer D is incorrect as the offence may also be committed if the manager assisted (or connived) in causing the obstruction. Answer B is incorrect, as the offence is not one of absolute liability in respect of an officer of the company.

Road Policing, para. 3.8.2

Answer 8.3

Answer **B** — Local highway authorities are empowered to make a stopping up order, under s. 118B, or a diversion order, under s. 119B, of the Highways Act 1980. The power allows the highway authority to either stop up or divert the relevant highway, where they are satisfied that premises adjoining or adjacent to the highway are affected by high levels of crime and that the existence of the highway is facilitating the persistent commission of criminal offences.

If the relevant highway crosses school land, an order can be made if it is expedient for the purposes of protecting the pupils or staff from violence or threats of violence, or from harassment, alarm or distress arising from unlawful activity. However, the power is not restricted to residential areas, or areas adjacent to educational premises. Answers A and C are therefore incorrect.

Neither a stopping up order nor a diversion order can be made until the highway authority has consulted the police authority for the area in which the highway lies. Answer D is therefore incorrect.

Road Policing, para. 3.8.2.1

Answer 8.4

Answer **A** — Under s. 22A(1) of the Road Traffic Act 1988, a person is guilty of an offence if he intentionally and without lawful authority or reasonable cause—

(a) causes anything to be *on or over* a road, or
(b) interferes with a motor vehicle, trailer or cycle, or
(c) interferes (directly or indirectly) with traffic equipment,
in such circumstances that it would be obvious to a reasonable person that to do so would be dangerous.

Answer D is incorrect, because the offence may be committed by placing something over the road, such as the rope referred to in this question.

However, while the section refers to activities which are committed on a 'road', a 'road' for the purposes of this offence does not include a footpath (or bridleway) (s. 22A(5)), neither does it include public places. Answers B and C are therefore incorrect.

Road Policing, para. 3.8.3

Answer 8.5

Answer **C** — Under s. 22A(1) of the Road Traffic Act 1988, a person is guilty of an offence if he intentionally and without lawful authority or reasonable cause—

(a) causes anything to be on or over a road, or
(b) interferes with a motor vehicle, trailer or cycle, or
(c) interferes (directly or indirectly) with traffic equipment,
   in such circumstances that it would be obvious to a reasonable person that to do so would be dangerous.

This offence requires a defendant to act both intentionally and without lawful authority. The intention in s. 22A only applies to the causing or interfering described. Since some element of intent must be shown, answer A is incorrect.

There is no need to show that the defendant *intended* to create danger (or was reckless as to whether it would be created)—only that it would have been obvious to a reasonable person that to do so would be dangerous. Answers B and D are therefore incorrect.

Road Policing, para. 3.8.3

Answer 8.6

Answer **C** — Under s. 161 of the Highways Act 1980, a person commits an offence if he or she discharges any firearm or firework within 15.24 metres (50 feet) of the centre of the highway, and in consequence a user of the highway is injured, interrupted or endangered.

As the offence took place on the pavement, which would be within 50 feet of the centre of the highway, answer A is incorrect.

Answer B is incorrect as a user of the highway must be injured, interrupted or endangered.

Answer D is incorrect as there must be a consequence, i.e. an injury, interruption or danger must occur as a result of the discharged firework.

Road Policing, para. 3.8.3.1

Answer 8.7

Answer **A** — Under s. 19 of the Road Traffic Act 1988, an offence is committed by a heavy commercial vehicle, which is parked wholly or in part on the verge of a road, or any land situated between two carriageways that is not a footway, or on a footway. Answer D is incorrect as the offence may be committed in the middle of the road also.

Answer B is incorrect as the vehicle was not a heavy commercial vehicle, i.e. one which exceeded 7.5 tonnes.

There is no requirement to prove that any danger was caused by the vehicle's presence. Answer C is therefore incorrect.

Road Policing, para. 3.8.4.1

Answer 8.8

Answer **A** — An offence may be committed under s. 22 of the Road Traffic Act 1988 if a person in charge of a vehicle causes or permits the vehicle or a trailer drawn by it to remain at rest on a road in such a position or in such condition or in such circumstances as to involve a danger of injury to other persons using the road. This suggests that although the offence applies to both motor vehicles and trailers, the trailer must be attached to the vehicle at the time of the offence (answer C is therefore incorrect).

This offence involves presenting a danger of injury to other road users by the position, condition or circumstances of the vehicle/trailer. Answer B is therefore incorrect.

The danger presented by the condition or circumstances of the vehicle is not confined to occasions when it is stationary, but will also apply to a vehicle/trailer which presents a danger by moving (such as where a driver fails to set the handbrake (*Maguire v Crouch* [1941] 1 KB 108)). Answer D is therefore incorrect.

Road Policing, para. 3.8.4.2

Answer 8.9

Answer **A** — Under reg. 8 of the Disabled Persons (Badges for Motor Vehicles) (England) Regulations 2000 (SI 2000/682), a local authority may require the return of a badge and may refuse to issue such a badge if the person concerned has held and subsequently misused it in a way which has led to a relevant conviction. Regulation 8 was amended by the Disabled Persons (Badges for Motor Vehicles) (England)

(Amendment) (No. 2) Regulations 2011 (SI 2011/2675), reg. 2(6)(a), which substituted 'at least three relevant convictions' with 'a relevant conviction'.

However, the power to require the return of a badge, or refuse to issue one, applies if the person concerned *has held and subsequently misused* it in a way which has led to a relevant conviction. The number of parking offences committed, or when they were committed, is irrelevant when the person has *not* previously held a badge. KWASHI has not misused a disabled badge, and is therefore not bound by this legislation.

Answers B, C and D are therefore incorrect.

Road Policing, para. 3.8.4.4

Answer 8.10

Answer **A** — Under s. 54(1) of the Protection of Freedoms Act 2012, a person commits an offence who, without lawful authority—

(a) immobilises a motor vehicle by the attachment to the vehicle, or a part of it, of an immobilising device, or

(b) moves, or restricts the movement of, such a vehicle by any means,

intending to prevent or inhibit the removal of the vehicle by a person otherwise entitled to remove it.

It is a criminal offence to immobilise a motor vehicle; the offence can be committed by attaching an immobilising device (typically a wheel clamp) to the vehicle or to a part of the vehicle, or to move it (e.g. by towing away) or to restrict the movement of a vehicle, which could be, for example, by using another vehicle to prevent it being driven away. Answer C is therefore incorrect.

The intent required for this offence is to 'prevent or inhibit the removal of the vehicle by a person otherwise entitled to remove it' (i.e. the owner); there is no requirement to prove that the person did so for monetary gain or otherwise and for that reason answer D is incorrect.

'Lawful authority' is restricted to bodies exercising a statutory authority in specified circumstances, such as the police, the DVLA, local authorities or the Vehicle and Operator Services Agency (VOSA), all of whom can clamp vehicles to enforce their respected lawful powers. This does not include a private individual acting in such a manner, regardless of whether the other party is trespassing; in fact, the Act was created to *prevent* such actions and in these circumstances, the affected party is expected to pursue parking on private property through civil remedies. Answer B is therefore incorrect.

(Note that the Removal and Disposal of Vehicles Regulations 1986 have been amended to allow police officers to remove vehicles from a road, place or 'other land', which effectively provides a power to remove a vehicle from private property which is parked in a way which creates a danger or major obstruction. This does not create a duty for the police to act, but allows them to use their discretion in any given situation to determine the appropriate action to take.)

Road Policing, para. 3.8.4.6

Answer 8.11

Answer **B** — An offence is committed under s. 25 of the Road Traffic Act 1988 when a person gets onto a vehicle, or tampers with the brake or mechanism of a vehicle. Since the offence may be committed in either of these circumstances, answer D is incorrect. Offences under this section may only be committed either on a road or in a car park owned by the local authority. The offence may not be committed in any public place, therefore answer C is incorrect. Since the offence is not restricted to vehicles parked on a road, answer A is also incorrect.

Road Policing, para. 3.8.5

Answer 8.12

Answer **D** — Section 26(1) of the Road Traffic Act 1988 states:

(1) If, for the purpose of being carried, a person without lawful authority or reasonable cause takes or retains hold of, or gets on to a motor vehicle or trailer while in motion on a road he is guilty of an offence.
(2) If, for the purpose of being drawn, a person takes or retains hold of a motor vehicle or trailer while in motion on a road he is guilty of an offence.

Therefore, the offence may be committed either by a person who gets on to a vehicle or trailer while in motion, or by a person who retains hold of one. Answer B is therefore incorrect.

The offence may only take place on a road; therefore, answers A and C are incorrect. (Note that the offence of tampering or getting onto vehicles, under s. 25 of the Act, may take place on a road or parking place provided by a local authority.)

Road Policing, para. 3.8.5

Answer 8.13

Answer **B** — An offence may be committed under s. 2 of the Refuse Disposal (Amenity) Act 1978 either by abandoning a motor vehicle or anything which formed part of a motor vehicle (s. 2(1)(a)), or by abandoning anything other than a motor vehicle (s. 2(1)(b)). Answers A and D are therefore incorrect.

The offence is complete when property, as referred to previously, is abandoned either on any land forming part of the highway, or on any land in the open air. Presumably this would include private property, if it is in the open air. Answer C is therefore incorrect.

Road Policing, para. 3.8.6

Answer 8.14

Answer **C** — Section 3(1) of the Refuse Disposal (Amenity) Act 1978 states that where it appears to a local authority that a motor vehicle in their area is abandoned without lawful authority on any land in the open air or on any other land forming part of a highway, it shall be the duty of the authority, subject to the following provisions of this section, to remove the vehicle. Before it can remove a vehicle under this section, a local authority must follow the requirements of the Act and of the Removal and Disposal of Vehicles Regulations (SI 1986/183) in relation to affixing of notices advising the owner (of both the vehicle, and the land if occupied) of its intention.

In order to combat the growing problem of abandoned cars, the notice period required to be given by a local authority in relation to a vehicle which appears to have been abandoned and ought to be destroyed is 24 hours (see reg. 10). Answers A, B and D are therefore incorrect.

Note also that if the local authority has taken possession of a vehicle which is in such good condition that it ought *not* to be destroyed, the owner will have 7 days in which to remove it (see reg. 14).

Road Policing, para. 3.8.6.1

Answer 8.15

Answer **C** — The Removal and Disposal of Vehicles Regulations 1986 allow for the removal of vehicles that are either causing a danger or obstruction. These Regulations were amended to allow police officers to remove vehicles from a road, place or other land, which effectively provides a power to remove a vehicle from private property (answer D is therefore incorrect). The inclusion of the phrase 'or other land' came as a consequence of the ban on clamping and towing and provides the police with an appropriate mechanism to allow the removal of vehicles obstructing or preventing a landowner's use of their land.

This extension to the Regulations does not create a duty for the police to act—it allows the police to use their discretion in any given situation to determine the appropriate action to take. However, the police should only use this power where a vehicle is considered to be parked in a way which creates a danger or a major obstruction (SI 2012/2277). Answers A and B are therefore incorrect.

Road Policing, para. 3.8.6.2

Answer 8.16

Answer **B** — Under s. 34 of the Road Traffic Act 1988, a person commits an offence who drives a *mechanically propelled vehicle* on any common land, moorland or land of any other description, not being part of a road. The offence is not restricted to motor vehicles. Answer A is therefore incorrect.

As soon as the person drives on the land, he or she commits the offence. Answer D is therefore incorrect.

A defence is provided for a person who has driven onto the land within 15 yards of the road in order to park the vehicle. There is no general defence of driving within 15 yards of the road only. Answer C is therefore incorrect.

Road Policing, para. 3.8.7, 3.8.7.1

Answer 8.17

Answer **B** — The arrangements for the removal, retention, release and disposal of vehicles are contained in the Police (Retention and Disposal of Motor Vehicles) Regulations 2002. They cover the seizure, retention and disposal of vehicles under s. 59 of the Police Reform Act 2002.

The Regulations provide that seizure notices must be served on the owner of a vehicle and where the authority is unable to serve a notice on the owner, or the person fails to remove the vehicle from its custody, it must take further steps to identify the owner. Where the person appearing to be the owner fails to comply with a seizure notice, or where the authority has not been able, having taken all reasonable steps, to give the seizure notice to a person, the relevant authority can (subject to specific time limits) dispose of the vehicle (see reg. 7).

Under reg. 8, if the vehicle is sold, the owner can claim the net proceeds (i.e. minus the storage fees) provided the claim is made within a year. It is immaterial that the owner failed to comply with the seizure notice (answer A is therefore incorrect). There is no requirement for the owner to show that the authority has failed to comply with the regulations before making such a claim, or to demonstrate that he or she was not aware of the use of the vehicle which resulted in it being seized. Answers C and D are therefore incorrect.

Road Policing, para. 3.8.7.2

Answer 8.18

Answer **B** — To exercise one of the powers under s. 59(3) of the Act, a constable in uniform must have reasonable grounds for believing that a motor vehicle is being used on any occasion in a manner which contravenes s. 3 or s. 34 of the Road Traffic Act 1988 (careless/inconsiderate driving and prohibition of off-road driving), and is causing/likely to cause alarm, distress or annoyance to members of the public (s. 59(1)). Under s. 59(2) of the Act, a constable may also exercise a power under s. 59(3) if he or she has reasonable grounds for believing a motor vehicle *has been* used in the circumstances outlined. Answer D is therefore incorrect.

The powers listed under s. 59(3) enable a constable in uniform to stop motor vehicles in contravention of s. 59(1) or (2), to seize and remove motor vehicles, enter any premises (except a dwelling) and use reasonable force if necessary. A vehicle may only be seized if a warning has previously been issued to the user of the vehicle that it will be seized if the use continues or is repeated and it appears to the officer that the use *has* continued or been repeated after the warning. The power to stop, seize and remove vehicles can be conferred on a PCSO, but he or she may not enter premises unless accompanied and supervised by a constable in uniform. Answers A and C are therefore incorrect.

Road Policing, para. 3.8.7.2

Answer 8.19

Answer **D** — Under s. 139(4)(a) of the Highways Act 1980, a skip which has been deposited on a road must be 'properly lighted' during the hours of darkness. Section 139(4) states that the owner of the skip will be responsible for ensuring that it complies with the conditions imposed under the Act. Answer A is therefore incorrect.

Section 139(11) of the Act states that if a skip is either hired, or made subject of a hire purchase agreement for not less than one month, the person in possession of it will become the 'owner'. Since the builder in the scenario hired it for three weeks, which is less than a month, the actual owner, BARRY, retains responsibility for it. Answers B and C are therefore incorrect.

Road Policing, para. 3.8.8

Answer 8.20

Answer **C** — The failure by a driver to stop at a crossing in contravention of the Regulations made under the Road Traffic Regulation Act 1984 is an absolute offence. There is no need to show any particular state of mind by the driver. Further, the failure by a driver to observe the crossing Regulations will not in itself provide sufficient proof that a person has driven without due care and attention (*Gibbons* v *Kahl* [1956] 1 QB 59). Further proof would be required, although such evidence may be presented as part of a case.

Consequently, answers A, B and D are incorrect.

Road Policing, para. 3.8.9.5

Answer 8.21

Answer **B** — Section 28 of the Road Traffic Regulation Act 1984 has been amended by the Transport Act 2000. There are no longer restrictions as to the time of day that an offence may be committed (formerly the hours were 0800 hrs to 1730 hrs). Answer A is therefore incorrect.

A further effect of the 2000 Act was that school crossing patrols are no longer restricted to stopping vehicles for children to cross. They may stop vehicles to allow anyone to cross safely. Answer C is therefore incorrect.

The offence may be committed by a person who is driving or propelling a vehicle. There is no requirement for a person to be driving a motor vehicle. Answer D is therefore incorrect.

Road Policing, para. 3.8.9.6

Answer 8.22

Answer **C** — Powers in the event of emergency are given to the Fire and Rescue Service by virtue of s. 44(2) of the Fire and Rescue Services Act 2004, which states:

(2) In particular, an employee of a fire and rescue authority who is authorised as mentioned in subsection (1) may under that subsection—
  (a) enter premises or a place, by force if necessary, without the consent of the owner or occupier of the premises or place;
  (b) move or break into a vehicle without the consent of its owner;
  (c) close a highway;
  (d) stop and regulate traffic;
  (e) restrict the access of persons to premises or a place...

These wide-ranging powers give fire and rescue personnel, who are authorised in writing, the practical authority to deal effectively with emergency situations. They need no consent of the owner of the property they enter (including motor vehicles); therefore answers A and B are incorrect. The power, however, does not extend to statutory removal of vehicles; answer D is therefore incorrect.

Although driving a motor vehicle without the owner's consent is an offence, this power gives the relevant personnel a defence to this and they may move it by driving it.

Road Policing, para. 3.8.10.1

QUESTIONS

Question 9.1

Constable HEINZE attended a road traffic collision, where STONELEY's unattended
car had rolled down a hill, colliding with another parked vehicle while STONELEY
was in a shop. STONELEY told the officer that the handbrake had been applied to the
vehicle; however, Constable HEINZE suspected that it was faulty. In order to test the
handbrake, the officer pushed STONELEY's vehicle along the road with the handbrake applied for 10 metres, forming the opinion that it was, in fact, defective. Constable HEINZE was not a qualified vehicle examiner.

If STONELEY were to be prosecuted for any offences, would Constable HEINZE's evidence in relation to the handbrake be admissible in court?

A No, the vehicle must be tested either by a qualified police officer trained to examine vehicles, or a qualified Department for Transport examiner.

B No, the vehicle must be tested by a qualified police officer trained to examine vehicles.

C No, the vehicle must be tested by a qualified Department for Transport examiner.

D Yes, the vehicle may be tested by a qualified examiner, but this is not absolutely necessary.

Question 9.2

CANTER was riding a motor cycle on a road and was stopped by Constable PARRY, an authorised vehicle examiner. On measuring the depth of tread on the tyres, Constable PARRY found that the grooves of the tread pattern on both tyres measured 1.1 mm.

Which of the following statements is correct in relation to the tyres on CANTER's vehicle, considering reg. 27 of the Road Vehicles (Construction and Use) Regulations 1986?

A The depth of tread on the tyres was lawful for the type of vehicle CANTER was riding.

B The depth of tread on the tyres was unlawful; for this type of vehicle, the depth of tread should have been at least 1.2 mm.

C The depth of tread on the tyres was unlawful; for this type of vehicle, the depth of tread should have been at least 1.5 mm.

D The depth of tread on the tyres was unlawful; for this type of vehicle, the depth of tread should have been at least 1.6 mm.

Question 9.3

CROFT was in the process of renovating an old Vauxhall motor vehicle which was parked on the road outside his house. Constable HEINEMAN passed the vehicle one day and noticed that two of the tyres were deflated and the officer felt that it made the vehicle unroadworthy. Constable HEINEMAN spoke to CROFT and established that the vehicle was fully taxed and insured and had an up-to-date MOT. CROFT stated that he hoped to have the vehicle working soon, but could not afford the new tyres yet. Constable HEINEMAN was considering reporting CROFT for the defective tyres, but the officer is not an authorised vehicle examiner.

Which of the following statements is correct in relation to the tyres on CROFT's vehicle, considering reg. 27 of the Road Vehicles (Construction and Use) Regulations 1986?

A The tyre must be inflated so as to make it fit for use in the future; Constable HEINEMAN does not need to be an authorised vehicle examiner to deal with this matter.

B The tyre must be inflated so as to make it fit for the use to which the vehicle is being put now; Constable HEINEMAN does not need to be an authorised vehicle examiner to deal with this matter.

C The tyre must be inflated so as to make it fit for use in the future; however, Constable HEINEMAN must arrange for it to be examined by an authorised vehicle examiner.

D The tyre must be inflated so as to make it fit for the use to which the vehicle is being put now; however, Constable HEINEMAN must arrange for it to be examined by an authorised vehicle examiner.

Question 9.4

POTTER was driving a car, while towing a trailer along the road. POTTER was stopped by Constable GILLANEY because the two rear tyres of the vehicle were so defective that the metal was in contact with the road, and sparks were flying as the vehicle was travelling along. POTTER was carrying wood in the trailer and his son was sitting on top of the load to stop it from falling off.

Ignoring any other offences that he may have committed, would POTTER be guilty of an offence under reg. 27 of the Road Vehicles (Construction and Use) Regulations 1986 (defective tyres)?

A Yes, if it could be shown there was danger to POTTER's son or that damage might have been caused to the road.

B Yes, if it could be shown there was danger to POTTER's son or that damage had been caused to the road.

C Yes, but only if it could be shown there was danger to other persons using the road, or that damage may have been caused to the road.

D No, this regulation applies only to the danger or damage caused by motor vehicles.

Question 9.5

WATSON is a taxi driver. One evening, WATSON pulled up outside a customer's house and sounded the taxi's horn several times, to attract the person's attention. The customer lived in a built up area and WATSON's taxi was stationary. The time was 11.35 pm.

Has WATSON committed an offence under reg. 99 of the Road Vehicles (Construction and Use) Regulations 1986?

A Yes, because it was after 11.00 pm and the vehicle was stationary.
B No, because it was not before 11.30 pm.
C Yes, because the vehicle was stationary.
D No, because the vehicle was stationary.

Question 9.6

PHEALAN was driving a dumper truck along the road from one building site to another. The vehicle, which was driven at a speed slightly over 20 mph, is not intended for use on the road and this was a one-off journey.

Which of the following statements is correct in relation to whether the vehicle should be fitted with an audible warning instrument, under the Road Vehicles (Construction and Use) Regulations 1986?

A Because the vehicle was used on a road, and has a maximum speed of more than 20 mph, it should be fitted with an audible warning instrument.
B The vehicle is exempt from the requirement, regardless of its use on the road, because it has a maximum speed below 25 mph.
C The vehicle is exempt from the requirement, regardless of its maximum speed, because it is not a motor vehicle.
D Any mechanically propelled vehicle used on a road must be fitted with an audible warning instrument, unless it is an agricultural vehicle.

Question 9.7

KIM was driving her car when she stopped at a cash point in a Waitrose car park. KIM was accompanied by CUMERFORD, a full licence holder, who was sitting in the front passenger seat. Before getting out of the car, KIM turned her engine off; however, she forgot to set the handbrake. Unfortunately for her, the car park was on a slope and her car rolled backwards into another parked car.

Has KIM committed the offence of 'quitting', contrary to reg. 107 of the Road Vehicles (Construction and Use) Regulations 1986, in these circumstances?

A No, even though KIM forgot to set the handbrake, she turned off the engine and both elements need to be present for the offence to be complete.

B Yes, a person must set the handbrake *and* turn off the engine to avoid prosecution for this offence.

C Yes, but she would have a defence; CUMERFORD was a full licence holder *and* was in a position to intervene; KIM could not be held responsible for the fact that he did not do so.

D No, the incident took place in a public place and not on a road.

Question 9.8

GRAY was driving a motor vehicle on a road, taking garden rubbish to a local tip. GRAY was towing an open trailer, which was also full of garden rubbish and GRAY's 10-year-old son, HARRY, was along for the trip. There was insufficient room in the car for HARRY and GRAY sat him on the trailer, telling him to hold on to a metal bar. GRAY drove slowly to the tip, and they arrived without any incident.

Would GRAY commit an offence under s. 40A of the Road Traffic Act 1988 (dangerous use of a vehicle) in these circumstances?

A No, HARRY was sitting on a trailer; the offence applies to motor vehicles only.

B No, HARRY did not encounter any danger during the journey.

C Yes, the offence applies to motor vehicles and trailers.

D Yes, the offence applies to any vehicle.

Question 9.9

YOUNG was a passenger in a motor vehicle that was travelling along a busy dual carriageway. At this time, he was supervising GLOVER, a learner driver. YOUNG received a text message on his mobile phone from his wife, telling him he had to pick up his children from school. It was not practicable to pull over due to the nature of the road, therefore YOUNG sent a text message to his wife saying that he would do so. YOUNG was not using a hands-free device at the time.

Who, if either, would commit an offence because of YOUNG's use of a mobile phone in these circumstances?

A YOUNG for using the phone and GLOVER for permitting its use.

B Only YOUNG commits the offence in these circumstances.

C Neither, as it was not practicable for GLOVER to stop in the circumstances.

D Neither, as YOUNG did not make a telephone call.

Question 9.10

FITZPATRICK was employed as a salesperson for a pharmaceutical company and was required to visit pharmacies in a region promoting the company's products. FITZ-PATRICK has been provided with a company car and a mobile telephone; however, the company has not installed a hands-free kit in the car because of the expense. FITZPATRICK is expected to regularly make and receive telephone calls while driving, using a headset which requires FITZPATRICK to hold the phone while dialling or answering the phone.

> Given that FITZPATRICK is using a hand-held mobile telephone while driving, which of the following statements is correct in respect of the offence under s. 41D of the Road Traffic Act 1988?

A Both FITZPATRICK and the employer may commit an offence, but FITZPATRICK could have a defence as using the mobile telephone while driving is a condition of employment.

B Only FITZPATRICK commits an offence, because a person may only be prosecuted for using a motor vehicle on a road under this section.

C Only FITZPATRICK commits an offence, because a driver is required to take responsibility for their own actions under this section.

D Both FITZPATRICK and the employer may commit an offence; FITZPATRICK for using a motor vehicle on a road contrary to this section and the employer for causing the offence.

Question 9.11

WHEELER was driving a motor vehicle along a dual carriageway during the hours of darkness with a defective headlamp. WHEELER was stopped by Constable SHARMER and given a Vehicle Defect Rectification Scheme (VDRS) form in respect of the defect.

> Regulation 23 of the Road Vehicles Lighting Regulations 1989 requires relevant lamps to be clean and in good working order. Which of the following statements is correct as to whether WHEELER could claim a defence to this offence?

A The only defence available to WHEELER is that she had no reason to believe that the defect had occurred.

B WHEELER would have a defence if she could show that the defect had only happened during the journey.

C WHEELER would have a defence if she could show that the defect had only happened during the journey, or that arrangements had been made to rectify it with all reasonable expedition.

D WHEELER would have no defence to this offence in these circumstances.

Question 9.12

DOMINGUEZ was driving his car on a road through a built up area at 1.00 pm, when he was stopped by Constable HIND. The officer examined DOMINGUEZ's car and discovered that the rear nearside light was defective.

What general exemption, under the Road Vehicles Lighting Regulations 1989, may DOMINGUEZ claim, to avoid prosecution for the defective light?

A None, as the exemption applies to headlamps only.

B That the defect occurred during the journey, or arrangements have been made to rectify it as soon as possible.

C That the defect occurred during the journey.

D That the defect has only recently occurred, and arrangements have been made to rectify it.

Question 9.13

Constable HANLON, an authorised vehicle examiner, has been working with the Vehicle and Operator Services Agency (VOSA) in relation to a garage owned by BREARLY. The garage is authorised as an MOT testing station, but is suspected of passing vehicles for their MOT tests, when they should have failed according to the testing standards. Constable HANLON is considering whether or not they could organise for a vehicle with defective brakes to be tested by BREARLY, with specific defects, to see whether or not staff at the garage would pass it.

Which of the following statements is correct, in relation to Constable HANLON's idea to conduct such a test?

A A vehicle may be driven to and from the garage by either a vehicle examiner from VOSA, or an authorised police vehicle examiner.

B Such a vehicle may not be driven to and from the garage, by either a vehicle examiner from VOSA or an authorised police vehicle examiner.

C A vehicle may only be driven to and from the garage by a vehicle examiner from VOSA.

D A vehicle may only be driven to and from the garage by an authorised police vehicle examiner.

Question 9.14

Information has been received that a local MOT testing station managed by DIXON is issuing test certificates to vehicles that have defects and which should have actually failed their tests. Consideration is being given to taking a vehicle with a defect to the garage, to see if the fault is identified.

Under what circumstances could the test take place, according to the Road Vehicles (Construction and Use) (Amendment) (No. 4) Regulations 2005 (SI 2005/3165)?

A Such a test may only take place with prior written authorisation from the Secretary of State.

B Such a test may only take place if it is reasonably believed that the defect will not cause a danger of injury to anyone.

C Such a test may only take place if the vehicle has failed a test at another authorised MOT testing station.

D Such a test may only take place if it is reasonably believed that DIXON's conduct may cause a danger of injury to any person.

Question 9.15

SETHI took her car to JEROME's garage as the test certificate was due for renewal. When SETHI returned for her vehicle, JEROME told her that her car had passed, but repairs had been necessary to the brakes and steering. SETHI paid JEROME £200, but as she was driving home, the steering felt unsteady. She took the car to another garage, where she was told that it was unroadworthy and required further repairs.

Would JEROME have committed an offence under s. 75 of the Road Traffic Act 1988 (supplying an unroadworthy vehicle), in these circumstances?

A No, as JEROME did not sell the vehicle to SETHI.

B Yes, the offence is complete in these circumstances.

C No, as SETHI is the owner of the vehicle, JEROME could not supply it to her.

D No, because SETHI had to pay JEROME for the repairs.

Question 9.16

CRAIG realised that the test certificate on his car had expired. His friend, WALSH, owned a garage and was authorised to issue MOT certificates. CRAIG drove his car to WALSH's garage, where it failed the MOT test. CRAIG made arrangements to return the car the next day for work to be carried out, in order to pass the test.

Has CRAIG committed an offence in relation to the vehicle in these circumstances, by driving it either to or from the garage?

A Yes, on his way there only, as he had not arranged a test for the vehicle in advance.

B Yes, on his way there and on his way home, as he had not arranged to test the vehicle in advance.

C No, as he was taking the vehicle to be tested, and returning it after it had been refused a certificate.

D Yes, on his way there only; he is exempt in relation to the return journey, as the vehicle had been refused a test certificate.

Question 9.17

Constable TAIT was dealing with a fail to stop road traffic accident, involving injury to a pedestrian on a zebra crossing. The offending vehicle was a medium-sized goods vehicle, which the officer discovered belonged to BARR. Through enquiries, Constable TAIT also discovered that BARR had failed to stop because he was concerned that the vehicle's brakes were defective and on examination, the vehicle may be taken off the road, which would affect his livelihood. Constable TAIT found the vehicle outside BARR's home address and contacted the Commercial Vehicle Unit to have it examined. There was no one available at the time and the officer was advised by the Unit to instruct BARR to take it to the examination centre, which was about three miles away.

Considering the power under s. 68 of the Road Traffic Act 1988, could Constable TAIT instruct BARR to do this?

A Yes, Constable TAIT may direct the vehicle to be taken to the examination centre in these circumstances.

B No, the examination centre is too far away to be able to use this power.

C No, only an authorised vehicle examiner can make such a request.

D No, there is no power to direct stationary vehicles in such a manner; this power applies to vehicles that have been stopped during an inspection.

Question 9.18

Constable KELLEHER, an authorised vehicle examiner, attended the scene of a road traffic collision, where GRANT had injured a child crossing the road. Witnesses told the officer that GRANT had stopped for a short while, and made a telephone call. GRANT was overheard shouting into the phone, 'I told you the brakes on this car were dangerous'. GRANT left the scene before the police arrived. Within five hours of the collision, Constable KELLEHER traced the vehicle to GRANT's home address. The vehicle was parked on the driveway and the officer wished to inspect the brakes. GRANT was not at home.

Under what circumstances could Constable KELLEHER examine the vehicle?

A There is no power to examine the vehicle without GRANT's permission.

B Constable KELLEHER may examine the vehicle without permission, because GRANT was involved in a road traffic collision involving injury.

C Constable KELLEHER may examine the vehicle without permission if GRANT is served with a notice, outlining the intention, within 48 hours of the collision.

D Constable KELLEHER may examine the vehicle without permission if the test takes place within 24 hours of the collision.

Question 9.19

Constable LAWRENCE was dealing with a road traffic collision involving a vehicle owned by KIM. The officer suspected that the vehicle's brakes were defective, because of comments made by KIM at the scene. KIM's vehicle was towed away from the scene by a friend and was being stored in the friend's garage. Constable LAWRENCE was an authorised vehicle examiner and attended the garage to test the brakes a few hours after the collision.

Would Constable LAWRENCE have the power to inspect the vehicle on premises, under reg. 74 of the Road Vehicles (Construction and Use) Regulations 1986?

A Yes, provided KIM consents to the examination.

B Yes, and she may enter by force if necessary.

C Yes, and she may enter by force if necessary if the garage owner is not present.

D Yes, provided the owner of the garage consents to the examination.

ANSWERS

Answer 9.1

Answer **D** — Regulations 15–18 of the Road Vehicles (Construction and Use) Regulations 1986 (SI 1986/1078) set out the requirements as to braking systems on vehicles, together with those for their maintenance. It is not absolutely necessary for the person testing the braking system of a vehicle to be a 'qualified examiner'—see *Stoneley* v *Richardson* [1973] RTR 229. In this case, a constable testified to being able to push the defendant's car along with the handbrake applied, and the evidence was accepted by the court. Since the officer was able to conduct this test, answers A, B and C are incorrect.

Road Policing, para. 3.9.4.1

Answer 9.2

Answer **A** — Generally, the requirement under reg. 27(1)(g) of the Road Vehicles (Construction and Use) Regulations 1986 is that the grooves of the tread pattern of a tyre must have a depth of at least 1 mm throughout a continuous band measuring at least three-quarters of the breadth of the tread and round the entire outer circumference of the tyre.

In the case of:

- passenger vehicles *other than motor cycles* constructed or adapted to carry no more than eight seated passengers in addition to the driver,
- goods vehicles with a maximum gross weight not exceeding 3,500 kg,
- light trailers

(first used on or after 3 January 1933 in each case), the depth of tread requirement is increased to 1.6 mm throughout a continuous band across the central three-quarters section of the tyre and around the entire circumference (see the Road Vehicles (Construction and Use) (Amendment) (No. 4) Regulations 1990 (SI 1990/1981)).

Therefore, a tyre on a motor cycle must have a depth of at least *1 mm* throughout a continuous band measuring at least three-quarters of the breadth of the tread and round the entire outer circumference of the tyre. Answers B, C and D are therefore incorrect.

Road Policing, para. 3.9.4.2

Answer 9.3

Answer **B** — Regulation 27 of the Road Vehicles (Construction and Use) Regulations 1986 sets out a number of specific defects that will make tyres unlawful. Under reg. 27(1)(b), a tyre will be unlawful if it is not so inflated as to make it fit for the use to which the motor vehicle or trailer is being put.

Under s. 41A(b) of the Road Traffic Act 1988, a person who uses on a road a motor vehicle or trailer which does not comply with such a requirement, or causes or permits a motor vehicle or trailer to be so used, is guilty of an offence.

To avoid the defect at reg. 27(1)(b), the tyre must be inflated so as to make it fit for the use to which the vehicle is being put *at the material time*; it does not have to be so inflated as to make it fit for some future use, however probable that use might be (*Connor* v *Graham* [1981] RTR 291). Answers A and C are therefore incorrect.

Evidence as to the defective condition of a tyre may be given by anyone who saw it and it is no defence to argue that the tyre was not examined by an authorised vehicle examiner (*Phillips* v *Thomas* [1974] RTR 28). Answers C and D are incorrect for this reason.

Road Policing, para. 3.9.4.2

Answer 9.4

Answer **A** — Regulation 27 of the Road Vehicles (Construction and Use) Regulations 1986 sets out a number of specific defects that will make tyres unlawful. Under reg. 27(1)(h), an offence is committed where the tyre is not maintained in such condition as to be fit for the use to which the vehicle or trailer is being put or has a defect which might in any way cause damage to the surface of the road or damage to persons on or in the vehicle or to other persons using the road. Since this regulation does not require actual damage to have been caused, answer B is incorrect. There is no requirement to show that other road users were endangered, or that people in or on the offending vehicle may have been placed in danger, therefore answer C is incorrect. Finally, the regulation applies either to vehicles or trailers—there is no mention of 'motor vehicles'; therefore, answer D is incorrect.

Road Policing, para. 3.9.4.2

Answer 9.5

Answer **C** — Under reg. 99 of the Road Vehicles (Construction and Use) Regulations 1986, a person commits an offence by using the audible warning instrument while the vehicle is stationary on the road or if it is used between 11.30 pm and 7 am. The offence is complete if one of these circumstances is met. Answer B is therefore incorrect.

Answer A is incorrect as the offence is committed after 11.30 pm, not 11 pm.

Answer D is incorrect as the offence was committed because the vehicle *was* stationary.

Road Policing, para. 3.9.4.4

Answer 9.6

Answer **C** — Regulations 37 and 99 regulate the fitting and use of audible warning instruments. Every *motor vehicle* which has a maximum speed of more than 20 mph shall be fitted with a horn, not being a reversing alarm or a two-tone horn. The dumper truck is not a motor vehicle; therefore, regardless of its maximum speed, it will not require an audible warning instrument. Answers A and D are therefore incorrect.

The Regulations do indeed apply to agricultural motor vehicles and these will require audible warning instruments if they are being driven at a speed of more than 20 mph. However, answer D is incorrect because the regulations only apply to motor vehicles.

If the dumper truck *was* a motor vehicle, it would require an audible warning instrument because it has a maximum speed *above* 20 mph, therefore, answer B is incorrect.

Road Policing, para. 3.9.4.4

Answer 9.7

Answer **D** — Regulation 107 of the Road Vehicles (Construction and Use) Regulations 1986 prohibits motorists from leaving a motor vehicle unattended on a road unless the engine has been stopped *and* the handbrake has been set (*Butterworth* v *Shorthouse* [1956] Crim LR 341). This means that the offence will be committed if the driver allows either of these circumstances to occur. Answer A is therefore incorrect.

A driver will not commit an offence if the vehicle is left 'attended'. For a person to be 'attending' a vehicle in these circumstances, he or she must be licensed to drive it and be in a position to intervene.

The crux of this question is the location of the incident, which occurred in a public place. Regulation 107 is clear that the offence may only be committed on a road.

Therefore, while answers B and C are seemingly correct, they are both incorrect because the incident did not occur on a road.

Road Policing, para. 3.9.4.5

Answer 9.8

Answer **C** — Section 40A of the Road Traffic Act 1988 creates an offence of:

- using, causing or permitting another to use on a road,
- a motor vehicle or trailer
- which, for whatever reason, involves a danger of injury to any person.

First, the offence applies to motor vehicles and trailers only; therefore, answers A and D are incorrect.

Secondly, the offence may be committed when the use of the vehicle involves a danger of injury to any person. In *Gray* v *DPP* [1999] RTR 339, the court held that a potential for injury would suffice to prove the offence. In this case, a 7-year-old boy was seen to be travelling in the open back of an uncovered jeep without any fitted restraints. The boy was steadying himself by holding on to the vehicle's roll-bars. The court held that, even though he had travelled in that way without incident many times in the past and that his father, the driver, was generally a responsible parent, the objective test as to the potential for injury meant that the offence had been committed. Answer B is therefore incorrect.

Road Policing, para. 3.9.4.11

Answer 9.9

Answer **B** — The unlawful use of hand-held mobile telephones while driving a motor vehicle on a road is prosecuted under s. 42 of the Road Traffic Act 1988. The three general offences are:

- driving a motor vehicle while using a hand-held mobile telephone;
- causing or permitting another person to drive a motor vehicle while using a hand-held mobile telephone; and
- using a hand-held mobile telephone while supervising a learner driver who is driving a motor vehicle on a road.

To commit the offence of 'permitting', you have to show the offender was permitting a person to use the hand-held device when *driving*. Since YOUNG was not driving the vehicle, GLOVER cannot be guilty of this offence and therefore answer A is incorrect.

The offence will be committed under *any* of the three subsections if the hand-held device is used either to make a telephone call *or* to *perform any other interactive communication function by transmitting and receiving data*, which will include sending a text message, fax, email or picture. Answer D is therefore incorrect.

Lastly, there is a specific defence to this offence, if the driver (or supervisor) can show that he or she was using the hand-held device to make an emergency call to the police, fire, ambulance or other emergency services, that he or she was acting in response to a genuine emergency *and* that it was impracticable to cease driving (or for the provisional licence holder to cease driving). All three of these circumstances must apply before the defence can be considered. Since YOUNG's text message was not an emergency, it is immaterial that it was not practicable to stop, and he would have no defence. Answer C is therefore incorrect.

Road Policing, para. 3.9.4.11

Answer 9.10

Answer **D** — The unlawful use of hand-held mobile telephones while driving a motor vehicle on a road is prosecuted under s. 42 of the Road Traffic Act 1988. The three general offences are:

- driving a motor vehicle while using a hand-held mobile telephone;
- causing or permitting another person to drive a motor vehicle while using a hand-held mobile telephone; and
- using a hand-held mobile telephone while supervising a learner driver who is driving a motor vehicle on a road.

Since the offence may be committed by 'causing' a motor vehicle to be driven on a road and the employers may be responsible in this respect, answers B and C are incorrect.

There is a very narrow defence to this offence; the driver would have to show that he or she was using the hand-held device to make an emergency call to the police, fire, ambulance or other emergency services *and* that he or she was acting in response to a genuine emergency *and* that it was impracticable to cease driving. All three of these circumstances must apply before the defence can be considered. FITZPATRICK does not have defence even if using the mobile telephone was a condition of employment. Answer A is therefore incorrect.

Road Policing, para. 3.9.4.11

Answer 9.11

Answer **D** — Regulation 23 of the Road Vehicles Lighting Regulations 1989 makes it an offence to use, or to cause or permit to be used, a vehicle on a road unless the relevant lamps and reflectors (including some optional ones) are clean and in good working order. Offences of contravening the lighting regulations are charged under s. 41 of the Road Traffic Act 1988.

The general exception to reg. 23 is if the vehicle is being used during daytime hours and the defect only happened during the journey or if arrangements have been made to rectify it with all reasonable expedition (reg. 23(3)). Since WHEELER was using the vehicle during the hours of darkness, this defence is not available to her—also, the defence is specific and not realising the defect had occurred would not be covered. Answers A, B and C are therefore incorrect.

Note that there is a separate offence under reg. 25 to use, or cause or permit to be used, a vehicle with obligatory headlamps on a road unless they are kept lit during the hours of darkness and in seriously reduced visibility. There is an exception to this requirement which applies to vehicles on 'restricted' roads per s. 81 of the Road Traffic Regulation Act 1984 where the street lights are on—but again, this would not provide a defence for WHEELER.

Road Policing, paras 3.9.5.6, 3.9.5.8

Answer 9.12

Answer **B** — It is an offence under reg. 23 of the Road Vehicles Lighting Regulations 1989 (SI 1989/1796) to use, cause or permit to be used a vehicle on a road unless the relevant lamps are clean and in good working order.

There is, however, an exemption under reg. 23(3): if the vehicle is being used during daytime hours and the defect only happened during the journey, or if arrangements have been made to rectify it with all reasonable expedition. Answers C and D are therefore incorrect.

The exemption applies to all relevant lamps, not just headlamps. Answer A is therefore incorrect.

Road Policing, para. 3.9.5.8

Answer 9.13

Answer **B** — The Road Vehicles (Construction and Use) (Amendment) (No. 4) Regulations 2005 and the Road Vehicles Lighting (Amendment) (No. 2) Regulations 2005 provide exemptions for vehicles used by Vehicle and Operator Services Agency (VOSA) examiners from having to comply with certain requirements of the Road Vehicles (Construction and Use) Regulations 1989 and the Road Vehicles Lighting Regulations 1989.

The exemptions allow VOSA examiners, posing as members of the public, to drive a vehicle with specific, recorded defects, to and from an MOT testing station, to ensure that the MOT tester applies the correct testing standards when conducting an MOT test.

Since the exemption applies to VOSA examiners, answers A and D are incorrect. However, in order to qualify for the exemptions, the examiner must:

- be authorised in writing by the Secretary of State to drive the defective vehicle; and
- reasonably believe that the defects will not cause a danger of injury to anyone while being so used.

This means that only minor defects may be present on the vehicles, such as horns or washers not working, or rear seat belts missing, as opposed to major defects, such as those to the brakes, steering or tyres of the vehicle. Since a vehicle examiner would not be entitled to drive a motor vehicle on a road with defective brakes: answers A, C and D are also incorrect for this reason.

Road Policing, para. 3.9.6

Answer 9.14

Answer **B** — The Road Vehicles (Construction and Use) (Amendment) (No. 4) Regulations 2005 and the Road Vehicles Lighting (Amendment) (No. 2) Regulations 2005 allow Vehicle and Operator Services Agency (VOSA) examiners to pose as members of the public and to drive a vehicle with specific, recorded defects, to and from an MOT testing station, in order to ensure that the MOT tester applies the correct testing standards when conducting an MOT test. In order to qualify for the exemptions, the examiner must:

- be authorised in writing by the Secretary of State to drive the defective vehicle *and*
- reasonably believe that the defects will not cause a danger of injury to anyone while being so used.

The risk assessment of whether the defects will cause a danger of injury to anyone relate to when the vehicle is being used to and from the test—it does not relate to the conduct of the testing station; therefore, answer D is incorrect. While the vehicle examiner must be authorised in writing by the Secretary of State to drive the defective vehicle, there is no requirement to seek authorisation for each test (answer A is therefore incorrect). Neither is there a requirement to test the vehicle at another authorised MOT testing station prior to it being used and therefore answer C is incorrect.

Road Policing, para. 3.9.6

Answer 9.15

Answer **B** — It has been held that where a garage returned a vehicle to an owner, after stating that it had been repaired and had passed its MOT, when in fact it was unroadworthy, the garage committed the offence of supplying an unroadworthy vehicle (*Devon County Council* v *DB Cars* [2001] EWHC Admin 521). In this case, the court held that 'supplying' involved a transfer of physical control of an item from one person to another (answer C is therefore incorrect). It is both immaterial that the owner had to pay for the repairs, and that the owner did not buy the vehicle from the offender, therefore answers A and D are incorrect.

Road Policing, para. 3.9.6

Answer 9.16

Answer **B** — There are exemptions to s. 47 of the Road Traffic Act 1988 (using a motor vehicle on a road without a test certificate), where a person is taking a vehicle to or from a testing station. However, a driver may only claim exemption if he or she is driving to or from a pre-arranged test. The key is whether the test was prearranged, and in this case it was not. Answer C is therefore incorrect.

Although they are worded differently, answers A and D are incorrect for the same reason. There is a further exemption for vehicles which have been refused test certificates. However, this exemption applies only when the vehicle is being driven, by prior arrangement, or brought from the relevant place where the work is being carried out. This exemption allows garage proprietors, who are not registered to supply test certificates, to take vehicles to and from testing stations, and again does not apply in these circumstances.

The last exemption, which again does not apply to the given facts, is where a vehicle is being towed to be broken up, following the refusal of a test certificate.

Road Policing, para. 3.9.6

Answer 9.17

Answer **A** — Section 68 of the Road Traffic Act 1988 provides a power for vehicle examiners to inspect goods vehicles, PSVs and some larger passenger-carrying vehicles. It also provides a power for a police officer in uniform to direct such a vehicle to a suitable place of inspection when found on a road, provided that that place of inspection is not more than five miles from the place where the requirement is made. Since Constable TAIT did not have to be an authorised vehicle examiner, and was directing the vehicle to a centre less than five miles away, answers B and C are incorrect.

The power conferred by s. 68 of the Road Traffic Act 1988 can be applied to stationary vehicles and answer D is incorrect.

Road Policing, para. 3.9.6.2

Answer 9.18

Answer **A** — Regulation 74 of the Road Vehicles (Construction and Use) Regulations 1986 provides a power to test and inspect the brakes, silencers, steering gear and tyres of any vehicle on any premises where that vehicle is located. The power applies to police officers in uniform and other authorised vehicle examiners, but may not take place unless:

- the owner of the vehicle consents;
- notice has been given to that owner (either personally or left at his or her address not less than 48 hours before the time of the proposed test/inspection, or sent to him or her by recorded delivery at least 72 hours before the proposed test/inspection); or
- the test or inspection is made within 48 hours of a reportable accident in which the vehicle was involved.

In ordinary circumstances, Constable KELLEHER could conduct an inspection without giving notice to the owner (as the inspection would take place within 48 hours of the collision) and therefore answer C is incorrect.

However, regardless of whether the person was involved in a personal injury road traffic collision, an inspection under this section must take place with the owner's permission. There is no power of entry to conduct such an examination and it was irrelevant, therefore, what time the officer arrived at the house; if the owner was not present to consent, the examination could not take place. Answers B and D are therefore incorrect.

Road Policing, para. 3.9.6.3

Answer 9.19

Answer **A** — The power applies to police officers in uniform and other authorised vehicle examiners (see reg. 74(1)(a)–(f)). Regulation 74 provides no power of entry and stipulates that the person empowered shall produce his or her authorisation if required to do so. Answers B and C are therefore incorrect.

Regulation 74 also provides that no such test or inspection shall be carried out unless the owner of the vehicle consents. There is no mention of the owner of the premises consenting to the examination, therefore answer D is incorrect.

Road Policing, para. 3.9.6.3

10 Driver Licensing

Please note that the questions in this chapter relate to material in the Blackstone's Police Manuals which has been excluded from the Inspectors' Exam syllabus for 2014.

STUDY PREPARATION

The law relating to driver licensing is of considerable practical significance.

You need to know how the licensing system works in terms of what licence is needed by what driver for what vehicle; you also need to know the relevant police powers in relation to licences and the attendant offences that can be committed.

Of particular importance is the offence of disqualified driving and the provisions that apply to learner drivers and their supervisors.

QUESTIONS

Question 10.1

SCOTT has secured employment with a haulage company to drive large goods vehicles to various locations in the UK. SCOTT has had to re-train after being made redundant and passed his driving test to drive large goods vehicles late, on his 39th birthday.

When will SCOTT's licence to drive large goods vehicles be due for renewal?

A The licence must be renewed annually.

B The licence must be renewed in five years.

C The licence will last until SCOTT's 45th birthday.

D The licence will last until SCOTT's 60th birthday.

Question 10.2

Section 121 of the Road Traffic Act 1988 contains the definition of a large passenger-carrying vehicle (PCV).

In relation to this definition, which of the following statements is correct?

A It will be a vehicle which is constructed or adapted to carry more than 16 passengers.

B It will be a vehicle which weighs more than 3.5 tonnes and is constructed or adapted to carry more than 16 passengers.

C It will be a vehicle which is constructed or adapted to carry more than 16 passengers for hire or reward.

D It will be a vehicle which is constructed or adapted to carry more than 16 passengers, including the driver.

Question 10.3

HOWLEY has bought a moped and intends signing up for an approved training course and passing a test of competence to ride it on a road.

In relation to the vehicle HOWLEY has bought, which of the following statements is correct, under s. 108(1) of the Road Traffic Act 1988?

A It may be a two-wheeled or three-wheeled vehicle and must have a maximum design speed of no more than 50 kilometres per hour.

B It must be a two-wheeled vehicle and must have a maximum design speed of no more than 50 kilometres per hour.

C It may be a two-wheeled or three-wheeled vehicle and must have a maximum design speed of no more than 45 kilometres per hour.

D It must be a two-wheeled vehicle and must have a maximum design speed of no more than 45 kilometres per hour.

Question 10.4

CASWELL is a provisional licence holder and has recently completed a compulsory basic training course to ride a motor bicycle.

Which of the following is correct in relation to the documentation CASWELL will require to prove the course has been passed?

A CASWELL will be issued with a certificate, which is valid for two years.

B CASWELL's provisional licence will be endorsed as proof that the course has been passed. The endorsement will be removed if a test is not passed within two years.

C CASWELL will be issued with a certificate, which is valid until a test has been passed—there is no time limit.

D CASWELL's provisional licence will be endorsed as proof that the course has been passed. The endorsement will be removed if a test is not passed within one year.

Question 10.5

SWEETMAN has passed a driving test and is classified as a 'new driver', as defined under s. 3 of the Road Traffic (New Drivers) Act 1995. SWEETMAN's driving licence has recently been revoked as a result of accumulating too many penalty points. SWEETMAN was stopped by Constable BELL while driving a motor vehicle on the road. At the time, SWEETMAN was displaying 'L' plates on the vehicle, but was not supervised by a qualified driver.

Is SWEETMAN guilty of an offence in these circumstances?

A Yes, of driving otherwise than in accordance with a licence.

B No; SWEETMAN has passed a driving test and must display 'L' plates, but does not have to be supervised by a qualified driver.

C Yes, of driving while disqualified.

D Yes, of driving when not supervised by a qualified driver.

Question 10.6

POTTER was supervising GREEN, who was learning to drive. As they were travelling along the road, GREEN collided with a parked car. GREEN panicked and drove off after the accident, without stopping.

Does POTTER have a responsibility for GREEN'S actions in these circumstances?

A Yes, but only if he encouraged the actions.

B No, he is only there to supervise GREEN's driving.

C No, he is only there to provide tuition for GREEN.

D Yes, he should have ensured that GREEN remained at the scene.

Question 10.7

FERDINAND was a passenger in a vehicle being driven by AZIZ, a provisional licence holder. The vehicle was fitted with L plates and FERDINAND, a full licence holder, was supervising AZIZ. The vehicle was stopped by Constable THAME, who observed that both FERDINAND and AZIZ smelled strongly of intoxicants.

In these circumstances, could a supervisor be found guilty of an offence under s. 5(1)(b) of the Road Traffic Act 1988 (in charge of a vehicle while over the prescribed limit)?

A No, they could only be guilty of aiding and abetting a driver who was over the prescribed limit.

B Yes, they could be in charge of the vehicle in these circumstances and be guilty of this offence.

C No, as the driver is in control of the vehicle, the supervisor could not also be in charge of it.

D Yes, but only if it could be proved that the driver was also over the prescribed limit.

Question 10.8

RANGER is the holder of a full driving licence, having passed a driving test three years ago. However, six months after passing the test, RANGER's licence was revoked as a result of accumulating too many penalty points. It took RANGER six months to regain the licence after passing a further test. RANGER has now held a driving licence for a continuous period of two years and an aggregate period of two years and six months.

Would RANGER be qualified to supervise learner drivers in line with reg. 17(1) of the Motor Vehicles (Driving Licences) Regulations 1999?

A No, RANGER has not held a relevant licence for a continuous period of at least three years.

B Yes, RANGER has held a relevant licence for a continuous period of at least two years.

C Yes, RANGER has held a relevant licence for a total period of at least two years.

D No, RANGER has not held a relevant licence for a total period of at least three years.

Question 10.9

KELLEHER is the holder of a provisional driving licence and has passed a driving test to drive motor vehicles on a road. KELLEHER has been issued with a certificate confirming that her test has been passed and is waiting for her full driving licence.

What restrictions, if any, are now placed on KELLEHER if she wishes to drive a motor vehicle on a road?

A KELLEHER will no longer have to display 'L' plates or be accompanied by a qualified driver.

B KELLEHER will no longer have to display 'L' plates; however, she will still have to be accompanied by a qualified driver, until she receives her full driving licence.

C KELLEHER will no longer have to be accompanied by a qualified driver; however, she will still have to display 'L' plates, until she receives her full driving licence.

D KELLEHER will have to continue displaying 'L' plates and be accompanied by a qualified driver, until she receives her full driving licence.

Question 10.10

BELL passed her driving test a year ago. Before passing her test, BELL had accumulated points on her provisional driving licence. She has recently been issued with an endorsable fixed penalty notice and is likely to accumulate penalty points on her full driving licence.

If the combined total of points that BELL has accumulated exceeds the limit set in s. 2 of the Road Traffic (New Drivers) Act 1995, is BELL likely to have her licence revoked?

A Yes, provided the second set of points was accumulated within two years of the first set of points.

B No, the first set of points was accumulated while BELL was a provisional licence holder.

C Yes, provided the first set of points was accumulated at least two years before BELL passed her driving test.

D Yes, the Secretary of State has no alternative but to revoke BELL's driving licence in these circumstances.

Question 10.11

HAY has been summonsed to appear in court for an offence under s. 87 of the Road Traffic Act 1988, of driving a motor vehicle on a road otherwise than in accordance with a licence. HAY intends pleading not guilty to the offence on two grounds: first that the vehicle had not actually been driven on a road, and secondly that the officer in the case had failed to issue her with an HORT/1 form for the production of her driving licence.

In relation to HAY's claim, which of the following statements is correct?

A It will be for HAY to prove that the vehicle was not being driven on a road, *and* that she had a licence to drive the vehicle.

B The failure of the officer in the case to issue HAY with an HORT/1 may be fatal to the case and would provide HAY with a defence to this offence.

C The prosecution need only show that HAY was driving on a road; HAY must show that she had a licence to do so.

D The prosecution must show that HAY was driving on a road *and* that she did not have a licence to do so.

Question 10.12

WILLEMS has been in a long-standing dispute with her neighbour, HEARN, over the parking spaces outside their respective houses. They share a common parking area, which is not a road or public place because the spaces are available only to them. WILLEMS was annoyed that HEARN's visitors constantly parked in her allocated space. One day, after coming home from work, there was a car parked in her space. WILLEMS lost her temper and deliberately drove at the car at speed, causing extensive damage to it. The police were called and, because of the location of the incident, WILLEMS was arrested for causing criminal damage. She pleaded not guilty to the offence, but was found guilty in court.

Would the Crown Prosecution Service (CPS) be entitled to apply for a disqualification period in respect of WILLEMS in these circumstances?

A Yes, the court may order a disqualification period instead of, or in addition to, the criminal conviction.

B Yes, the court may order a disqualification period, but this must replace the criminal conviction, to avoid duplicity.

C No, a person may only be disqualified on conviction in these circumstances when the crime involves an injury to another person.

D Yes, the court may order a disqualification period provided the damage caused to the other vehicle amounts to 'serious' damage.

Question 10.13

A gang was involved in cash-in-transit robberies, which resulted in several security guards being seriously assaulted. The gang used stolen vehicles to commit the crimes, which they later abandoned at different locations. CHAPMAN did not take part in the robberies, but was paid to pick up the gang members in various places and take them safely back to their homes. When the police caught the principal offenders they also arrested CHAPMAN, who claimed that he was unaware of the crimes the gang had committed and was simply a driver. Ten people were charged and convicted in Crown Court with conspiracy to commit five robberies, including CHAPMAN. The court accepted that CHAPMAN had played a lesser part than the principal offenders and the Crown Prosecution Service (CPS) anticipated that he would receive a lesser sentence.

Would the CPS be entitled to apply for a disqualification period in respect of CHAPMAN in these circumstances?

A No, CHAPMAN's vehicle was not used in the commission of the robberies themselves.

B Yes, but only if it can be shown that CHAPMAN's vehicle was used to assist the gang to avoid apprehension after the offence.

C Yes, but only if it can be shown that CHAPMAN's vehicle was used to dispose of evidence related to the offence.

D Yes, if it can be shown that CHAPMAN's vehicle was used to assist the gang to avoid apprehension, or to dispose of evidence related to the offence.

Question 10.14

Constable BUDIANSKI was on mobile patrol in a police vehicle. The officer was stationary at a set of traffic lights and saw a vehicle on the opposite side of the road, waiting for the lights to change. Constable BUDIANSKI recognised GOODE sitting in the driver's seat and knew that he was a disqualified driver. The officer approached the vehicle and arrested GOODE for that offence.

Given that GOODE is actually disqualified from driving, which of the following would be the key considerations as to whether he could be prosecuted, under s. 103 of the Road Traffic Act 1988, in these circumstances?

A There must be evidence to show that the vehicle had been seen in motion in order to prosecute GOODE.

B GOODE could not be prosecuted as he was not seen driving.

C In these circumstances, the prosecution could convince the court that he had stopped driving and intended carrying on when the lights changed.

D Evidence that a person has been driving would be insufficient for this offence; the person must be stopped while driving.

Question 10.15

KLINE was driving a motor vehicle on a road, when he was stopped by Constable POPE. KLINE admitted that he was only 16 and did not possess a licence to drive the vehicle.

What power would Constable POPE have to arrest KLINE in these circumstances?

A KLINE can be arrested, where the officer believes it necessary, for driving other than in accordance with a licence.

B KLINE can be arrested, where the officer believes it necessary, for driving while disqualified in these circumstances.

C None at all, KLINE should be reported for summons for driving other than in accordance with a licence.

D KLINE can be arrested, where the officer believes it necessary, for driving while disqualified by reason of his age.

Question 10.16

MEARS is due to appear in court, having been charged with an offence of driving while disqualified. However, MEARS intends using the defence that she was not aware that she was disqualified from driving.

Which of the following statements is correct in relation to the proof that is required to prove an offence of driving while disqualified under s. 103 of the Road Traffic Act 1988?

A MEARS will need to show that she was not disqualified, or alternatively that she was not aware of this fact.

B MEARS will need to show that she was not disqualified *and* that she was not aware of this fact.

C The prosecution will need to show that MEARS was disqualified *and* that she was aware of this fact.

D The prosecution will need to show that MEARS was disqualified, but not that she was aware of this fact.

Question 10.17

VERDI was convicted of failing to cooperate with a preliminary breath test and failing to stop for the police. VERDI had attempted to escape from the police, but was eventually stopped. VERDI refused to provide a roadside breath test, but provided a sample later at the station, which proved negative. The court was considering using its discretion to implement a period of disqualification, until VERDI passed an appropriate driving test.

Which of the following statements is correct, in relation to the court's considerations?

A Because the offence involves a discretionary disqualification, VERDI may be made to sit a regular driving test.

B Because the offence involves a discretionary disqualification, VERDI may not be made to re-sit a driving test.

C Because the offence involves a breath test offence, VERDI may be made to sit an extended driving test.

D Regardless of the offence, an extended driving test will always be the appropriate test when the court makes such an order.

Question 10.18

JELF was driving a motor vehicle on a road and was stopped by Constable STACEY. A Police National Computer (PNC) check revealed that JELF had recently been convicted of speeding, and had been disqualified from driving until passing a driving test. JELF was in possession of a provisional driving licence and was accompanied by FERDINAND, a fully qualified driver. The vehicle was not displaying 'L' plates.

Has JELF committed an offence in these circumstances?

A Yes, of failing to display 'L' plates.

B Yes, of driving while disqualified.

C Yes, of driving other than in accordance with a licence.

D No, JELF was accompanied by a fully qualified driver.

Question 10.19

BARKER has been disqualified from driving by the court until she passes her driving test. BARKER is due to attend court in relation to an offence where the prosecution allege that she failed to comply with the terms of a provisional licence holder when driving a motor vehicle on a road. BARKER intends pleading not guilty to the offence and is disputing the fact that she has failed to comply with the conditions of her licence.

Which of the following statements is correct, in relation to the burden of proof for this offence?

A The prosecution must show that BARKER was driving a motor vehicle on a road; BARKER must show she had a provisional licence and that she was driving in accordance with that licence.

B The prosecution must show that BARKER was driving a motor vehicle on a road, that she had a provisional licence and that she was not driving in accordance with that licence.

C BARKER will have to show either that she was not driving a motor vehicle on a road, or that she had a provisional licence and that she was driving in accordance with that licence.

D The prosecution must show that BARKER was driving a motor vehicle on a road and that she had a provisional licence; BARKER must show that she was driving in accordance with that licence.

Question 10.20

SHELFORD was disqualified from driving by the court just over 12 months ago. At the end of the disqualification period, SHELFORD was free to apply for a new full driving licence and did so. However, two weeks after submitting the application, it has still not been sent by the DVLA. SHELFORD has been offered employment as a delivery driver and rather than losing the position, has started the job before receiving the licence from the DVLA. SHELFORD has been stopped by the police while driving a motor vehicle on a road.

What are SHELFORD's liabilities under the Road Traffic Act 1988 in these circumstances?

A SHELFORD is not entitled to drive a motor vehicle on a road until receiving the licence from the DVLA and has committed the offence of disqualified driving.

B SHELFORD is entitled to drive a motor vehicle on a road if the application has been received by the DVLA and may not have committed an offence in these circumstances.

C SHELFORD has applied for a driving licence after a disqualification period has ended and has no liability once the application is submitted.

D SHELFORD is not entitled to drive a motor vehicle on a road until receiving the licence from the DVLA and has committed the offence of driving otherwise than in accordance with a licence.

Question 10.21

HARVEY appeared in court and was convicted of driving a motor vehicle on a motorway at a speed of 101 mph. The prosecution asked the court to disqualify HARVEY from driving. The defence managed to convince the court that a long period of disqualification would have a significant impact on HARVEY's business and family life. HARVEY was eventually disqualified from driving for a period of a month, having agreed to take part in a community road safety scheme.

Which of the following statements is correct, in relation to HARVEY's driving licence following this disqualification?

A The driving licence will be retained by the DVLA; HARVEY will need to apply for its return when the disqualification period expires.

B The driving licence will be retained by the court; HARVEY will need to apply for its return when the disqualification period expires.

C The driving licence will be returned to HARVEY; it will become valid again the day after the disqualification period expires.

D The driving licence will be returned to HARVEY; it will become valid again if HARVEY makes an application to the DVLA, after the disqualification period expires.

Question 10.22

FLAHERTY and his wife are American nationals who moved to live permanently in this country two months ago. FLAHERTY is 30 years of age and has been the holder of a full American driving permit for 10 years, but his wife has not passed a driving test in any country. FLAHERTY's wife would like to learn to drive and pass her driving test in this country.

Under what circumstances could FLAHERTY supervise his wife as she learns to drive?

A FLAHERTY may only supervise his wife when he has passed a driving test in this country.

B Because of his age and relevant driving experience, FLAHERTY is a qualified driver and may supervise his wife automatically.

C FLAHERTY may only supervise his wife when he has applied for a provisional driving licence in this country to accompany his full driving licence.

D FLAHERTY may only supervise his wife when he has passed a driving test in this country and then demonstrated the relevant driving experience in this country.

Question 10.23

WEBBER is an Australian national who has recently immigrated to the UK. Six months before coming to this country, WEBBER was convicted of a drink driving offence in Australia and was disqualified from driving in that country. WEBBER is seeking advice as to whether the disqualification also applies in the UK.

Section 97(1) of the Road Traffic Act 1988 (amended by Motor Vehicles (Driving Licence) (Amendment) Regulations 2012) deals with disqualified drivers from other countries. Which of the following statements is correct in relation to WEBBER's situation?

A This section means that WEBBER may not apply for a full licence, or a provisional driving licence.

B This section does not apply to WEBBER in these circumstances.

C This section means that WEBBER may not apply for a full licence, but may apply for a provisional licence.

D This section means that WEBBER is automatically disqualified from driving in the UK.

Question 10.24

DUBOIS is a Canadian national who has moved to live permanently in the UK. DUBOIS has been the holder of a full Canadian driving permit for five years and wishes to drive in this country. DUBOIS is considering applying to the DVLA for a provisional driving licence.

Which of the following statements is correct, in relation to any restrictions there may be on DUBOIS driving in the UK?

A DUBOIS may use a provisional licence to drive in the UK for 12 months and abide by its conditions, but must take a test during this period otherwise the licence will expire.

B DUBOIS may use a provisional licence to drive in the UK for 12 months; the conditions of the provisional licence will only apply at the end of this period if DUBOIS does not pass a test.

C DUBOIS may use a provisional licence to drive in the UK for 12 months; the conditions of the provisional licence will only apply at the end of this period if DUBOIS has not exchanged the Canadian licence for a UK licence.

D DUBOIS may immediately exchange the Canadian licence for a UK licence and does not require a provisional licence to drive in the UK.

Question 10.25

AMIR was involved in a road accident during the hours of darkness. A witness stated that AMIR had caused the accident by failing to comply with a 'Give Way' sign. AMIR admitted to Constable WARE that he normally wore contact lenses, but had forgotten to wear them that night.

Under what conditions may Constable WARE require AMIR to submit to an eyesight test?

A In daylight conditions, while wearing his contact lenses.
B In darkness, without his contact lenses.
C In darkness, while wearing his contact lenses.
D In daylight conditions, without his contact lenses.

Question 10.26

Constable MORSE attended a road traffic collision in which HAMILTON had failed to give way at a junction and had driven into the path of GIBSON, who was driving on the main road. GIBSON had swerved to avoid HAMILTON and had collided with a parked car. There was no damage to HAMILTON's vehicle and he admitted to Constable MORSE that he had not seen the Give Way markings at the junction. The officer suspected that HAMILTON's eyesight was defective and submitted him to a test, which he failed. HAMILTON did not wear any corrective lenses for his eyesight and Constable MORSE strongly believed he represented a danger to other motorists, especially as HAMILTON's vehicle was undamaged and he had stated that he would continue to drive.

Given that HAMILTON has committed an offence under s. 96(1) of the Road Traffic Act 1988 (driving with defective eyesight), how should Constable MORSE proceed to prevent him from continuing to commit this offence?

A Constable MORSE must confiscate HAMILTON's driving licence and forward it to the DVLA as soon as reasonably practicable.
B Constable MORSE must notify the DVLA in writing as soon as reasonably practicable, allowing the DVLA to revoke HAMILTON's licence as soon as possible.
C Constable MORSE should notify the DVLA electronically, allowing the DVLA to revoke HAMILTON's licence as soon as possible.
D Constable MORSE should notify the DVLA electronically, allowing the DVLA to apply to the court for HAMILTON's licence to be revoked as soon as reasonably practicable.

ANSWERS

Answer 10.1

Answer **C** — Licences will generally last until the holder's 70th birthday or for three years, whichever is the longer (see s. 99 of the Road Traffic Act 1988). However, the case is different in respect of large goods vehicles and large passenger-carrying vehicles licences. These licences last until a driver's 45th birthday or five years, whichever is the *longer*. If the driver is between 45 and 65, they last for five years or until the holder's 66th birthday, whichever is the *shorter*.

Therefore, in SCOTT's case, he was 39 when he passed his test to drive large goods vehicles and the *longest* period between passing the test and the requirement for renewal is six years (as opposed to five years) and the licence will expire on his 45th birthday.

Answers A, B and D are therefore incorrect.

Road Policing, para. 3.10.2.1

Answer 10.2

Answer **A** — Under s. 121 of the Road Traffic Act 1988, a large passenger-carrying vehicle (PCV) is one which is constructed or adapted for carrying more than 16 passengers.

The definition does not mention the weight of the vehicle (weights are contained in the definition of goods vehicles) and therefore answer B is incorrect.

If a vehicle is designed to carry more than 16 passengers, it will be classed as a large PCV, *regardless* of whether the passengers are being carried for hire or reward. This condition applies to a small PCV (which is constructed or adapted to carry more than eight but not more than 16 passengers). Answer C is therefore incorrect.

Finally, the 16 passengers *do not* include the driver of a large PCV; therefore, answer D is incorrect.

Road Policing, para. 3.10.2.1

Answer 10.3

Answer **C** — Under s. 108(1) of the Road Traffic Act 1988, a 'moped' is defined as a two-wheeled or three-wheeled vehicle which must have a maximum design speed of no more than 45 kilometres per hour.

Answer C contains the only correct combination, therefore, answers A, B and D are incorrect.

Road Policing, para. 3.10.3.1

Answer 10.4

Answer **A** — When a person completes a compulsory basic training course, he or she is issued with a certificate which is valid for two years, therefore answers B, C and D are incorrect.

Road Policing, para. 3.10.3.1

Answer 10.5

Answer **D** — If a person is a 'new driver' and has his or her driving licence revoked after accumulating six penalty points (under s. 3 of the Road Traffic (New Drivers) Act 1995), he or she will not be counted as 'disqualified'. He or she will revert to the position of a learner driver and will have to abide by the conditions of the Motor Vehicles (Driving Licences) Regulations 1999, by displaying 'L' plates and being supervised by a qualified driver when driving a motor vehicle on a road. Answer B is therefore incorrect.

If a provisional licence holder fails to observe these conditions, he or she may be prosecuted for an offence under s. 91 of the Road Traffic Offenders Act 1988 for breaching the Regulations (in SWEETMAN's case, reg. 16(2)(a)). He or she will not be guilty of driving otherwise than in accordance with a licence, or driving while disqualified: therefore answers A and C are incorrect.

Road Policing, para. 3.10.3.3

Answer 10.6

Answer **D** — A person supervising a learner driver is required not to provide tuition for the learner, but to 'supervise'. That means doing whatever might reasonably be expected to prevent the learner driver from acting carelessly or endangering others (see *Rubie* v *Faulkner* [1940] 1 All ER 285). Answer C is therefore incorrect.

Supervising requires some positive action on behalf of the supervisor, and these duties extend to ensuring compliance with other legislative requirements, such as remaining at the scene of an accident (*Bentley* v *Mullen* [1986] RTR 7), or remaining sober when doing so (*DPP* v *Janman* [2004] EWHC 101). Answer B is therefore incorrect. There is no need to show encouragement to commit the offence, merely that the supervisor did not act to prevent the actions. Answer A is therefore incorrect.

Road Policing, para. 3.10.4

Answer 10.7

Answer **B** — The situation of a passenger being drunk while supervising a learner driver was considered by the Divisional Court in *DPP* v *Janman* [2004] EWHC 101. There it was held that, in any ordinary case, the person supervising a learner driver was in control of the vehicle and this was the obvious and normal consequence of their role. Therefore, if the supervisor's blood/alcohol level exceeded the prescribed limit, he or she would commit the offence under s. 5(1)(b) of the Road Traffic Act 1988 simply by supervising a learner driver on a road or in a public place.

Additionally, the contingent role of the supervisor, whereby he or she has to be ready to take actual control of the vehicle at any point, means that it is almost impossible for him or her to argue the defence under s. 5(2) of the Act—because that defence requires the defendant to show that there was no likelihood of his or her driving while still over the limit. The whole purpose of supervising a learner is to intervene as and when it becomes necessary and therefore there is every likelihood of the supervisor having to drive during the journey. Answer C is therefore incorrect.

A 'supervisor' can also be convicted of aiding and abetting where the learner driver is over the prescribed limit or unfit through drink or drugs (*Crampton* v *Fish* [1970] Crim LR 235). This is a separate issue from the *Janman* case, which shows that a supervisor could commit *either* offence, depending on the circumstances, and one is not dependent upon the other. Answers A and D are therefore incorrect.

Road Policing, para. 3.10.4

Answer 10.8

Answer **D** — Under reg. 17(1) of the Motor Vehicles (Driving Licences) Regulations 1999, a person is a 'qualified driver' for the purpose of the Regulations if he or she is 21 years of age or over, holds a relevant licence and has the relevant driving experience.

A 'relevant licence' means a full licence (including a Northern Ireland or Community licence) authorising the driving of vehicles of the same class as the vehicle being driven by the provisional licence holder (reg. 17(3)(c)).

'Relevant driving experience' is defined at reg. 17(3)(e). Generally a person will have relevant driving experience if they have held the relevant full licence for a continuous *or* aggregate period of not less than three years. Since there may be a break, and the period is three years, answers A, B and C are incorrect.

Road Policing, para. 3.10.4

Answer 10.9

Answer **A** — Regulation 16(10) of the Motor Vehicles (Driving Licences) Regulations 1999 (SI 1999/2864) makes provision for the situation where a provisional licence holder has been issued the relevant certificate stating that he or she has passed a driving test but has not yet received his or her full licence.

In such cases, the requirements to display 'L' (or 'D') plates and to be supervised do not apply.

Answers B, C and D are therefore incorrect.

Road Policing, para. 3.10.6.1

Answer 10.10

Answer **D** — The Road Traffic (New Drivers) Act 1995 sets out a probationary period of two years, during which a person may have his or her driving licence revoked by the Secretary of State after accumulating six or more penalty points. In *R (On the application of Adebowale)* v *Bradford Crown Court* [2004] EWHC 1741 (Admin), the Divisional Court held that if a driver attracts penalty points on a provisional driving licence, and then receives further points in the first two years of holding a full licence, taking him or her to six or more points in all, the Secretary of State has no alternative but to revoke the licence under the provisions of s. 3 of the Act. Answer B is therefore incorrect.

The Divisional Court's ruling does not state that the points on the full driving licence have to be accumulated within two years of any other points (therefore answer A is incorrect). Additionally, the ruling does not state that the points on the provisional driving licence have to be accumulated at least two years before a person passes their driving test. Answer C is therefore incorrect.

Road Policing, para. 3.10.7

Answer 10.11

Answer **C** — In proving the offence under s. 87 of the Road Traffic Act 1988, it is for the *prosecution* to show that the defendant was driving on a road. Answer A is therefore incorrect.

It is for the defendant to show that he or she had a licence to drive that class of vehicle (*John* v *Humphreys* [1955] 1 WLR 325). In spite of this, it would be prudent for the prosecution to gather such evidence as is available to them, such as DVLA records. This was confirmed in *DPP* v *Hay* [2005] EWHC 1395 (Admin), where the court held that once the prosecution had proved the defendant had driven on a public highway, it is for him or her to show that he or she had a driving licence and insurance as those matters were within the defendant's knowledge. Answer D is therefore incorrect.

It was also held in *Hay* that there is no obligation for the police to serve a request for production of the relevant driving documents (e.g. by issuing an HORT/1 form). Answer B is therefore incorrect.

Road Policing, para. 3.10.10

Answer 10.12

Answer **A** — The Powers of Criminal Courts (Sentencing) Act 2000 gives courts the power to disqualify any defendant from holding or obtaining a driving licence when convicting that person of any criminal offence (and not merely those involving injury to another person). Answer C is therefore incorrect. There is no requirement for the incident (or in this case the damage) to be 'serious' and therefore answer D is incorrect.

Other than in very serious cases, this disqualification may be made instead of, or in addition to, any other penalty and the disqualification can be for any period. Answer B is therefore incorrect.

Road Policing, para. 3.10.11

Answer 10.13

Answer **D** — The Powers of Criminal Courts (Sentencing) Act 2000 gives courts the power to disqualify any defendant from holding or obtaining a driving licence when convicting that person of any criminal offence (see s. 146). Other than in very serious cases, this disqualification may be made instead of, as well as in addition to, any other penalty and the disqualification can be for any period.

In the case of the Crown Court, if it is satisfied that a motor vehicle was used by the person convicted or by anyone else for the purpose of committing, or facilitating the commission of, the offence in question, the court may order the person convicted to be disqualified (see s. 147).

Facilitating the commission of an offence includes the taking of any steps *after* the offence has been committed for the purpose of disposing of any property to which it relates or of avoiding apprehension or detection (s. 147(6)).

Answers A, B and C are therefore incorrect.

Road Policing, para. 3.10.11

Answer 10.14

Answer **C** — Under s. 103 of the Road Traffic Act 1988, a person is guilty of an offence if, while disqualified for holding or obtaining a licence, he drives a motor vehicle on a road. Generally, the person must be driving to commit the offence, but the courts have allowed some leeway in respect of the evidence that the person has been driving.

Case law has allowed for the meaning of 'driving' to include occasions where a person *has* been driving but has temporarily ceased (see *Shackleton* v *Chief Constable of Lancashire Police* [2001] EWCA Civ 1975, when a police officer saw a disqualified driver 'jogging' away from a car). Answer D is therefore incorrect.

In *Pinner* v *Everett* [1969] 1 WLR 1266, the House of Lords found that each case should be taken on its merits. Their Lordships held that there was no requirement for the vehicle to be in motion (answer A is therefore incorrect) and that the key considerations in assessing each case on its merits were whether the defendant:

- had actually stopped driving or intended carrying on (e.g. at a set of traffic lights);
- was still driving;
- had arrived at his or her destination or intended to continue to a further location;
- had been prevented or dissuaded from driving by someone else.

These cases demonstrate that to require a witness to have actually *seen* the person driving would be too restrictive and that the courts would consider other circumstantial evidence when deliberating whether to convict a defendant of this offence. Answer B is therefore incorrect.

Road Policing, para. 3.10.11

Answer 10.15

Answer **A** — Even though a person who drives a certain class of vehicle under age will be 'disqualified' from holding a licence, that person will not commit an offence of disqualified driving under s. 103 of the Road Traffic Act 1988. They will commit an offence of driving other than in accordance with a licence, under s. 87(1) of the Act. Answers B and D are incorrect for this reason.

As all offences are now potentially arrestable, it is wrong to say that there is no power of arrest at all; answer C is therefore incorrect. The officer can arrest, but would have to show it was necessary within the strict criteria laid down in s. 24 of the Police and Criminal Evidence Act 1984.

Road Policing, para. 3.10.11

Answer 10.16

Answer **D** — The offence under s. 103 of the Road Traffic Act 1988 is one of strict liability. However, the prosecution will still need to prove that the defendant was, in fact, a disqualified driver. As the onus is on the prosecution, answers A and B are incorrect.

However, there is no need for the prosecution to prove that the defendant knew of the disqualification (*Taylor* v *Kenyon* [1952] 2 All ER 726). Answer C is therefore incorrect.

Road Policing, para. 3.10.11

Answer 10.17

Answer **A** — Section 36 of the Road Traffic Offenders Act 1988 gives the court the power to disqualify a person from holding or obtaining a licence until the person passes an 'appropriate' test.

If the person is disqualified under the provisions for 'totting up' penalty points or is found guilty of an offence involving obligatory disqualification; the 'appropriate' test is an *extended* test as defined in s. 36(5)(b).

In other cases the 'appropriate' test will be a regular driving test under s. 89(3) of the Road Traffic Act 1988.

Answers B, C and D are therefore incorrect.

Road Policing, para. 3.10.11.1

Answer 10.18

Answer **B** — Where a person has been disqualified by the court until a test is passed, he or she has to comply with the requirements of a provisional licence holder. This will include driving with 'L' plates and being accompanied by a qualified passenger. Answer D is therefore incorrect.

If a person fails to comply with these requirements, he or she commits the offence of disqualified driving under s. 103 of the Road Traffic Act 1988 (*Scott* v *Jelf* [1974] RTR 256). Answers A and C are therefore incorrect.

Road Policing, para. 3.10.11.1

Answer 10.19

Answer **A** — A person disqualified from holding a licence until he or she has passed another driving test is a disqualified person for the purposes of s. 103 of the Road Traffic Act 1988. That person may only drive a motor vehicle on a road if he or she obtains a provisional driving licence and drives in accordance with the terms of that licence (i.e. being accompanied by a qualified passenger and using 'L' plates).

It will fall to the driver to show that, not only did he or she have a provisional driving licence at the time, but that he or she was driving in accordance with the conditions of that licence (see *DPP* v *Barker* [2004] EWHC 2502 (Admin)). Answers B and D are therefore incorrect. The burden is on the prosecution to show that a defendant was the driver of the vehicle at a particular time; it is not down to the defendant to prove the opposite, therefore answer C is incorrect.

Road Policing, para. 3.10.11.1

Answer 10.20

Answer **B** — Once a period of disqualification ends, the person may apply for another licence. On application for another licence the person falls within the category of someone who 'has held and is entitled to obtain' a licence under s. 88 of the Road Traffic Act 1988.

Section 88 provides an exemption to the offence of driving otherwise than in accordance with a licence (s. 87)—the person can begin to drive again as soon as a proper application has been received by the Driver and Vehicle Licensing Agency (DVLA). The exception applies when the application is received by the DVLA and not when the application is submitted (or when it is returned) and therefore answers A, C and D are incorrect.

If a person drives before applying for a new licence, they commit the offence under s. 87 of the Act and answer A is also incorrect for this reason.

Road Policing, para. 3.10.11.2

Answer 10.21

Answer **C** — A person who receives a disqualification period of less than 56 days (called a Short Period Disqualification) will have his or her counterpart licence stamped by the court with details of the disqualification and the licence will be handed back to them. Answers A and B are therefore incorrect.

The licence will become valid again the day after the expiry of the disqualification and they can then drive again *without the need to apply to the DVLA for return of their licence*. Answer D is therefore incorrect.

Road Policing, para. 3.10.11.2

Answer 10.22

Answer **A** — The entitlement of drivers living outside the United Kingdom to drive here under the authority of their overseas permits is governed by the Motor Vehicles (International Circulation) Order 1975 (SI 1975/1208). If such drivers hold a domestic or Convention driving permit issued abroad or a British Forces driving licence, they may drive the vehicles covered by those authorities in Great Britain for one year (Art. 2). Regulation 80 of the Motor Vehicles (Driving Licences) Regulations 1999 makes similar provisions in relation to people who become resident in the United Kingdom. That permit allows the holder to take a driving test in that 12-month period. If they do not do so successfully then they will need a GB provisional licence.

However, the permit alone does *not* allow them to supervise learner drivers. Therefore, if FLAHERTY wanted to supervise his wife as she learns to drive in this country, he would have to pass a driving test in this country and abide by the regulations relating to 'qualified drivers' supervising others. Answers B and C are therefore incorrect.

There is no mention of the person having to further qualify once the test is passed by demonstrating the relevant driving experience (three years) in this country. Answer D is therefore incorrect.

Road Policing, para. 3.10.12

Answer 10.23

Answer **B** — Section 97(1) of the Road Traffic Act 1988 has been modified by the Motor Vehicles (Driving Licence) (Amendment) Regulations 2012 to prevent a driver disqualified in a European Economic Area State where they formerly held a licence from being granted a licence in Great Britain (including a provisional licence).

Because of WEBBER's nationality, s. 97(1) does not apply, therefore answers A, C and D are incorrect.

Road Policing, para. 3.10.12

Answer 10.24

Answer **B** — Regulation 80 of the Motor Vehicles (Driving Licences) Regulations 1999 makes provisions in relation to people who become resident in the United Kingdom. The driving permit from their original country allows the holder to take a driving test in that 12-month period. If they do not do so successfully, then they will need a GB provisional licence. Visitors and new residents holding a valid driving licence may also use that licence during the first 12 months and, if they apply for a GB provisional licence during that period, they will be exempt from the conditions imposed on provisional licence holders (reg. 18). The conditions of the provisional licence will apply at the end of the 12-month period and the licence will not expire if a test is not passed; DUBOIS would simply have to abide by the provisional licence conditions in these circumstances. Answer A is therefore incorrect.

The law governing drivers from EU Member States is slightly different and can be found in the Driving Licences (Community Driving Licence) Regulations 1996 (SI 1996/1974). Drivers from such countries must meet the fitness requirements of British drivers and, provided they are not disqualified, drivers meeting those physical requirements may exchange their licence for a part III licence if they have become normally resident in Great Britain (s. 89 of the Road Traffic Act 1988). Since these provisions are only available to drivers from EU Member States, they do not apply to DUBOIS and therefore answers C and D are incorrect.

Road Policing, para. 3.10.12

Answer 10.25

Answer **D** — Under s. 96(1) of the Road Traffic Act 1988, a person commits an offence if he or she drives a motor vehicle on a road while his or her eyesight is such (whether through a defect which cannot be or one which is not for the time being sufficiently corrected) that he or she cannot comply with any requirement as to eyesight pre-scribed under this Part of this Act for the purposes of tests of competence to drive.

Where a constable has reason to suspect that a person may be guilty of driving a motor vehicle on a road with defective eyesight, he or she may require the driver to submit to an eyesight test (s. 96(2)).

The specific requirements as to eyesight are set out at regs 72–73 and Sch. 8 to the Motor Vehicles (Driving Licences) Regulations 1999 (SI 1999/2864) and include the ability to read characters 79 mm high and 57 mm wide on a registra-tion mark fixed to a motor vehicle from 20.5 metres (or if the registration mark is the new type with narrower characters, 20 metres). Refusing to do so is an offence under s. 96(3).

The driver must be given the eyesight test in good light, while wearing corrective lenses, if they were worn when the person drove the motor vehicle on a road. This means that if the person was not wearing corrective lenses, they must take the test without them. Answers A and C are therefore incorrect. Even if the offence took place in darkness, the driver must take the test in good light. Answers B and C are incorrect for this reason.

Road Policing, para. 3.10.13.1

Answer 10.26

Answer **C** — The agreement with the DVLA allows for the fast-tracking of a revoca-tion of a licence from a motorist who fails a roadside eye test. Under the agreement, a licence can be revoked in a matter of hours rather than days. The system enables the police to notify the DVLA electronically with details of eyesight test failures, allowing a notice of revocation of the licence to be issued to motorists within hours (the police are able to contact the DVLA between 8 am and 9 pm). Previously, the police notified DVLA in writing or by fax, which in some cases meant that the revoca-tion could take up to four days. Answer B is therefore incorrect.

A motorist who commits the offence under s. 96(1) will have their licence revoked and it will not be returned until a driver can demonstrate that their eyesight meets the required standard; however, this process belongs to the DVLA and not the courts. Answer D is therefore incorrect.

This agreement does not provide the police with a power to confiscate a driving licence (therefore answer A is incorrect). In the circumstances outlined, it is suggested that the officer could use his or her powers to impose bail conditions (under s. 30A of PACE) if the circumstances merit immediate action. This could include requiring the person not to drive and if the person broke the condition, they could be taken to court to reconsider the question of bail.

Road Policing, para. 3.10.13.1

11 | Fixed Penalty System

Please note that the questions in this chapter relate to material in the Blackstone's Police Manuals which has been excluded from the Inspectors' Exam syllabus for 2014.

STUDY PREPARATION

The fixed penalty notice (FPN) system is pretty straightforward. Understand the principles behind it and you will realise that the system is simply designed to speed up the administration of some common offences which won't result in disqualification.

The Road Safety Act 2006 allows for financial deposits to be taken from drivers in certain circumstances, where an offence has been committed which may be dealt with by an FPN. The 2006 Act also extends the power to issue an FPN and demand the production of a driving licence to authorised vehicle examiners.

QUESTIONS

Question 11.1

Where a fixed penalty offence has been committed, s. 52(3)(a) of the Road Traffic Offenders Act 1988 allows for a procedure other than prosecution to be followed during a specified period, known as the 'suspended enforcement period'.

Which of the following statements is correct in relation to the length of this period?

A The suspended enforcement period will be at least 14 days.
B The suspended enforcement period will be at least 21 days, unless otherwise specified.
C The suspended enforcement period will be at least 21 days.
D The suspended enforcement period will be at least 28 days.

Question 11.2

Together with colleagues from the Vehicle and Operator Services Agency (VOSA), Constable PARKER was conducting road checks aimed at examining drivers' hours. They stopped MURPHY, a UK national, who was driving a large passenger-carrying vehicle (PCV). MURPHY was on the way to a ferry to take his passengers to France for a ten-day tour. On examining the vehicle's tachograph, Constable PARKER noticed that MURPHY had exceeded his driver's working hours. The officer intended issuing MURPHY with a fixed penalty notice for the offence.

Would Constable PARKER be entitled to require a deposit for the fixed penalty notice, under s. 90A of the Road Traffic Offenders Act 1988, in these circumstances?

A Yes, because MURPHY has indicated that he will be leaving the UK for a period longer than seven days.
B No, this power is only available in relation to drivers who are not citizens of the UK.
C No, because MURPHY has not indicated that he will be leaving the UK for a period longer than 28 days.
D Yes, but only if Constable PARKER is satisfied that MURPHY could not be found at an address in the UK.

Question 11.3

FISHER works for the Vehicle and Operator Services Agency (VOSA) and has stopped BUSCH, a German national, during a road check. BUSCH was driving a heavy goods vehicle and FISHER detected that he was committing an offence under s. 64(2) of the Road Traffic Act 1988, of using a goods vehicle with an unauthorised weight. FISHER intended issuing the driver with a fixed penalty notice for the offence. BUSCH was on the way to the ferry port and was leaving the UK within the next 24 hours and FISHER was not satisfied that he could be found if the penalty was not paid. FISHER asked the driver for a financial deposit relating to the notice, however BUSCH stated that he did not have enough money to pay a deposit.

In relation to the fixed penalty notice, what powers does FISHER have to remove the vehicle to another place, using powers under s. 90A of the Road Traffic Offenders Act 1988?

A FISHER may not remove the vehicle; this power is only given to a constable.

B FISHER may detain the vehicle at the scene until a deposit is paid, but there are no powers to remove a vehicle under this section.

C FISHER may remove the vehicle if the deposit is not paid immediately.

D FISHER may remove the vehicle if the deposit is not paid, but must allow a reasonable time for BUSCH to pay the deposit before removing it.

Question 11.4

Constable KERR stopped GROGAN, who was driving a motor vehicle on a road. Upon examining the vehicle, Constable KERR noticed that the tread on one of the front tyres fitted to the vehicle was below the legal limit. Constable KERR intended issuing GROGAN with an endorsable fixed penalty notice, but GROGAN stated that the vehicle belonged to his brother and that he was using it with his permission. He claimed that his brother was responsible for maintaining the vehicle.

Could Constable KERR issue a fixed penalty notice to GROGAN's brother for permitting the use of the vehicle, in these circumstances?

A Yes, a notice could be given to the driver for using and to the owner for permitting.

B No, a fixed penalty notice may only be issued to the driver of a vehicle.

C No, a fixed penalty notice may not be issued to a person who is guilty of permitting an offence.

D No, the officer would only have been able to do so if it could be proved that his brother *caused* GROGAN to drive the vehicle.

Question 11.5

SAXTON was stopped by Constable TALLY for a speeding offence. Constable TALLY intended issuing SAXTON with a fixed penalty notice for the offence. SAXTON was not in possession of a driving licence at the time and was required by Constable TALLY to produce it at a police station.

To whom must SAXTON produce the licence at the station?

A It must be produced to any constable or an authorised person at the station.

B It must be produced to any constable in uniform or an authorised person at the station.

C   It must be produced to any person at the station.

D   It must be produced to any constable in uniform at the station.

Question 11.6

Constable LEVINE stopped HOPKINS for driving through a red light and intended issuing a fixed penalty notice for the offence. HOPKINS was unable to produce a driving licence, but thought that there were already eight penalty points on it. Constable LEVINE was unable to confirm the number of penalty points on the driving licence at that time.

Given that this offence involves an obligatory endorsement, is Constable LEVINE precluded from issuing HOPKINS with a fixed penalty notice in these circumstances?

A   No, as the number of penalty points on the driving licence will not exceed 12.

B   Yes, as the number of penalty points on the driving licence will reach 11.

C   No, because the number of penalty points on the driving licence will not exceed 11.

D   Yes, because the number of penalty points on the driving licence cannot be confirmed.

Question 11.7

Constable FOSTER is in uniform and working on a joint exercise with SCOTT, a vehicle examiner from the Vehicle and Operator Services Agency (VOSA). They are stopping and examining motor vehicles for safety purposes and BOZMAN has been stopped as part of the exercise. SCOTT has discovered that BOZMAN's vehicle has a defective tyre. BOZMAN is not in possession of a driving licence at this time.

Which of the following statements is correct, in relation to whether SCOTT was able to issue a fixed penalty notice for the offence?

A   SCOTT has the power to issue a notice, because she is accompanied by a police constable in uniform.

B   SCOTT does not have the power to issue a notice, because BOZMAN is not in possession of a driving licence.

C   SCOTT has the power to issue a notice, provided the number of points for this offence would not render BOZMAN liable to disqualification.

D   SCOTT has the power to issue a notice in these circumstances alone, provided she produces her authority to do so.

Question 11.8

HILL has been issued with a fixed penalty notice for an offence by HAHN, a qualified vehicle examiner who works for the Vehicle and Operator Services Agency (VOSA). HILL was not in possession of a driving licence at the time the notice was issued.

How long does HILL have to produce a driving licence, in order to comply with the fixed penalty notice?

A 7 days.

B 14 days.

C 21 days.

D 28 days.

Question 11.9

SAGGERS was sent a letter by the Clerk to the Justices in his area that a vehicle regis-tered to him had been issued with a fixed penalty notice, and that the notice had not been paid. The letter stated that a request had been made to the court to increase the sum payable on the fixed penalty notice. SAGGERS had sold the vehicle recently to a neighbour, but had forgotten to notify the DVLA. His intention was to return the notice to the Clerk, declaring that he was not the person given the fixed penalty notice.

What period of time is allowed for SAGGERS to return such a declaration to the court?

A Within 21 days from the time the notice was sent by the Clerk.

B Within 14 days of receiving the notice from the Clerk.

C Within 14 days from the time the notice was sent from the Clerk.

D Within 21 days of receiving the notice from the Clerk.

Question 11.10

SCHIFFER is an Austrian national who is a temporary resident in the UK and is using an Austrian permit as a driving licence in this country. SCHIFFER has received a condi-tional offer of a fixed penalty notice for activating a speed camera.

Which of the following statements is correct, as to whether or not the DVLA will be able to allocate SCHIFFER with penalty points for this offence?

A SCHIFFER will not receive penalty points on the Austrian driving licence; the DVLA will only be able to create a computer record of the offence.

B SCHIFFER will receive penalty points on the Austrian driving licence for this offence.

C The DVLA may not allocate penalty points on a foreign driving licence; they will have to notify Austrian officials who will deal with the matter as they would for a driver convicted in that country.

D The DVLA may not allocate penalty points on a foreign driving licence; they will have to issue SCHIFFER with a provisional licence with the points on it.

Question 11.11

KELNER has been charged with an offence of removing a fixed penalty notice, which had been fixed to a vehicle outside the premises where she worked. KELNER is pleading not guilty to the offence.

What defence, if any, might be available to KELNER to this offence, contrary to s. 62(2) of the Road Traffic Offenders Act 1988?

A There is no defence to this particular offence.

B KELNER must show that she removed the fixed penalty notice on behalf of the person who parked the vehicle at the location.

C KELNER must show that she removed the fixed penalty notice on behalf of the owner of the vehicle.

D KELNER must show that she removed the fixed penalty notice on behalf of the driver, the person in charge of the vehicle or the person liable for the offence.

Question 11.12

WALLIS has been issued with a conditional offer of a fixed penalty notice after activating a speed camera.

How long does WALLIS have to make a payment in order to avoid attending court?

A 14 days.

B 21 days.

C 28 days.

D 1 month.

Question 11.13

LARSEN, having activated a camera at a set of traffic lights after driving through a red light, was sent a conditional offer of a fixed penalty notice through the post.

However, being concerned about the potential sanction for the offence, LARSEN did not reply to the offer.

What action is likely to happen now under s. 76(5) of the Road Traffic Offenders Act 1988, as a result of LARSEN's failure to respond to the conditional offer?

A The administrating office will notify the police that the penalty notice has not been paid.

B The administrating office will notify the clerk of the court for the relevant area that the penalty notice has not been paid.

C The administrating office should apply to the clerk of the court for the relevant area to issue a summons to be served on LARSEN.

D The administrating office will issue a notice to LARSEN, which will amount to a summons to appear in court.

ANSWERS

Answer 11.1

Answer **B** — Where a fixed penalty offence has been committed, the system allows for a procedure other than prosecution to be followed during a specified period. This period, known as the 'suspended enforcement period', *is at least 21 days following the date of the fixed penalty notice or such longer period as may be specified in it.*

Answers A, C and D are therefore incorrect.

Road Policing, para. 3.11.2

Answer 11.2

Answer **D** — Under s. 90A of the Road Traffic Offenders Act 1988, where any driver cannot satisfy a police officer or vehicle examiner that he or she can be found in the UK when necessary in connection with fixed penalty notice procedures, a deposit may be taken and the deposit may be used to pay any uncontested fixed penalty notice.

This power is available in relation to *any* driver, whether or not they are a UK citizen—the test is whether or not they can be found after the notice has been issued. Answer B is therefore incorrect.

Similarly, the fact that MURPHY is leaving the UK for a period of time is irrelevant, provided he can be found when he returns. Answers A and C are therefore incorrect.

Road Policing, para. 3.11.2.1

Answer 11.3

Answer **C** — Under s. 90A of the Road Traffic Offenders Act 1988, where any driver cannot satisfy a police officer *or vehicle examiner* that he or she can be found in the UK when necessary in connection with fixed penalty notice procedures, a deposit may be taken and the deposit may be used to pay any uncontested fixed penalty notice. Answer A is therefore incorrect.

Under s. 90D, if the deposit is not paid immediately, the police officer or vehicle examiner may prohibit the removal of the vehicle, or move it to another specified place. There is no requirement to allow a reasonable time for a person to pay the deposit before removing a vehicle under this section. Answers B and D are therefore incorrect.

Road Policing, para. 3.11.2.1

Answer 11.4

Answer **C** — Section 51(2) of the Road Traffic Offenders Act 1988 specifies that a person may be issued only with a fixed penalty notice if the offence relates to the 'use' of the vehicle on a road. The system does not apply to those who 'cause' or 'permit' the use of a vehicle on a road while an offence is being committed. Answers A and D are therefore incorrect.

Fixed penalty notices may be issued to a person not driving a vehicle—most nonendorsable notices are issued to stationary vehicles, and even though an endorsable notice may not be fixed to a stationary vehicle, there is nothing to prevent one being issued to the owner of a vehicle which is, for example, parked outside a house and committing an offence. Answer B is therefore incorrect.

Road Policing, para. 3.11.3

Answer 11.5

Answer **A** — A person may be issued with a fixed penalty notice (FPN) if he or she commits an offence to which the procedure applies (in this case, an endorsable offence). If a constable intends issuing such an FPN and the person is not in possession of a driving licence, he or she may be required under s. 54(4) of the Road Traffic Offenders Act 1988 to produce it at a police station within seven days. Once the licence is produced at the police station, provided it appears likely to the person receiving the licence that the driver will not be liable to disqualification by the issuing of points for this particular offence, the person may be given an FPN.

The driving licence may be produced either to a constable (whether in uniform or not) or to an authorised person, such as an enquiry clerk at a police station. Answers B, C and D are therefore incorrect.

Road Policing, para. 3.11.4.1

Answer 11.6

Answer **C** — A person may be issued with a fixed penalty notice (FPN) if he or she commits an offence to which the procedure applies (in this case, an endorsable offence). If a constable intends issuing such an FPN and the person is not in possession of a driving licence, he or she may be required under s. 54(4) of the Road Traffic Offenders Act 1988 to produce it at a police station within seven days.

Once the licence is produced at the police station, the person may not be issued with an FPN if he or she would be liable for disqualification if convicted for the offence. Therefore, even if a person does not have his or her driving licence at the time of the offence, he or she may still be required to produce it, even if it is unclear at the time of the offence how many penalty points are on the licence. The safeguard built into the process is that the person at the station will have to examine the driving licence for any penalty points and make the decision at that time whether or not the number of penalty points is likely to reach 12. If this is the case, the member of staff will not issue the notice. Answer D is therefore incorrect.

A person will be liable for disqualification under the 'totting up' procedure if his or her driving licence shows 12 points or more. Answer A is incorrect as an FPN may not be issued if the points are likely to exceed 11, not 12. Answer B is incorrect, as the process can continue if the number of penalty points on a person's driving licence reaches 11.

Road Policing, para. 3.11.4.1

Answer 11.7

Answer **D** — Section 54(1) and (2) of the Road Traffic Offenders Act 1988 states that where a constable in uniform, *or a vehicle examiner who produces his or her authority*, has reason to believe that a person he or she finds is committing or has on that occasion committed a fixed penalty offence, he or she may give the person a fixed penalty notice in respect of the offence. There is no requirement for the authorised vehicle examiner to be accompanied by a police constable in uniform in order to exercise this power and therefore answer A is incorrect.

If the person is not in possession of a driving licence, the authorised vehicle examiner has the same power to require the person, under s. 54(4), to produce it at a police station (within 14 days as opposed to seven days when issued by a police constable), and therefore answer B is incorrect. This is regardless of how many points are currently on the licence (answer C is therefore incorrect).

Road Policing, para. 3.11.4.1

Answer 11.8

Answer **B** — Under s. 54(4A)(a) of the Road Traffic Offenders Act 1988, if a fixed penalty notice is issued by a constable in uniform, delivery of the driving licence must be made in person, within seven days after the notice is given, to a constable or authorised person at the police station specified in the notice (being a police station chosen by the person concerned).

However, under s. 54(4A)(b), where the notice is given *by a vehicle examiner*, delivery of the driving licence may be made (either by post or in person), within 14 days after the notice is given, to the Secretary of State at the place specified in the notice. Answers A, C and D are therefore incorrect.

Road Policing, para. 3.11.4.1

Answer 11.9

Answer **D** — If a person receives a notice stating that a fixed penalty notice (FPN) has not been paid, he or she may serve a statutory declaration to the court to the effect either that he or she was not the person who was given the FPN, or that he or she has given a notice requesting a court hearing. In either case, the statutory notice must be made and served within 21 days of receiving the notice from the Clerk (and not 21 days from the time the notice was sent). Answers A, B and C are therefore incorrect.

Road Policing, para. 3.11.4.1

Answer 11.10

Answer **B** — Section 54 of the Road Traffic Offenders Act 1988 has been amended to facilitate the endorsement of a driver's record held at the DVLA for unlicensed and foreign drivers. Previously a fixed penalty notice could only be issued to a person who held a licence issued in Great Britain. The new system enables a fixed penalty notice which carries an endorsement to be issued to anyone provided that they are not liable to be disqualified under s. 35 of the Road Traffic Offenders Act 1988.

Answers A, C and D are therefore incorrect.

Road Policing, para. 3.11.4.1

Answer 11.11

Answer **D** — Section 62(2) of the Road Traffic Offenders Act 1988 states that a person is guilty of an offence if he or she removes or interferes with any notice fixed to a vehicle under this section, unless he or she does so by or under the authority of the *driver or person in charge of the vehicle or the person liable for the fixed penalty offence in question*.

Answers A, B and C are therefore incorrect.

Road Policing, para. 3.11.4.3

Answer 11.12

Answer **C** — Under s. 75(8)(a) of the Road Traffic Offenders Act 1988, the specified period is 28 days and therefore answers A, B and D are incorrect.

Road Policing, para. 3.11.5

Answer 11.13

Answer **A** — If the defendant fails to pay the fixed penalty and, where appropriate, surrender their licence, the police will be notified (s. 76(5) of the Road Traffic Offenders Act 1988). This will allow the agents acting on behalf of the police to decide how to proceed against the defendant. Answers B, C and D are therefore incorrect.

Road Policing, para. 3.11.5

Notices of Intended Prosecution

Please note that the questions in this chapter relate to material in the Blackstone's Police Manuals which has been excluded from the Inspectors' Exam syllabus for 2014.

STUDY PREPARATION

Like much road traffic legislation, the law governing notices of intended prosecution (NIPs) is concerned with procedural detail. Once you know which offences are generally covered by the NIP procedure, you then need to learn the procedure required for proper service to be accepted by the courts and any exceptions provided for.

Understanding the purpose behind NIPs will help you in learning all this important procedural detail.

QUESTIONS

Question 12.1

Constable DURSTOW had been trying to trace PHELPS whom the officer knew well, having had dealings with him on several occasions. Constable DURSTOW saw PHELPS driving a vehicle dangerously in a housing estate yesterday; the officer is not pursuit trained and lost sight of the vehicle, which was unregistered. Constable DURSTOW tried several addresses yesterday without success, but saw PHELPS walking down the street today and arrested him for the offence. Constable DURSTOW interviewed PHELPS at the station and a decision has been made by the Crown Prosecution Service (CPS) that the defendant should be charged with dangerous driving.

What action should Constable DURSTOW take, to comply with s. 1 of the Road Traffic Offenders Act 1988 (notice of intended prosecution (NIP))?

A Constable DURSTOW should serve a written NIP on PHELPS at the time of charging him.

B Constable DURSTOW should give PHELPS a verbal NIP at the time of charging him.

C Constable DURSTOW should identify PHELPS's address (or last known address) while he is in police detention and arrange for a written NIP to be sent there.

D Constable DURSTOW is not required to serve any type of NIP on PHELPS, as he is being charged with the offence.

Question 12.2

Constable McKEE stopped HODGESON for driving through a 'No Entry' sign. The officer reported HODGESON for the offence at the time of the incident. However, when she returned to the station, Constable McKEE realised she had forgotten to give HODGESON a verbal notice of intended prosecution (NIP). The officer took a period of leave, returning to work today, six days after the driving incident.

What type of NIP should Constable McKEE now issue, to comply with s. 1 of the Road Traffic Offenders Act 1988?

A Constable McKEE could attend HODGESON's home address and issue a verbal NIP, provided this is done before tomorrow.

B Constable McKEE should ensure a written NIP is sent to HODGESON within eight days.

C There is no action Constable McKEE can take to comply with s. 1, because she failed to issue a verbal NIP at the time of the offence.

D Constable McKEE should give a verbal NIP today, and ensure a written NIP is sent to HODGESON within 14 days from the time it is given.

Question 12.3

ALLAN has been given a verbal warning, at the time she committed an offence, of a notice of intended prosecution (NIP).

What proof is required that she understood the notice?

A It is for the prosecution to prove that the defendant understood the notice on every occasion.

B If the defendant claims he or she did not understand a verbal notice, it is for the defence to prove this fact.

C It is for the prosecution to prove that the defendant understood the notice, if a written notice was not given at a later date.

D It is for the prosecution to prove that the defendant understood the notice, if the defendant disputes this fact.

Question 12.4

A vehicle was caught activating a speed detection camera in the Eastshire area. A notice under s. 172 of the Road Traffic Act 1988 was sent to the registered keeper, YOUNG, who lived in the Westshire area, requesting the driver details. YOUNG was, in fact, the driver of the vehicle at the time of the offence, but decided to ignore the request and failed to reply to the notice.

Considering the original offence (exceeding the speed limit) took place in East-shire, could both cases be heard in Westshire where the second offence (failing to reply to the notice) took place?

A No, as the two offences were not part of an ongoing incident.

B Yes, but only if the court considers the second offence to be more serious.

C Yes, the cases may be heard in either court.

D No, the cases must be heard in a court where the original offence took place.

Question 12.5

PCSO GREENING was on foot patrol in uniform, walking along a one-way street, when he saw a vehicle being driven by BURGESS enter the street the wrong way, passing through a 'No Entry' sign. BURGESS spotted PCSO GREENING and stopped the vehicle. PCSO GREENING approached BURGESS and told her that she had committed an offence. Due to a lack of experience, PCSO GREENING could not state exactly which offence, but stated he would be reporting the matter to his sergeant, who would make a decision as to whether BURGESS would be prosecuted.

Would PCSO GREENING's warning that BURGESS could be prosecuted amount to a notice of intended prosecution (NIP) in these circumstances?

A No, BURGESS would have to have been told exactly which offence is being considered for prosecution.

B Yes, provided BURGESS understood the nature of the offence being considered for prosecution.

C No, PCSO GREENING is not empowered to make a decision whether or not to prosecute BURGESS.

D Yes, BURGESS has been made aware of the likelihood of prosecution; there is no requirement to make her aware of the nature of the offence.

Question 12.6

Constable PELLERITO had been attempting to trace CONLEY to deal with him for a driving offence. The officer called at CONLEY's address, but his mother stated he was not there very often and suggested Constable PELLERITO called at a local garage, where CONLEY worked. Three days after the alleged incident took place, Constable PELLERITO attended the premises in possession of a written notice of intended prosecution (NIP), intending to serve it on CONLEY.

Which of the following statements is correct, in relation to Constable PELLERITO's intention to serve a written NIP on CONLEY in these circumstances?

A Constable PELLERITO could serve a verbal NIP on CONLEY in these circumstances; there is no requirement for it to be in writing.

B Constable PELLERITO is correct in serving a written NIP personally on CONLEY in these circumstances.

C Constable PELLERITO should have sent a written NIP to the last known residential premises frequented by CONLEY; there is no facility to serve a written notice personally.

D Constable PELLERITO should have sent a written NIP to an address known to be frequented by CONLEY, such as the garage premises; there is no facility to serve a written notice personally.

Question 12.7

Constable NEWTON attended an accident where CONRAD, who was riding a pedal cycle on the pavement, had knocked over a child. The child did not suffer serious injuries and Constable NEWTON decided to report CONRAD for the offence of careless or inconsiderate cycling.

Should Constable NEWTON serve CONRAD a verbal notice of intended prosecution (NIP), in these circumstances?

A No, NIPs are not required where an offence has been committed involving a pedal cycle.

B No, but an NIP would have been required if CONRAD had been reported for dangerous cycling.

C Yes, an NIP is required as the accident involved a pedal cycle and not a motor vehicle.

D No, NIPs are generally required when a person has been reported for this offence, but there is no requirement to serve one in these circumstances.

Question 12.8

MUIR was dealt with by Constable ROCHELLE for an offence of parking a vehicle on the grass verge of a busy main road. The vehicle was not left in a dangerous position, but the officer considered that its location was causing an inconvenience to pedestrians. Constable ROCHELLE reported MUIR for an offence under s. 19 of the Road Traffic Act 1988. The officer believed that a notice of intended prosecution (NIP) would have been required for leaving a vehicle in a dangerous position, but was uncertain as to whether one was required for this particular offence.

Should Constable ROCHELLE issue MUIR with an NIP in these circumstances?

A Yes; unless the exceptions under s. 2(1) of the Road Traffic Offenders Act 1988 apply, an NIP is required for all offences under the Road Traffic Act 1988.

B Yes; an NIP is required for specific offences under the Road Traffic Act 1988, such as leaving a vehicle in a dangerous position, or those similar to them.

C No; even though the offence is similar to leaving a vehicle in a dangerous position, an NIP is not required for this particular offence.

D No; an NIP is not required for either of these offences.

Question 12.9

CLAYTON was in detention for an offence of causing death by dangerous driving and was charged with this offence on the advice of the out-of-hours Crown Prosecutor. However, a month later, after reviewing the evidence, the CPS decided that the evidence connecting CLAYTON with the death of the victim was not strong and recommended an alternative charge be put to the defendant of dangerous driving. CLAYTON was not served with a notice of intended prosecution (NIP) when charged with the original offence.

Which of the following is correct in relation to the service of an NIP for the alternative offence of dangerous driving, in these circumstances?

A A verbal NIP should now be served on CLAYTON for this offence, otherwise the prosecution will fail.

B There is no requirement to serve an NIP on CLAYTON, and the prosecution may proceed.

C A written NIP should now be served on CLAYTON for this offence, otherwise the prosecution will fail.

D An NIP may not be served on CLAYTON because of time limits, and the prosecution may fail as a result of failing to serve one sooner.

Question 12.10

HAWKLEY was responsible for failing to stop after an accident in a supermarket car park, when he damaged another car and drove off. A witness took his registration number and reported the accident to Constable DAVIES. The officer sent a notice of intended prosecution (NIP) to HAWKLEY's address as shown on the Police National Computer (PNC). However, HAWKLEY had moved. HAWKLEY was traced two months later and, when interviewed, stated he had never received the NIP.

What effect would the failure to serve the NIP have on any future prosecution against HAWKLEY?

A None, as HAWKLEY was at fault for the failure of the service.

B The NIP was not served in time and therefore the case cannot proceed.

C None, an NIP was not required as the offence occurred at the time of an accident.

D None, an NIP was not required as the accident did not occur on a road.

Question 12.11

LEWINSKI was driving his motor vehicle along a main road, approaching a set of traffic lights at a junction. Due to a lack of concentration, LEWINSKI drove through a red light and collided with a heavy goods vehicle. LEWINSKI suffered severe head injuries as a result of the accident and was taken to hospital, where he remained for several weeks. Because of his injuries, LEWINSKI was not able to recall being involved in the accident. The officer in the case is contemplating whether or not a notice of intended prosecution (NIP) should be served on LEWINSKI, for driving through the red light.

Would the officer be correct in serving an NIP because of the serious injuries, in these circumstances?

A Yes, as LEWINSKI was severely injured as a result of the accident.

B No, an NIP is never required when the driver has been involved in an accident.

C It is immaterial whether he was injured or not, because the accident was not of a minor nature.

D Yes, an NIP is always required when the driver is injured as a result of an accident.

Question 12.12

GODDARD has been summonsed to court for an offence of careless driving.

What evidential proof will be required by the court that GODDARD has been served with a notice of intended prosecution (NIP), under s. 1(1) of the Road Traffic Offenders Act 1988?

A The prosecution must show that the requirements of s. 1(1) of the 1988 Act have been complied with through oral testimony.

B The prosecution must show that the requirements of s. 1(1) of the 1988 Act have been complied with through documentary evidence.

C The court will always assume that the requirements of s. 1(1) of the 1988 Act have been complied with.

D The court will always assume that the requirements of s. 1(1) of the 1988 Act have been complied with until the contrary is proved.

Question 12.13

Constable HAMILTON has been attempting to serve a notice of intended prosecution (NIP) on KUBICA, whom the officer witnessed driving dangerously. Constable HAMILTON attended KUBICA's home address, but was told that the suspect was staying in France for six weeks. Constable HAMILTON returned to KUBICA's home address the following day and served a written NIP on the suspect's father.

Has an NIP been served correctly in these circumstances?

A Yes, the NIP has been served in these circumstances.

B No, the NIP should only be served on the person who was believed to be the driver.

C No, Constable HAMILTON was aware that KUBICA would not be at the address to receive the NIP.

D No, Constable HAMILTON should have arranged for a written NIP to be sent to KUBICA's home address by recorded delivery.

Question 12.14

COSTAS is facing prosecution for an offence of dangerous driving, contrary to s. 2 of the Road Traffic Act 1988. COSTAS is pleading not guilty, citing a technical reason: that the notice of intended prosecution (NIP) was not served correctly. COSTAS admits to having received a written NIP by post, but claims not to have received it within the required timescales. The prosecution will claim that the NIP was sent by registered post within the required timescales.

Which of the following statements is correct, in relation to a driver being properly warned of a prosecution, under s. 1 of the Road Traffic Offenders Act 1988?

A There is a presumption that if an NIP was sent by registered post or recorded delivery, it was served within 14 days.

B There is a presumption that if an NIP was sent by registered post or recorded delivery, it was served within two days.

C There is a presumption that if an NIP was sent by registered post or recorded delivery, it was served within five days.

D There is a presumption that if an NIP was sent by registered post or recorded delivery, it was served within seven days.

Question 12.15

HARDING is appearing in court for a speeding offence. HARDING is pleading not guilty, claiming that a notice of intended prosecution (NIP) was never served on him with the details of the offence, in accordance with s. 1 of the Road Traffic Offenders Act 1988. It has been established that an NIP was sent to HARDING, by second class post.

Which of the following statements is correct in relation to whether HARDING was correctly served with an NIP?

A The NIP was sent to HARDING by second class post; therefore it was not served correctly.

B The NIP was sent to HARDING by second class post; it must be sent by first class post on every occasion, therefore, it was not served correctly.

C The NIP has been correctly served on HARDING; any postal service may be used to serve such a notice.

D The NIP was sent to HARDING by second class post; it must be sent either by registered post or recorded delivery on every occasion; therefore it was not served correctly.

ANSWERS

Answer 12.1

Answer **D** — Under s. 1 of the Road Traffic Offenders Act 1988, before certain offences can be prosecuted the defendant must have *either* been:

1. warned of the possibility of prosecution at the time of the offence; or
2. served with a summons (or charged) within 14 days of the offence; or
3. a notice of intended prosecution (NIP) must have been sent to the registered keeper within 14 days of the offence.

Therefore, as PHELPS is being charged with the offence, the provisions of s. 1 do not apply and an NIP is not required.

Answers A, B and C are therefore incorrect.

Road Policing, para. 3.12.1

Answer 12.2

Answer **B** — Under s. 1 of the Road Traffic Offenders Act 1988, before certain offences can be prosecuted, the defendant must have *either* been:

1. warned of the possibility of prosecution at the time of the offence, *or*
2. served with a summons (or charged) within 14 days of the offence, *or*
3. a notice of intended prosecution (NIP) must have been sent to the registered keeper within 14 days of the offence.

Therefore, even if a verbal NIP is not given at the time, the officer can recover the situation provided a notice is sent to the registered keeper within 14 days of the offence. Answer C is incorrect because a written NIP can still be sent.

Answers A and D are incorrect as a verbal NIP may only be given at the time of the offence. If this is not possible, the prosecution is able to send a written one to the keeper's last known address.

Road Policing, para. 3.12.1

Answer 12.3

Answer **A** — If a verbal warning is given at the time of the offence, it must be shown that the defendant understood it (*Gibson* v *Dalton* [1980] RTR 410). Proof that the defendant understood the warning will lie with the prosecution. Answer B is therefore incorrect. The prosecution must show this on *every* occasion, whether or not the defendant claims he or she did not understand, or whether a written notice of intended prosecution (NIP) was given at a later date. Answers C and D are therefore incorrect.

Road Policing, para. 3.12.1

Answer 12.4

Answer **C** — When an offence is committed partly within the jurisdiction of two different courts, it may be heard in *either* court (*Kennet DC* v *Young* [1999] RTR 235). Answers A, B and D are therefore incorrect.

Road Policing, para. 3.12.1

Answer 12.5

Answer **C** — Under s. 1 of the Road Traffic Offenders Act 1988, before certain offences can be prosecuted, the defendant must have either been:

1. warned of the possibility of prosecution at the time of the offence, *or*
2. served with a summons (or charged) within 14 days of the offence, *or*
3. a notice of intended prosecution (NIP) must have been sent to the registered keeper within 14 days of the offence.

As the purpose of the warning or notice is to alert the defendant to the likelihood of prosecution, it is not necessary to specify exactly which offence is being considered (answer A is therefore incorrect). However, the defendant should be made aware of the *nature* of the offence (*Pope* v *Clarke* [1953] 2 All ER 704). Answer D is therefore incorrect.

Answers B and D are incorrect because, if the person giving the NIP is not empowered to make a decision whether or not to prosecute (such as a vehicle examiner employed by the vehicle inspectorate or, in this case, a PCSO), the warning or notice will not be deemed to have been served (*Swan* v *Vehicle Inspectorate* [1997] RTR 187).

Road Policing, paras 3.12.1, 3.12.5

Answer 12.6

Answer **B** — Under s. 1(1A) of the Road Traffic Offenders Act 1988, a notice required by this section to be served on any person may be served on that person—

(a) by delivering it to him;
(b) by addressing it to him and leaving it at his last known address; or
(c) by sending it by registered post, recorded delivery service or first class post addressed to him at his last known address.

A written notice *may* be served personally, provided the defendant fully understands what is said to them—in fact, if neither the defendant nor the registered keeper have a fixed abode, reasonable efforts must be made to serve the notice of intended prosecution (NIP) personally. Answers C and D are therefore incorrect. Also, nothing in s. 1 requires an NIP to be served at a residential premises and answer C is also incorrect for this reason.

Finally, for a verbal NIP to be given, the defendant must have been warned of the possibility of that prosecution *at the time of the offence* (s. 1(1)(a)). Answer A is therefore incorrect.

Road Policing, paras 3.12.1, 3.12.5

Answer 12.7

Answer **D** — There is a list of offences which require a notice of intended prosecution (NIP) contained in Sch. 1 to the Road Traffic Offenders Act 1988 and these include dangerous, careless or inconsiderate cycling. Answer A is therefore incorrect.

Section 2(1) of the Road Traffic Offenders Act 1988 lists the exemption from the requirement to serve an NIP, namely, the requirement to serve an NIP does not apply in relation to an offence if, at the time, or immediately afterwards and owing to the presence of the *vehicle* concerned on a road an accident occurred. The exemption is not restricted to motor vehicles, which means that since CONRAD was involved in an accident while riding a vehicle on a road, an NIP would not be required (even if the offence reported was dangerous cycling). Answers B and C are incorrect for this reason.

Road Policing, paras 3.12.2, 3.12.3

Answer 12.8

Answer **C** — The offences which require a notice of intended prosecution (NIP) are listed in Sch. 1 to the Road Traffic Offenders Act 1988 and include:

• Dangerous, careless or inconsiderate driving.
• Dangerous, careless or inconsiderate cycling.
• Failing to comply with traffic signs and directions.

- Leaving a vehicle in a dangerous position.
- Speeding offences under ss. 16 and 17 of the Road Traffic Regulation Act 1984.

The list of offences in Sch. 1 is exhaustive and does not apply to *all* offences under the Road Traffic Act 1988. Neither does it include offences under s. 19 of the Road Traffic Act 1988. Answer A is therefore incorrect.

However, an NIP *is* required for the offence of leaving a vehicle in a dangerous position and answer D is incorrect.

Other offences, even if similar in nature to those in the list, will *not* be covered by the requirements of s. 1(1) of the Road Traffic Offenders Act 1988 and will not require an NIP (see *Sulston* v *Hammond* [1970] 1 WLR 1164). Answer B is therefore incorrect.

Road Policing, para. 3.12.2

Answer 12.9

Answer **B** — Under s. 1(1) of the Road Traffic Offenders Act 1988, before an offence to which the section applies can be prosecuted, the defendant must have been warned of the possibility of that prosecution at the time of the offence. If this is not done, he or she must be notified by way of summons (or charge) within 14 days, or a notice setting out the possibility of that prosecution must have been sent to the driver or registered keeper of the vehicle within 14 days of the offence. Section 1(1) does not allow for notices of intended prosecution (NIPs) to be served outside these timescales, therefore, answers A and C are incorrect.

Section 2(4) of the Act outlines that a failure to observe the requirements of s. 1(1) will not necessarily bar an alternative conviction, where the original offence prosecuted was not one requiring an NIP, but where the alternative offence *would* ordinarily require such a notice. Section 24 contains a list of such alternatives, which includes an alternative charge of dangerous driving, where the defendant was originally charged with causing death by dangerous driving. Therefore, although the CPS decision in this particular case fell outside the normal 14 days' time limit for serving an NIP, the prosecution may still proceed on the grounds that the defendant has been charged in the alternative. Answer D is therefore incorrect.

Road Policing, paras 3.12.2, 3.12.3

Answer 12.10

Answer **A** — Section 2(1) of the Road Traffic Offenders Act 1988 states that a notice of intended prosecution (NIP) does not need to be served if at the time or immediately afterwards and owing to the presence of the motor vehicle concerned *on a road* an accident occurred. This means that where an accident occurs on a road, an NIP is not required for a due care offence; however, where an accident occurs in a public place an NIP *will be* required. Answers C and D are therefore incorrect.

An NIP must be served on the defendant within 14 days of the offence, if it was not given verbally at the time. However, under s. 2(3) of the 1988 Act, if the defendant contributes to the failure to serve the NIP, then that will not be a bar to his or her conviction. Answer B is therefore incorrect.

Road Policing, para. 3.12.3

Answer 12.11

Answer **C** — Generally, a notice of intended prosecution (NIP) is *not* required if at the time of the offence, or immediately afterwards, an accident occurred owing to the presence of a motor vehicle on a road (s. 2(1) of the Road Traffic Offenders Act 1988). However, there is an exception to this rule. Where the driver of a motor vehicle is unaware that an accident has taken place because it is so minor, there *will* be a need to serve an NIP (*Bentley* v *Dickinson* [1983] RTR 356). Answer B is incorrect as the exception shows that sometimes an NIP may be required following an accident.

When the accident is so severe that the driver of the vehicle is unable to recall it, an NIP is *not* required (*DPP* v *Pidhajeckyj* [1991] RTR 136). Answer A is incorrect because of the ruling in this case. Answer D is incorrect as there is nothing in the Act stating that an NIP is required every time a driver is injured in an accident.

Answer C is *correct* because it is *not* relevant whether the driver was injured, as the accident was not of a minor nature (and *Bentley* does not apply), and therefore it falls within the scope of s. 2(1).

Road Policing, para. 3.12.3

Answer 12.12

Answer **D** — Section 1 of the Road Traffic Offenders Act 1988 relates to the notice or warning in relation to notices of intended prosecution (NIP).

Subsection (3) of this section relates to a presumption in relation to NIPs, in that:

(3) The requirement of subsection (1) above shall in every case be deemed to have been complied with unless and until the contrary is proved.

The effect of s. 1(3), therefore, is to place the burden of proving failure to comply with the section on the defence on a balance of probabilities. Answer C is therefore incorrect. The prosecution have no such evidential burden. Answers A and B are therefore incorrect.

Road Policing, para. 3.12.4

Answer 12.13

Answer **A** — Section 1 of the Road Traffic Offenders Act 1988 states:

(1A) A notice required by this section to be served on any person may be served on that person—
  (a) by delivering it to him;
  (b) by addressing it to him and leaving it at his last known address; or
  (c) by sending it by registered post, recorded delivery service or first class post addressed to him at his last known address.

In the case of *Hosier* v *Goodall* [1962] 2 QB 401, a notice of intended prosecution (NIP) served on the defendant's spouse or partner was sufficient. Answer B is therefore incorrect.

In the case of *Phipps* v *McCormick* [1972] Crim LR 540, it was found that if the defendant is not at his or her home address, for instance because he or she is in hospital or on holiday, service to his or her last known address will suffice, even if the police are aware of that fact. Answer C is therefore incorrect.

Under s. 1(1A), any method of service of an NIP will suffice, therefore, provided the NIP has been served correctly, the method of service is unimportant. Answer D is therefore incorrect.

Road Policing, para. 3.12.5

Answer 12.14

Answer **B** — Under s. 1 of the Road Traffic Offenders Act 1988, before certain offences can be prosecuted, the defendant must have either been:

• warned of the possibility of prosecution at the time of the offence, *or*
• served with a summons (or charged) within 14 days of the offence, *or*

- a notice of intended prosecution (NIP) must have been sent to the registered keeper within 14 days of the offence.

If the driver is not warned of the possibility of prosecution at the time of the offence, then a notice must be sent to the registered keeper of the vehicle, in writing, within 14 days of the offence.

The Road Traffic Offenders Act 1988, s. 1(1A)(c) states that a notice required by this section to be served on any person may be served on that person—

by sending it by registered post, recorded delivery service or first class post addressed to him at his last known address.

Generally, proof is required that the NIP was sent to the registered keeper of the vehicle within 14 days of the offence; however, there is an irrebuttable presumption that if an NIP is sent by registered post or recorded delivery then it has been served within *two* days.

Answers A, C and D are therefore incorrect.

Road Policing, para. 3.12.5

Answer 12.15

Answer **A** — Under s. 1 of the Road Traffic Offenders Act 1988, before certain offences can be prosecuted, the defendant must have either been:

- warned of the possibility of prosecution at the time of the offence, *or*
- served with a summons (or charged) within 14 days of the offence, *or*
- a notice of intended prosecution (NIP) must have been sent to the registered keeper within 14 days of the offence.

If the driver is not warned of the possibility of prosecution at the time of the offence, then a notice must be sent to the registered keeper of the vehicle, in writing, within 14 days of the offence. Section 1(1A)(c) of the Road Traffic Offenders Act 1988 states that a notice required by this section to be served on any person may be served on that person—

by sending it by registered post, recorded delivery service or first class post addressed to him at his last known address.

Since the NIP can be sent by any of these methods, answers B and D are incorrect.

However, such a notice may be sent to the person by registered post, recorded delivery service or first class post addressed to him or her at his or her last known address. This means that an NIP will *not* be correctly served if it is sent by second class post (answer C is therefore incorrect).

Note that there is a rebuttable presumption that service by first class post would not suffice, if the defence can give evidence that the notice was received after the 14-day period (*Gidden* v *Chief Constable of Humberside* [2009] EWHC 2924 (Admin)).

Road Policing, para. 3.12.5

13 Forgery and Falsification of Documents

STUDY PREPARATION

The end of the road—or at least for road policing!

There are relatively few offences involving forgery and falsification, although as much road traffic law—and its enforcement—relies upon records, these offences are more relevant than they may at first appear. The following deals with occasions where a defendant has, or uses, false documentation.

QUESTIONS

Question 13.1

UNION was stopped while driving PIPER's car on a road and was asked to produce his driving documents. UNION did not have his own policy of insurance. PIPER did not have insurance either, as he had failed to keep up his monthly payments and his insurance company had cancelled the policy. PIPER was still in possession of the insurance certificate, and he lent this to UNION for him to produce it. UNION was aware of the situation when he produced the documents.

Has either UNION or PIPER committed the offence of forgery of documents under s. 173 of the Road Traffic Act 1988?

A Yes, UNION only commits this offence in these circumstances.

B Yes, UNION and PIPER both commit this offence in these circumstances.

C Yes, PIPER only commits this offence in these circumstances.

D Yes, UNION commits this offence; PIPER is guilty of aiding and abetting.

Question 13.2

STANGER runs an international road haulage company and has recently married. He wishes to start another business in his wife's name and applies for an international road haulage permit for her. His wife has a recent conviction for drink driving, although she is currently not disqualified. STANGER is unaware of this, as his wife does not wish him to know, and he claims on the application form that neither he nor his wife have any previous convictions. As a result, a permit is issued, when it may not have been had the conviction been declared.

Has an offence of making a false statement to obtain the grant of an international road haulage permit been committed?

A Yes, as a false statement has been made; STANGER's wife knows it to be false and it is an application on her behalf.

B Yes, as STANGER has gained an advantage by not declaring the conviction in that a permit was issued that may not have been.

C No, because STANGER had no intention of deceiving the issuers of the permit when he made the declaration.

D No, because STANGER did not knowingly make a false statement as he was unaware of the conviction.

Question 13.3

FRANCIS is the transport manager of a haulage company. Before going on holiday, FRANCIS was aware that five of the company's vehicles were due to be submitted for goods vehicle tests while he was away. When FRANCIS returned, all five had been tested and issued with certificates. When FRANCIS examined the certificates, he suspected that they were forgeries. FRANCIS turned a blind eye, knowing the company was in financial difficulty. He provided one of the certificates to a driver, which was then produced to the police.

Under what circumstances could an offence be proved against FRANCIS, under s. 174(2) of the Road Traffic Act 1988 (producing documents which are false)?

A If it can be shown FRANCIS either knew the certificate was false, or was reckless as to whether or not it was.

B If it can be shown FRANCIS either knew the certificate was false, or was reckless as to whether or not it was and that someone gained by the transaction, though not necessarily him.

C If it can be shown FRANCIS knew the certificate was false.

D If it can be shown FRANCIS knew the certificate was false and that someone gained by the transaction, though not necessarily him.

Question 13.4

ROSS was involved in a road traffic collision, during which she knocked a pedestrian over. There was no damage to her vehicle; however, the police dealt with the incident and issued ROSS with an HORT/1. When she got home, ROSS realised that her test certificate had expired the day before. Knowing she could be prosecuted, ROSS contacted her friend, CRUTCHER, who ran a testing station, and asked him to put her car through an MOT and to backdate her test certificate. CRUTCHER agreed to do so and ROSS was issued with a test certificate backdated to the day before.

Has CRUTCHER committed an offence under s. 175 of the Road Traffic Act 1988 (issuing false documents), in these circumstances?

A No, the offence under this section applies to documents that have been altered; it would be necessary to prosecute CRUTCHER for conspiracy instead.

B Yes, provided it can be proved that CRUTCHER knew why ROSS had made this request.

C Yes, provided it can be proved that CRUTCHER either knew why ROSS had made this request, or was reckless as to why she had done so.

D Yes, CRUTCHER could be prosecuted, because he issued a false document, whether he knew ROSS's intentions or not.

Question 13.5

While on mobile patrol, Constable FRENCH stopped a large goods vehicle being driven by PARSONS. Constable FRENCH was not an authorised vehicle examiner, but had recently been studying to go on a traffic officer's course and decided to examine the vehicle. The officer noticed that the plate attached to the vehicle authorising its 'plated' weight had been interfered with in that the characters and words had been scratched out. Constable FRENCH suspected that the plate had been fraudulently altered.

What powers would Constable FRENCH have in respect of the vehicle and the plate attached to it, under s. 176 of the Road Traffic Act 1988?

A Constable FRENCH may seize the vehicle to which the plate is attached until it has been examined.

B None, Constable FRENCH will have to call an authorised vehicle examiner, who may detach the plate from the vehicle.

C Constable FRENCH may detach the plate, and cause it to be examined by an authorised vehicle examiner.

D None, the power under this section relates to seizing documents and a plate is not a document.

Question 13.6

MARTIN and STOUT own car showrooms next to each other. Often, they park cars on the road while moving other vehicles around in the showrooms. Occasionally, when doing this, both MARTIN and STOUT have been reported for keeping vehicles on the road without an excise licence. To try to avoid being booked again, they now park vehicles outside with trade plates fitted. One day, all of STOUT's trade plates were being used on other vehicles, therefore MARTIN lent him several sets of trade plates to park some vehicles on the road.

Which of the following statements is correct in relation to either MARTIN's or STOUT's liability for an offence, of forgery, under s. 44(1) of the Vehicle Excise and Registration Act 1994?

A Both persons could be guilty of this offence provided it can be shown that they intended to deceive someone.

B Both persons could be guilty of this offence in these circumstances alone; there is no requirement to show intent on either person's behalf.

C Both persons could be guilty of this offence, provided it can be shown that they intended to cause economic loss.

D Only STOUT could be guilty of the offence; s. 44(1) does not cover circumstances of lending anything to another person.

Question 13.7

NOLAN works in the admin department of a haulage company and is responsible for filing tacograph records submitted by the drivers. NOLAN is aware that drivers frequently alter their drivers' hours because they make regular jokes about it, but she shares the common view that it is done in the best interests of the company in respect of profit margins. NOLAN is not directly involved in changing any records, but is aware of what is happening and is prepared to produce the false records on behalf of the company should an inspection take place.

Section 38 of the Goods Vehicles (Licensing of Operators) Act 1995 deals with offences of forgery or alteration of documents relating to goods vehicle operators. Would NOLAN be liable for such an offence in these circumstances?

A No, while documents have been forged or altered, they have not been used to deceive any person at this stage.

B Yes, NOLAN is in possession of documents that have been forged or altered and are calculated to deceive.

C No, NOLAN is not in possession of documents or other things that are covered by this Act, even though they have been forged or altered.

D No, the documents NOLAN possessed were altered by another person.

Question 13.8

GARDNER parked in a pay-and-display car park and went shopping, paying for three hours' parking. After an hour, GARDNER decided to go home and returned to the car park. As GARDNER was leaving, LASSITER parked in the vacant space. GARDNER stopped and gave LASSITER the pay-and-display parking ticket, which was still valid for another hour. LASSITER displayed the ticket on the car windscreen and went shopping.

Has either GARDNER or LASSITER committed an offence contrary to s. 115 of the Road Traffic Regulation Act 1984 (misuse of parking documents) in these circumstances?

A Only LASSITER could be guilty of the offence, provided it can be proved that the owner of the car park suffered some economic loss.

B No, this is a civil matter between the owner of the car park and LASSITER, who has not paid to park in the car park.

C Yes, both persons could be guilty of this offence; it can be proved that they intended to deceive someone.

D Yes, both persons could be guilty of this offence in these circumstances alone; there is no requirement to show intent on either person's behalf.

ANSWERS

Answer 13.1

Answer **B** — Under s. 173(1)(b) of the Road Traffic Act 1988, a person commits an offence if, with intent to deceive, he or she lends to, or allows to be used by, any other person, a document or other thing to which the section applies. Certificates of insurance are covered, and where a person produced a certificate of insurance issued under a policy which had expired, the offence is made out (*R v Cleghorn* [1938] 3 All ER 398). Therefore, PIPER is guilty of the full offence, by lending/allowing UNION to use the insurance certificate.

Under s. 173(1)(a) of the Road Traffic Act 1988, a person is guilty of an offence if, with intent to deceive, he or she 'uses' a document to which this section applies. UNION is guilty of 'using' the document when he produces it. Answers A, C and D are therefore incorrect.

Road Policing, para. 3.13.2.1

Answer 13.2

Answer **D** — There is a specific offence under s. 174(1)(e) of the Road Traffic Act 1988, of knowingly making a false statement for the purpose of obtaining the grant of an international road haulage permit.

However, such an offence must be committed knowingly whether the application is for the applicant himself or another person. Knowingly is very different from intent, and this offence requires no intent; answer C is therefore incorrect. Without the 'knowingly' the offence is not complete, even though STANGER's wife knew about the conviction (although this may negate the legality of the actual permit); answers A and B are therefore incorrect.

Road Policing, para. 3.13.2.2

Answer 13.3

Answer **A** — Under s. 174(2) of the Road Traffic Act 1988:

A person who, in supplying information or producing documents for the purposes either of sections 53 to 60 and 63 of this Act or of regulations made under sections 49 to 51, 61, 62 and 66(3) of this Act—

(a) makes a statement which he knows to be false in a material particular or recklessly makes a statement which is false in a material particular, or

(b) produces, provides, sends or otherwise makes use of a document which he knows to be false in a material particular or recklessly produces, provides, sends or otherwise makes use of a document which is false in a material particular,

is guilty of an offence.

FRANCIS's actions are covered by s. 174(2)(b), in that he provided a false goods vehicle test certificate, which was required to be produced under s. 53 of the Act. Section 174(2)(b) is clear that the offence can be committed by a person who produces, provides etc. any document which he or she either knows to be false in a material particular or is reckless as to this fact. Answers C and D are therefore incorrect.

There is no need to show that the person actually gained anything, or brought about the desired consequences (see *Jones* v *Meatyard* [1939] 1 All ER 140). Answers B and D are incorrect for this reason.

Road Policing, para. 3.13.2.2

Answer 13.4

Answer **D** — Section 175 of the Road Traffic Act 1988 states that if a person issues:

(a) any such document as referred to in section 174(5)(a) or (b) of this Act, or

(b) a test certificate or certificate of conformity and the document or certificate so issued is to his knowledge false in a material particular,

he/she is guilty of an offence.

The offence under this section is complete when the document is issued falsely—there is only a requirement to show that the person issuing the documents *knew that they were false* (see *Ocean Accident etc. Co* v *Cole* (1932) 96 JP 191). There is no requirement to show that the defendant knew what the documents would be used for (or was reckless as to their use). Answers B and C are therefore incorrect.

Test certificates bearing a false stamp *or ones which have been backdated* are 'false in a material particular' (see *Murphy* v *Griffiths* [1967] 1 WLR 333). Answer A is incorrect for that reason.

Road Policing, para. 3.13.2.3

Answer 13.5

Answer **B** — Section 176(4) of the Road Traffic Act 1988 provides a power to seize either a document or a plate from a vehicle where the constable reasonably believes that an offence under s. 173 (forgery or falsification) has occurred. Since the power also applies to plates on a vehicle, answer D is incorrect. However, the officer removing the plate must be an examiner appointed under s. 66A of the Act. Since Constable FRENCH is not an authorised vehicle examiner, one must be called to the scene to detach the plate and therefore answer C is incorrect. The power under this section relates to seizing documents (or plates) and does not allow the seizure of a vehicle by the officer. Answer A is therefore incorrect.

Road Policing, para. 3.13.2.4

Answer 13.6

Answer **B** — Section 44(1) of the Vehicle Excise and Registration Act 1994 states that a person is guilty of an offence if he or she forges, fraudulently alters, fraudulently uses, *fraudulently lends* or fraudulently allows to be used by another person anything to which subs. (2) applies. Section 44(2) applies to a trade plate (including a replacement trade plate) and since the offence under s. 44(1) does cover the circumstances of lending anything to another person, answer D is incorrect.

Section 44(1) does not require the prosecution to show an intent to deceive on behalf of the person fraudulently using or lending the trade plates. Answer A is therefore incorrect. Similarly, in *R* v *Terry* [1984] AC 374, the court decided that there is no need to prove any intent to cause economic loss (and answer C is therefore incorrect).

Road Policing, para. 3.13.3

Answer 13.7

Answer **C** — Under s. 38(1) of the Goods Vehicles (Licensing of Operators) Act 1995, a person is guilty of an offence if, with intent to deceive, he or she—

(a) forges, alters or uses a document or other thing to which this section applies;
(b) lends to, or allows to be used by, any other person a document or other thing to which this section applies; or
(c) makes or has in his possession any document or other thing so closely resembling a document or other thing to which this section applies as to be calculated to deceive.

The offence may be committed by a person who is simply in possession of a document which is calculated to deceive; therefore, answers A and D are incorrect.

However, s. 38(2) of the Act is specific about the documents to which the section applies (which are similar to those covered in the main offence under s. 173 of the Road Traffic Act 1988), which are:

- any operator's licence;
- any document, plate, mark or other thing by which, in pursuance of regulations, a vehicle is to be identified as being authorised to be used, or as being used, under an operator's licence;
- any document evidencing the authorisation of any person for the purposes of ss. 40 and 41;
- any certificate of qualification under s. 49; and
- any certificate or diploma such as is mentioned in para. 13(1) or (1A) of Sch. 3.

Tachographs are not covered; therefore, answer B is incorrect. (Note that offences relating to drivers' hours and accurate recording of such are covered by the Transport Act 1968 and the people in this scenario would most likely be liable under this Act.)

Road Policing, para. 3.13.3

Answer 13.8

Answer **C** — Section 115(1)(a) of the Road Traffic Regulation Act 1984 states that a person shall be guilty of an offence who, with intent to deceive, uses, or lends to, or allows to be used by, any other person any parking device or apparatus designed to be used in connection with parking devices, *or* any ticket issued by a parking meter, parking device or apparatus designed to be used in connection with parking devices.

It would surprise many people that this is an offence, as it is common practice between people parking in pay-and-display car parks. Many car park owners try to combat such fraud by forcing the customer to input their registration number in the machine, which is then displayed on the ticket. In summary, this is a criminal offence (and not a civil matter), which can be committed by a person who uses or lends to another person, a parking ticket with *intent to deceive* (the deceit being that the ticket was paid for by the person displaying it). Answers B and D are therefore incorrect. There is no requirement in this section to prove that a person intended to cause economic loss, or that economic loss was caused (although this would obviously be useful in any court case if the loser is claiming compensation). Answer A is therefore incorrect.

Road Policing, para. 3.13.3

Question Checklist

The following checklist is designed to help you keep track of your progress when answering the multiple-choice questions. If you fill this in after one attempt at each question, you will be able to check how many you have got right and which questions you need to revisit a second time. Also available online, to download visit www.blackstonespolicemanuals.com.

	First attempt Correct (✓)	Second attempt Correct (✓)
1 Definitions and Principles		
1.1		
1.2		
1.3		
1.4		
1.5		
1.6		
1.7		
1.8		
1.9		
1.10		
1.11		
1.12		
1.13		
1.14		
1.15		
1.16		
1.17		
1.18		
1.19		
1.20		
1.21		

	First attempt Correct (✓)	Second attempt Correct (✓)
1.22		
1.23		
1.24		
1.25		
2 Key Police Powers		
2.1		
2.2		
2.3		
2.4		
2.5		
2.6		
2.7		
2.8		
2.9		
2.10		
2.11		
2.12		
3 Offences Involving Standards of Driving		
3.1		
3.2		
3.3		

	First attempt Correct (✓)	Second attempt Correct (✓)
3.4		
3.5		
3.6		
3.7		
3.8		
3.9		
3.10		
3.11		
3.12		
3.13		
3.14		
3.15		
3.16		
3.17		
3.18		

4 Reportable Accidents

	First attempt Correct (✓)	Second attempt Correct (✓)
4.1		
4.2		
4.3		
4.4		
4.5		
4.6		
4.7		
4.8		
4.9		
4.10		
4.11		
4.12		
4.13		
4.14		
4.15		

5 Drink, Drugs and Driving

	First attempt Correct (✓)	Second attempt Correct (✓)
5.1		
5.2		
5.3		
5.4		
5.5		

	First attempt Correct (✓)	Second attempt Correct (✓)
5.6		
5.7		
5.8		
5.9		
5.10		
5.11		
5.12		
5.13		
5.14		
5.15		
5.16		
5.17		
5.18		
5.19		
5.20		
5.21		
5.22		
5.23		
5.24		
5.25		
5.26		
5.27		
5.28		
5.29		
5.30		
5.31		
5.32		
5.33		
5.34		
5.35		
5.36		
5.37		

6 Insurance

	First attempt Correct (✓)	Second attempt Correct (✓)
6.1		
6.2		
6.3		
6.4		
6.5		

	First attempt Correct (✔)	Second attempt Correct (✔)
6.6		
6.7		
6.8		
6.9		
6.10		

7 Protection of Drivers, Riders and Passengers

7.1		
7.2		
7.3		
7.4		
7.5		
7.6		
7.7		
7.8		
7.9		
7.10		
7.11		
7.12		
7.13		
7.14		
7.15		
7.16		

8 Highways and Safety Measures

8.1		
8.2		
8.3		
8.4		
8.5		
8.6		
8.7		
8.8		
8.9		
8.10		
8.11		
8.12		
8.13		
8.14		

	First attempt Correct (✔)	Second attempt Correct (✔)
8.15		
8.16		
8.17		
8.18		
8.19		
8.20		
8.21		
8.22		

9 Construction and Use

9.1		
9.2		
9.3		
9.4		
9.5		
9.6		
9.7		
9.8		
9.9		
9.10		
9.11		
9.12		
9.13		
9.14		
9.15		
9.16		
9.17		
9.18		
9.19		

10 Driver Licensing

10.1		
10.2		
10.3		
10.4		
10.5		
10.6		
10.7		
10.8		

Question Checklist

	First attempt Correct (✔)	Second attempt Correct (✔)
10.9		
10.10		
10.11		
10.12		
10.13		
10.14		
10.15		
10.16		
10.17		
10.18		
10.19		
10.20		
10.21		
10.22		
10.23		
10.24		
10.25		
10.26		

11 Fixed Penalty System

	First attempt Correct (✔)	Second attempt Correct (✔)
11.1		
11.2		
11.3		
11.4		
11.5		
11.6		
11.7		
11.8		
11.9		
11.10		

	First attempt Correct (✔)	Second attempt Correct (✔)
11.11		
11.12		
11.13		

12 Notices of Intended Prosecution

	First attempt Correct (✔)	Second attempt Correct (✔)
12.1		
12.2		
12.3		
12.4		
12.5		
12.6		
12.7		
12.8		
12.9		
12.10		
12.11		
12.12		
12.13		
12.14		
12.15		

13 Forgery and Falsification of Documents

	First attempt Correct (✔)	Second attempt Correct (✔)
13.1		
13.2		
13.3		
13.4		
13.5		
13.6		
13.7		
13.8		

BLACKSTONE'S POLICE MANUALS 2014: FOUR VOLUME SET

Paul Connor, David Johnston, Glenn Hutton, and Gavin McKinnon

- The only official study guide for the Police Promotion Examinations endorsed by the College of Policing

- If it's not in the book, it won't be in the exam - questions are only drawn from the 2014 Manuals

- Contains the latest case law and legislation - don't risk losing marks studying with out-of-date materials

- New for this year - coverage of the Legal Aid, Sentencing and Punishment of Offenders Act 2012, the Protection of Freedoms Act 2012, th[e] Criminal Procedure Rules 2012, the Terrorism Act 2000, as well as revised PACE Codes C, G and H

- Written by experienced law specialists and professionally reviewed by the College of Policing, giving you confidence in the products

AUGUST 2013 | 1,280 PAGES | 978-0-19-968052-8 | PACK

OXFORD
UNIVERSITY PRESS

For more information visit
www.oup.com